Self-Mutilation
Theory, Research, and Treatment

Barent W. Walsh, DSW
Paul M. Rosen, PhD

The Guilford Press
New York   London

© 1988 The Guilford Press
A Division of Guilford Publications, Inc.
72 Spring Street, New York, NY 10012

Printed in the United States of America

Last digit is print number: 9 8 7 6 5 4 3 2 1

Library of Congress Cataloging-in-Publication Data
Walsh, Barent W.
  Self-mutilation: theory, research, and treatment.

  Bibliography: p.
  Includes index.
  1. Self-mutilation. I. Rosen, Paul M. II. Title.
[DNLM: 1. Self Mutilation. WM 100 W223s]
RC552.S4W35 1988   616.85'82   88-5154
ISBN 0-89862-731-1

To two Fathers who have taught me a great deal:
E. A. W. and W. J. R.
    —*Barent W. Walsh*

To Karen.
    —*Paul M. Rosen*

Preface

As befits an enterprise of this type, we begin this book-length discussion with a basic question: What is self-mutilation? And our initial response is this: Self-mutilation, at its most elemental, self-evident, even tautological level, is a mutilation of the self. For some of its perpetrators, self-mutilative behavior (abbreviated in this book as SMB) is an intentional self-defacement, a disfigurement, an expression of self-abhorrence. For others, it is an implosion within the self, a means of reducing intolerable tension or venting inexpressible anger. Some use it as a form of self-stimulation, to escape frightening feelings of emptiness, deadness, or depersonalization—that is, to escape a perceived loss of the self. And others use it out of self-preoccupation, in order to influence and coerce family, friends, and involved clinicians.

Of course, these comments lead only to an additional series of questions and unresolved issues. These are the questions and issues that have intrigued us and that we have attempted to address throughout this book. Part I of the book focuses on the scope of the problem of self-mutilation. This entails reviewing the forms of SMB that have been reported in the literature. It also involves discussing why SMB is viewed as a serious clinical problem. In addition, reviewing the scope of self-mutilation requires a look at the incidence of the behavior as it has been reported in a number of Western countries.

One topic that we emphasize in Part I is making the distinction between self-mutilation and suicide. Here we address whether self-mutilation is a variant of suicide or a separate and distinct problem. In discussing this issue, we begin by reviewing the previous attempts to distinguish between these two forms of self-harm. We also describe a study of our own that pertains to making this distinction. The section concludes with an extended theoretical discussion of the definitions of self-mutilation versus suicide.

In Part II of the book, self-mutilation is discussed as it occurs in different clinical populations. First, we report findings from a recent study regarding conditions and experiences associated with self-mutilation in disturbed adolescents. Next, we discuss the problem of contagion (or self-mutilative epidemics), which has frequently been reported in clinical settings. As part of this discussion, we provide empirical findings from a recent study of ours that documents the existence of a contagion phenomenon. In this section, we also examine SMB as it occurs in different types of client groups, including borderline personalities, psychotics, and retarded and autistic individuals. In this section, emphasis is placed on the determinants of the behavior that are specific to a particular client group.

In the third and final section of the book, the focus is on treatment. Here we review some of the therapeutic techniques that have been used by others, and we present a number of our own. We also identify clinical strategies or responses that we believe are likely to be especially counterproductive. In this treatment section, the focus is on four types of interventions: cognitive–behavioral, psychoanalytic, family therapy, and group treatment. In addition, we also present a concluding chapter on multimodal, integrative treatment.

The approach we use throughout this book is decidedly pluralistic. In some chapters, the discussion is on an entirely theoretical, even a speculative, level. In others, the focus is on the results of various empirical studies. Finally, we also share, in primarily anecdotal form, our clinical experience in dealing with many self-mutilators. This pluralistic approach has been selected because, as the ensuing chapters indicate, we believe that self-mutilation is an especially complex problem. We view it as one of the more puzzling and intriguing riddles that clinicians encounter. As a result, we feel that to look at self-mutilation in a reasonably comprehensive fashion, it is necessary to employ multiple perspectives and methodologies.

Reflective of this pluralistic approach is the fact that we consulted many others in the completion of this book. First of all, we wish to acknowledge the patience and cooperation of our colleagues at the Community Treatment Complex (CTC) in Worcester, Massachusetts. Special thanks are due to the CTC Board of Directors and to Jeanne Barboni, Dan Bridgeo, John Doyle, Dr. Linda Jamieson, Donna Lis,

Beth Post, and Judy Barkus. Our research assistants, Patti Lucas
Johnson and Debbie Raybold, were vitally important in collecting
data for the empirical studies reported here. We also wish to thank
those who were involved in preparing the manuscript, including Judy
Brewster, Chris Mahoney, Tina Bermingham, and especially Denise
Castello.

We wish to acknowledge the assistance with editorial and substantive matters that a number of professional colleagues provided. Those
reviewing and suggesting improvements to various chapters of this
book included Dr. Vincent Lynch and Dr. Richard Mackey, both of
Boston College; Dr. Lawrence Peterson of Worcester State Hospital;
Dr. Lionel Hersov of the University of Massachusetts Department of
Psychiatry; and Dr. Inge Broverman of the Fielding Institute in Santa
Barbara, California. Finally, we want to thank Seymour Weingarten,
Editor-in-Chief of The Guilford Press, for his considerable patience
and his many helpful editorial suggestions.

Contents

I
The Scope of the Problem

Chapter 1

The Spectrum of Self-Mutilative Behavior: An Introduction and Overview

Self-mutilative behavior (SMB) is among those acts that seem to delimit human experience. Like acts of suicide, homicide, and the sexual abuse of children, self-mutilation carries with it an implicit connotation of "This is human behavior at its worst" or "These are examples of human beings gone wrong—as wrong as is conceivable."

As with most extremes, there is something fascinating about encountering self-mutilators—both in the literature and in person. It is a fascination, however, that is tempered by anguish and recoil, by shock and sometimes disgust, and (for those who are clinically minded) by a desire to comprehend and to help.

Many authors have referred to the anguish-provoking, complex nature of self-mutilation. Crabtree (1967) has described self-mutilative behavior as a "most distressing, challenging psychotherapeutic problem" (p. 91). Nelson and Grunebaum (1971) have referred to such behavior as "a major psychiatric and surgical problem" (p. 1345). Carr (1977) has termed the related problem of self-injurious behavior "perhaps the most dramatic and extreme form of chronic human pathology" (p. 800). Maclean and Robertson (1976) have argued that "self-mutilation is . . . more alarming and repugnant than suicide" (p. 242).

What is it about self-mutilation that provokes such aversive responses in others? The most obvious answer is that we inevitably experience discomfort when encountering fellow human beings so intensely distressed that they cause themselves concrete physical harm. Beyond this response, we also experience shock both in reacting to individual acts of self-mutilation and in learning of the broad spectrum of self-mutilative behaviors that have been performed. It would seem that the creativity human beings have shown over the centuries in adorning their bodies and enhancing their beauty has been entirely matched by the ingenuity mutilators have shown in damaging and disfiguring themselves.

Forms of Self-Mutilative Behavior

The most common examples of SMB, such as self-inflicted wrist cuts, tattoos, and cigarette burns, are familiar enough to most clinicians. Other examples of SMB are relatively rare in most clinical populations. These include such behaviors as self-excoriation and inoculation of the skin (Krupp, 1977; Herzberg, 1977); self-mutilation of the nose (Gilgotti & Waring, 1967; Akhtar & Hastings, 1978); chronic hair pulling and scalp irritation (trichotillomania) (Holdin-Davis, 1914; Delgado & Mannino, 1969); self-mutilation of the tongue (Neil, 1958); and self-inflicted conjunctivitis (Roper-Hall, 1950). This list does not even include the more extreme forms of self-mutilation, such as self-blinding or self-enucleation (Rosen & Hoffman, 1972; Maclean & Robertson, 1976; Griffin, Webb, & Parker, 1982); autocannibalism (Mintz, 1960; Betts, 1964); female genital self-mutilation (French & Nelson, 1972; Goldney & Simpson, 1975); self-castration (Stroch, 1901; Blacker & Wong, 1963; Pabis, Mirza, & Tozman, 1980; Clark, 1981; Krieger, McAninch, & Weimer, 1982); and self-inflicted penis removal (Greilsheimer & Groves, 1979).

For those interested in a complete listing of the forms of SMB, including a variety of clinical examples, Ross and McKay's (1979) book is highly recommended. Since Ross and McKay (1979), Lester (1972), and others have already presented thorough compilations of the forms of SMB, a complete inventory of these acts is not repeated here.

Categorization

Inevitably, as researchers and clinicians have studied self-mutilation, they have attempted to develop categories. The earliest attempt was Menninger's, published in 1935. He discussed self-mutilation in terms of six categories: (1) "neurotic self-mutilations," which included such behavior as nail biting, skin picking, disfiguring hair removal, and the obtaining of unnecessary surgery; (2) "religious self-mutilations," such as ascetic self-flagellation and genital self-mutilation; (3) "puberty rites," such as hymen removal, clitoral alteration, and circumcision; (4) "self-mutilation in psychotic patients," such as self-enucleation, ear removal, genital self-mutilation, and extremity amputation; (5) "self-mutilations in organic diseases," such as intentional fracturing of fingers and self-enucleation in patients suffering from encephalitis; and finally (6) "self-mutilation in normal people: customary and conventional forms," which included such acts as nail clipping, trimming of hair, and the shaving of beards.

As one can see from this list, Menninger's schema was multidimensional in scope. His formulation emphasized the interrelationship of at least four factors: (1) the extent and type of the psychological or physiological dysfunction of the mutilator; (2) the subcultural context of the mutilator and the meaning of the self-mutilative act within that context; (3) the degree of self-harm and its physical location on the body; and (4) the specific psychodynamic determinants of the SMB.

Like any nosology, Menninger's schema had its problems. For instance, referring to common practices such as nail clipping, hair trimming, and beard shaving as "self-mutilations" was a curious and questionable use of language. *The Merriam–Webster Dictionary* (1974) defines "to mutilate" as "to maim, cripple" or "to cut up or alter radically so as to make imperfect" (p. 463). The word, therefore, connotes a degree of self-damage and disfigurement that normal practices such as nail clipping and hair trimming clearly lack. Also, Menninger's categories were not mutually exclusive. For example, "religious self-mutilations" and "puberty rites" have often been interrelated. One other problem is that in developing his categories, Menninger failed to include an important group of individuals who inflict self-harm: self-injuring retardates. Despite these criticisms, it is without question that Menninger's formulations were ground-breaking in significance. The fact that his categories are still discussed 50 years after he first proposed them indicates their enduring value.

A more recent attempt at categorization has taken a different direction. Ross and McKay (1979) have used a behavioral–descriptive approach in dividing all types of self-mutilative acts into nine categories. Each category refers to the type of action employed in producing the self-harm. Their categories include (1) cutting, (2) biting, (3) abrading, (4) severing, (5) inserting, (6) burning, (7) ingesting or inhaling, (8) hitting, and (9) constricting. This way of describing SMB is couched exclusively in behavioral terms. No attempt is made to categorize behaviors according to level of disturbance, subcultural context, or psychodynamic determinants. Ross and McKay have explained their approach as an antidote to most previous attempts to explain SMB:

> The mind-boggling array of explanations offered for self-mutilating behavior not only reflect the host of disciplines which have studied this phenomenon but often represent the rigid loyalty of the investigator to a particular school of thought. There is a distinct lack of any coherent theory, even less an attempt to integrate the hodgepodge of conjectures, hypotheses, speculation, post hoc interpretation, suggestions, and commentaries. Further confusion is added to this bewildering scene when some authors choose to employ both different explanations and different levels of explanation for the same behavior. Correlations are proposed and presented without data. Data are presented without statistical test or interpretation. Very few of the hypotheses have been derived from theory, data or some form of fuctional analysis of the behavior. (Ross & McKay, 1979, p. 75)

Although the accuracy of Ross and McKay's polemic must be conceded (at least within the empiricist's world view), we have chosen to employ a categorical schema in this book that goes beyond the behavioral–descriptive. In our schema, we have developed a compromise position between Menninger's level of speculation and Ross and McKay's restrictiveness. This stance permits the use of a multidimensional model (like Menninger's), which nonetheless does not include speculations about psychodynamics (like Ross & McKay's).

What we present in Table 1.1 is intended to be a heuristic schema rather than a formal typology or nosology. We use the term "self-alteration of physical form" in order to avoid calling such behaviors as nail biting and ear piercing "self-mutilations." The schema indicates that there is a rather wide spectrum of human behavior that entails the alteration of physical appearance and body configuration. We propose that what makes some of these alterations self-mutilative (Types III and IV) and others not self-mutilative (Types I and II) are the interre-

TABLE 1.1
Self-Alteration of Physical Form: A Continuum

Type	Examples of behavior	Degree of physical damage	Psychological state	Social acceptability
I	Ear piercing; nail biting; small, professionally applied tattoos; cosmetic plastic surgery	Superficial to mild	Benign	Acceptable in all or most social groups
II	Punk rock piercings; saber scars among 19th-century Prussian students; ritualistic scarring among Polynesian and African clans; large tattoos among sailors, motorcycle gangs	Mild to moderate	Benign to agitated	Acceptable only within a specific subculture
III	Wrist and body cutting; self-inflicted cigarette burns; self-inflicted tattoos; wound excoriation	Mild to moderate	Psychic crisis	Generally unacceptable in all social groups; may be acceptable with a few like-minded peers
IV	Autocastration; self-enucleation; amputation	Severe	Psychotic decompensation	Entirely unacceptable with all peers and in all social groups

lated dimensions of (1) severity of physical damage, (2) psychological
state at the time of the self-altering act, and (3) the social acceptability
of the behavior.

As the table indicates, the most common forms of self-effected
bodily alteration are termed Type I. This category includes such behaviors as simple ear piercing, nail biting, and the professional application of small tattoos. These behaviors are not considered self-mutilative because the physical damage is superficial to mild, the psychic
state at the time of the act is benign, and the social acceptability of the
behavior is broad. The situation is somewhat more complex regarding
Type II self-alterations, such as punk rock piercings and ritualistic
scarrings among African and Polynesian clans. These behaviors may
entail more substantial physical damage and may be performed in a
group-induced state of excitement. Nonetheless, since these behaviors
are considered to be beauty-enhancing or symbolically meaningful
within a specific subculture, they are not considered truly self-mutilative.

In order for a behavior to be termed self-mutilative in this schema,
all three dimensions must be in some sense deviant. Thus, Type III
self-alterations are considered self-mutilative because the physical
damage is mild to moderate, the psychic state is one of crisis, and the
social acceptability is limited to a few similarly *dysfunctional* individuals. Finally, for Type IV self-alterations, the behavior is without
question self-mutilative and pathological, since the physical damage
is severe, the psychic state is usually one of psychotic decompensation,
and the social response of others is one of universal condemnation.

The present book concerns Type III and Type IV alterations of
physical form. Nonetheless, it is important to place SMB in its broader
context. Placing SMB on a continuum permits understanding of the
specific dimensions that cause the behavior to be viewed as dysfunctional. Moreover, in some cases, self-mutilative patterns of behavior
begin as culturally acceptable forms of self-alteration. In such cases,
individuals intensify or exaggerate normative forms of self-alteration
until the behaviors reach extreme self-mutilative proportions.

For an example of this progression, consider the following case: A
young housewife becomes convinced that her eyebrows are too bushy.
Initially, she plucks her eyebrows in a way that enhances or at least
maintains her attractiveness. Over time, she becomes fascinated and
preoccupied with the appearance of her eyes. When she becomes anx-

ious about a fight with her husband or a future social engagement, she distracts herself by plucking her eyebrows. One day she is surprised to discover that she has removed *all* of her eyebrows. Still, she is unable to stop the behavior. Neighborhood friends notice the change in her appearance; they begin to avoid her because she looks so unusual. This makes the young woman even more anxious. She begins to remove her eyelashes as well. The area around her eyes becomes inflamed and subject to infection. She eventually is referred for psychiatric treatment.

In this example, we see behavior that begins as normal, socially acceptable alteration of physical form and culminates in bizarre, socially condemned disfigurement. In order to understand this extreme form of self-mutilation, one needs to understand the psychological state and social milieu that have produced it.

Definition

In addition to the attempts to develop categories of SMB, the literature contains a number of formal definitions of the behavior. Some writers have emphasized the physical damage performed: for example, "[S]elf-mutilation . . . denotes those measures carried out by the individual, upon himself, which tend to cut off, to render imperfect some part of the body" (Phillips & Alkan, 1961, p. 421). Others have stressed the intentionality and nonlethality of the act, describing SMB as "nonfatal, deliberate self-harm" (Morgan, Burns-Cox, Pocock, & Pottle, 1975, p. 564). Both Lester (1972) and Ross and McKay (1979) have emphasized the distinction between SMB and suicidal behavior:

> There is in the action of the self-mutilator seldom an intent to die and often very little risk of dying. Although a self-mutilator could engender his own death by his behavior, in the vast majority of cases, this does not happen. His behavior is actually counter-intentional to suicide rather than suicidal. (Ross & McKay, 1979, p. 15)

Others have referred to the social consequences of SMB, underscoring that SMB is a "socially unacceptable alteration of physical form" (Phillips & Alkan, 1961, p. 421). Incorporating all of these features into a single statement has resulted in our developing the following definition: *Self-mutilative behavior is deliberate, non-life-threatening, self-effected bodily harm or disfigurement of a socially unacceptable nature.* We also provide more detailed formulations regarding definition in the next two chapters. However, the one provided above is sufficient for the purposes of this chapter.

Self-Mutilation as a Clinical Problem

Thus far, we have reviewed the forms of SMB, presented a schema for categorizing the behavior, and proposed a concise definition. In this introductory chapter, it is also important to identify the types of clinical settings in which SMB has been reported and to indicate how SMB has been a problem in those settings.

The majority of settings in which SMB has been reported have been adult inpatient psychiatric facilities (e.g., Grunebaum & Klerman, 1967; Graff & Mallin, 1967; Pao, 1969; Simpson, 1975; Gardner & Gardner, 1975; Roy, 1978; Kroll, 1978; Carroll, Schaffer, Spensley, & Abramowitz, 1980) and institutions for the retarded (McKerracher, Loughnane, & Watson, 1968; Ballinger, 1971). The phenomenon has also been reported in several prisons (Panton, 1962; Johnson, 1973; Bach-y-Rita, 1974; Yaroshevsky, 1975) and a general hospital emergency room (Weissman, 1975). In addition, SMB has been described in a few treatment settings for children and adolescents (Offer & Barglow, 1961; Green, 1968; Ross & McKay, 1979; Walsh & Rosen, 1985).

One theme that emerges in reviewing these clinical reports is that SMB has posed multiple problems for professionals. Stated concisely, these problems can be identified as generally consisting of the following:

1. SMB is inherently troublesome because people cause themselves concrete physical harm.

2. SMB is highly disruptive in treatment settings. Since these settings are designed to alleviate problems and protect clients, SMB represents a temporary setback or failure in the provision of effective treatment.

3. SMB is also upsetting to program staff and to the family members of clients. Families feel threatened and lose confidence in programs where SMB occurs. Staff morale can also be affected, with

"confusion, guilt, heated arguments and breakdowns in communication resulting in an untherapeutic environment" (Offer & Barglow, 1960, p. 194).

4. Adding to these difficulties is that self-mutilation is frequently reported to occur in "epidemics" in treatment settings (see Chapters 5 and 12 for detailed discussions of this phenomenon). When epidemics or contagion of SMB occurs, the problems cited in items 1, 2, and 3 are present for a number of clients simultaneously.

5. Some clients mutilate themselves for the first time while in treatment settings. This suggests undesirable iatrogenic effects of supposedly therapeutic environments.

6. SMB is difficult to understand, since it runs counter to the normal human preference to avoid pain and seek pleasure. The obscurity of the etiology of SMB has led to a proliferation of theories to explain it and techniques to treat it. The result is that clinicians are often faced with multiple and conflicting models of theory and practice. The guidelines for choosing among these diverse models are frequently unclear; yet the professional must choose intervention strategies.

7. Finally, SMB has proven difficult to treat. Many reports describe self-mutilators who become chronic repeaters (Graff & Mallin, 1967; Bach-y-Rita, 1974; Gardner & Gardner, 1975; Ross & McKay, 1979). Some self-mutilating clients have injured themselves as many as several hundred or even thousands of times (Azrin, Gottlieb, Hughart, Wesolowski, & Rahn, 1975).

In sum, SMB has presented clinicians with a complex array of problems. Each of these clinical problems is discussed throughout this book, particularly in Parts II and III.

Incidence

An additional cause for concern regarding self-mutilation is that its incidence has increased markedly since the 1960s. Epidemiological studies from Canada (Johnson, Ferrence, & Whitehead, 1973; Johnson, Frankel, Ferrence, Jarvis, & Whitehead, 1975), England (Smith & Davison, 1971; Morgan, 1979), Denmark (Bille-Brahe, 1982), and the United States (Clendenin & Murphy, 1971; Weissman, 1975) have consistently cited an increased incidence of self-harm behaviors, including SMB.

Johnson *et al.* (1975), for example, stated, "This rising incidence of self-injury is a medical, social and economic problem of major proportions and has implications for the planning of adequate medical, psychiatric and other counseling services" (p. 307).

Determining precisely the incidence of self-mutilation is difficult if not impossible at present. One reason is that self-harm behaviors such as SMB have been shown to be seriously underreported (Whitehead, Johnson, & Ferrence, 1973). The behavior tends to go unreported, in part, because mutilators frequently choose to commit their acts in private. Mutilators are aware that their acts are socially stigmatizing and can result in restrictive psychiatric interventions. As a result, some mutilators choose to conceal their wounds or to reveal them only to confidants or family members who are unlikely to tell others. Other mutilators who perform seriously damaging acts may mislead medical personnel into believing that their wounds are the result of accidents or attacks from others. Thus, professionals who are responsible for collecting data on self-mutilation may be forced to rely on the self-reports of individuals who have multiple reasons for concealing their actual intentions.

Another difficulty in determining the incidence of SMB pertains to the nature of the studies that have examined incidence. Previous studies have tended to be either overinclusive or underinclusive with regard to SMB. For example, the epidemiological studies of Whitehead *et al.* (1973) and Johnson *et al.* (1973, 1975) looked at rates of what they termed "self-injury." Self-injury was comprised of a broad spectrum of nonfatal self-harm behaviors, including not only self-mutilations but also intentional drug overdoses, self-poisonings, and asphyxiations. Similarly, the studies by Morgan (1979) and Myers (1982) focused on rates of occurrence for what they called "deliberate self-harm" (DSH). DSH included an even broader range of self-destructive behaviors: failed suicides, overdoses, self-poisonings, and gas inhalations, as well as self-mutilations.

Although it may be understandable why epidemiologists would want to study self-harm behaviors within broadly defined categories, this is not very useful from a clinical perspective. As we stress in the next chapter and throughout Part I, we consider self-mutilation to be substantially different from other forms of self-harm (e.g., overdose, self-poisoning, hanging, and asphyxiation). Stated briefly, SMB is generally different from these other forms of self-harm in terms of intent, method, risk to life, and degree of physical damage and disfigurement. Thus, from our perspective at least, to study self-mutilation in combination with a number of other largely dissimilar acts is likely to result in considerable confusion.

A related problem is that a number of other epidemiological studies have been *underinclusive* with regard to self-mutilation. For example, Clendenin and Murphy (1971) and Weissman (1975) focused exclusively on the behavior of wrist cutting. Both of these studies were methodologically sophisticated and yielded important information about the characteristics of wrist slashers. Nonetheless, since these studies focused on only this single form of SMB, one cannot derive from their findings any conclusions regarding the broader category of SMB itself.

Because of either the overinclusiveness or the underinclusiveness of previous studies, what is reported below is decidedly incomplete. The best data that can be presently provided are rough estimates of incidence, generally based on findings regarding wrist-cutting behavior alone. Since there are many other forms of self-mutilation for which the incidence is unknown, the figures provided below can only serve as a general guideline regarding the extent of the problem.

The epidemiological literature suggests that the incidence of self-mutilation during the 1970s and early 1980s ranged between 14 and 600 persons per 100,000 population per year. We arrived at this very imprecise estimate in the following manner. The low end of the range was gleaned from Morgan's studies, performed in the Bristol, England area. He reported in his 1979 book, *Death Wishes?*, that the incidence of what he called "DSH" during 1972–1974 averaged about 275 persons per 100,000 population. Of these individuals, 95% had used the methods of self-poisoning, overdosing, inhaling gas, attempting to jump from a height, or attempting to drown themselves. The remaining 5% had employed what Morgan termed "self-laceration." Of the DSH behaviors listed by Morgan, we would classify only self-laceration as self-mutilative. And since lacerations comprised 5% of the total, this would yield an incidence of 14 persons per 100,000 population per year. Presumably, the incidence for the more inclusive category of self-mutilation would have been higher, but no other data were reported.

When we performed similar calculations using data from other epidemiological studies, we were able to make some additional approximations. Hawton, Fagg, Marsack, and Wells (1982) presented findings from a study of nonlethal forms of self-harm in the Oxford, England area. They reported an incidence of 351 persons per 100,000 population per year. Of these, 37 persons per 100,000 were individuals who had cut their wrists. Other forms of SMB were not reported. In an earlier study, Johnson *et al.* (1973) reported a much higher incidence of wrist cutting. They found that in London, Ontario, during 1970–1971, the incidence of wrist cutting was 131 persons per 100,000.

Finally, on the high end of the range is the incidence of 400–600 persons per 100,000 population reported in nearly identical papers by Pattison and Kahan (1983) and Kahan and Pattison (1984). Unlike the other papers, their reports concerned multiple forms of self-mutilation. Unfortunately, their papers do not reveal the source of their figure. This rate seems unusually high in comparison with those found in the epidemiological studies described above. It may be that including the additional forms of SMB accounts for the substantially higher incidence. An alternative explanation may be that Pattison and Kahan's figure is an approximate one based on findings of previous epidemiological studies (regarding the more inclusive category of non-lethal self-injury). If the latter case is true, the figure is inflated and incorrect, since both the Pattison and Kahan (1983) and Kahan and Pattison (1984) papers purported to exclude such acts as overdosing and self-poisoning from their discussion.

In conclusion, any attempt to determine the incidence of self-mutilation at this time is fraught with problems. The best that can be said currently is that the range in incidence is probably between 14 and 600 persons per 100,000 population per year. To state this in somewhat more meaningful terms, in the United States at this time (with a population of 240 million) there are probably somewhere between 33,600 and 1,440,00 people who mutilate themselves during a given year. Although this range is extremely broad, it nonetheless begins to indicate the magnitude of the problem of self-mutilation today. Even if the lower end of the range is accepted as the correct figure, this incidence indicates a problem of serious proportions.

Chapter 2

Distinguishing Self-Mutilation
from Suicide: A Review
and Commentary

Over the past 50 years, researchers and clinicians interested in self-harm behaviors have made numerous attempts to distinguish SMB from suicide. These professionals have generally shared the conviction that self-mutilation is somehow different from suicidal behavior, but they have been hard pressed to determine exactly how it is different. This chapter reviews a number of the attempts to distinguish between self-mutilation and suicide. As the chapter indicates, slow but gradual progress has been made in this area. At the outset, the reader is advised to proceed at his or her own risk, since, as Kreitman, Philip, Greer, and Bagley (1969) have indicated, "The problem of nomenclature in studies of so-called 'attempted suicide' has certain affinities with migraine: both are recurrent, are associated with headache, and induce difficulties focusing clearly" (pp. 746–747).

Background

Table 2.1 presents a concise review of attempts to distinguish self-mutilation (and related behaviors) from suicide. The citations presented in the table are not intended to provide an exhaustive, complete list. Rather, the intent has been to select the key or at least representative efforts at differentiating self-mutilation from suicide. As even a quick perusal of the table indicates, a mind-boggling number of terms, con-

TABLE 2.1
Representative Attempts to Distinguish Self-Mutilation from Other Forms of Self-Harm

Publication	Key terms	Types of behavior discussed	Conclusions/findings
Menninger (1935, 1938)	Focal suicide	Self-mutilation in neurotics, psychotics, the organically injured, and members of religious sects.	Explained self-mutilation as a focal suicide in which the perpetrator unconsciously indulges a forbidden indulgence at the expense of an act of self-harm. The SMB is a compromise, a partial or focal suicide.
Hendin (1950)	Attempted suicide	Self-assault occurring in hospitalized patients.	Proposed three categories of self-assaultive behavior, based on intent to die.
Schmidt, O'Neal, & Robbins (1954)	Suicide attempts	Broad range of self-destructive behaviors	Differentiated between medically serious physical harm and psychiatrically serious intent to die.
Stengel (1964)	Suicide vs. attempted suicide	Broad range of self-destructive behaviors.	Distinguished between completed "successful" suicides and all other attempts at self-harm that entailed some risk of life. Distinguished between seriousness of intent and degree of physical dangerousness.
Graff & Mallin (1967); Grunebaum & Klerman (1967); Nelson & Grunebaum (1971); Rosenthal, Rinzler, Walsh, & Klausner (1972)	"Wrist-cutting syndrome," wrist slashing	Wrist cutting occurring in inpatient psychiatric settings.	Proposed "wrist-cutting syndrome," based on small-sample, single-setting studies. Cutting was seen as a means to reduce tension and not as a suicide attempt. The syndrome was thought to be comprised primarily of young, single women.

Study	Term	Population/Focus	Findings
Pao (1969)	"Delicate self-cutting syndrome"	Self-cutting behavior in an inpatient psychiatric setting.	Distinguished "delicate cutters" from "coarse cutters." Syndrome was seen as comprised of females who used cutting as an obsessive device to reduce tension. Such behavior was differentiated from suicide attempts.
Cohen (1969)	Suicidation, self-assault	Broad range of self-destructive acts presenting at a mental health clinic.	Proposed classifying self-assaultive acts in terms of the phases of (1) ideation, (2) preparation, and (3) the act itself and related physical trauma.
Kreitman, Philip, Greer, & Bagley (1969)	Parasuicide	Self-poisoning and other forms of self-injury.	Proposed the new term "parasuicide" as a way to avoid confusions associated with the term "attempted suicide." The authors selected "parasuicide" because they saw such behaviors as self-poisoning and SMB as simulating or mimicking suicide.
Clendenin & Murphy (1971); Weissman (1975)	Wrist cutters, suicide attempters	Wrist cutting as reported by police (Clendenin & Murphy) and as presenting at a medical complex (Weissman). Cutters were compared with "other suicide attempters" using epidemiologically sized samples.	Found evidence that the idea of a distinct wrist-cutting syndrome is unwarranted. Weissman found that cutters posed significantly less risk to life, were less likely to require medical attention, had more paranoid delusions, and had fewer secondary signs of depression than the "other suicide attempters."

(continued)

TABLE 2.1
(*Continued*)

Publication	Key terms	Types of behavior discussed	Conclusions/findings
Freidman, Glasser, Laufer, Laufer, & Whol (1972)	Self-mutilation *vs.* attempted suicide	Self-mutilation and suicide attempts occurring in adolescents.	Distinguished between mutilators, who attacked part of the body and experienced psychic relief following their acts, and suicide attempters, who attacked the entire body and experienced relief prior to their acts.
Litman, Farberow, & Wold (1974)	Acute suicidal behavior *vs.* chronic repetitive self-injury	Broad range of self-destructive acts in diverse populations.	Distinguished between those who committed a single act of self-harm while in acute crisis and those who were chronic repeaters of acts of self-injury.
Simpson (1976, 1980)	Self-mutilation, antisuicide	A range of self destructive acts, with primary emphasis on wrist cutting.	Termed self-mutilation, especially wrist cutting, an "antisuicide," since it was viewed as an attempt to end feelings of deadness and a state of depersonalization, rather than an attempt to die.
Morgan, Burns-Cox, Pocock, & Potle (1975); Morgan, Barton, Potle, & Burns-Cox (1976); Morgan (1979)	Non-fatal deliberate self-harm (DSH)	Various forms of self-harm, especially self-poisoning and drug over-doses, as presented in epidemiologically sized samples. A small percentage of self-lacerators were also included.	Proposed that DSH can be distinguished from suicide in terms of the low lethality of the acts, absence of suicidal ideas, use of overdose as primary method, and various demographic characteristics.

Ross & McKay (1979)	Self-mutilation, carving	Self-mutilation, especially cutting or "carving," which occurred in 86% of the girls detained in a residential school for delinquents.	Contended that self-mutilation is "counter-intentional to suicide." The authors proposed that self-mutilation is different from suicide, in that with the former there is "seldom an intent to die and often very little risk of dying."
Farberow (1980)	Indirect self-destructive behavior	Wide range of harmful or potentially harmful forms of nonsuicidal behavior, including substance abuse, over-eating, smoking, risk taking, self-mutilation, noncompliance with medical treatments, etc.	Indicated complex nature of distinguishing between direct, overt suicidal behaviors and indirect forms of self-harm. Suggested that key variables include (1) verbal vs. active behavior; (2) time as a dimension (i.e., short-term vs. long-term effects); (3) intent (i.e. conscious vs. unconscious intent to commit self-harm); and (4) passivity vs. activity.
Pattison & Kahan (1983); Kahan & Pattison (1984)	Deliberate self-harm syndrome (DSH)	Reviewed 33 reports in the literature, which described 56 cases of DSH. Cases reviewed were of patients who directly harmed themselves using low-lethality methods. Cases of drug and alcohol overdose were excluded, as were forms of indirect self-harm.	Proposed that a new and distinct DSH syndrome be included in DSM-IV. Suggested that DSH can be distinguished from suicide in terms of lethality, repetition, use of multiple methods, absence of death-oriented thoughts, and other variables.
Shneidman (1985)	Suicide vs. parasuicide	Suicidal acts in general, with some reference to other forms of self-harm, including parasuicide.	Presented 10 commonalities of suicide and compared and contrasted these with 10 commonalities of parasuicide. Delineated eight points of contradistinction.

cepts, definitions, and variables have been proposed as being crucial to making this distinction. Rather than attempting a thoroughgoing, chronological review of each publication listed in the table, we focus on key trends in conceptualization, terminology, and methodology.

Self-Mutilation as a Variant of Suicide

Beginning with Menninger in 1935, the earliest efforts to discuss self-mutilation and suicide emphasized the interrelatedness of these two forms of behavior. As the terms "partial suicide," "focal suicide" (Menninger, 1935, 1938), "attempted suicide" (Hendin, 1950; Schmidt, O'Neal, & Robbins, 1954; Stengel, 1964), and even the more recent "parasuicide" (Kreitman *et al.*, 1969) indicate, these authors viewed self-mutilation as a variant of suicide. For example, Menninger (1935) stated,

> [S]elf-mutilation is the net result of a conflict between (1) the aggressive destructive impulses aided by the superego and (2) the will to live, whereby a partial or local self-destruction serves the purpose of gratifying irresistible urges and at the same time averting the prelogical but antici-pated consequences thereof. . . . [W]hile apparently a form of attenuated suicide, self-mutilation is actually a compromise formation to avert total annihilation, that is to say, suicide. In this sense it represents a victory, sometimes a Pyrrhic victory, of the life instinct over the death instinct. (pp. 465–466)

Thus, we see in this formulation that self-mutilation is conceptualized as derived from suicide and as a psychic compromise that prevents or forestalls suicide.

In utter disagreement with this position is Simpson's (1976, 1980) statement that self-mutilation is actually an "antisuicide." Simpson contended that acts such as wrist cutting are the opposite of suicide, in that they serve to alleviate feelings of deadness and depersonalization and assist in regaining a sense of being alive. In a similar vein, Ross and McKay (1979) have written,

> There is in the action of the self-mutilator seldom an intent to die and often very little risk of dying. Although a self-mutilator could engender his own death by his behavior, in the vast majority of cases, this does not

happen. *His behavior is actually counter-intentional to suicide rather than suicidal.* To view self-mutilation as a subtype or a variant of suicide is to encourage attempts to explain the behavior in terms of explanations of suicide . . . to do so would impede progress in understanding self-mutilation since we simply do not know enough about the nature of the relationship between self-mutilation and suicide. (p. 15, emphasis added)

Most authors since the 1960s appear to agree with the position articulated by Simpson (1976, 1980) and Ross and McKay (1979), since they have avoided the use of the word "suicide" in their terminology. Two recent exceptions are Pabis *et al.* (1980), who have discussed a case of autocastration using Menninger's term, "focal suicide"; and, more importantly, Shneidman, who has employed Kreitman's term "parasuicide" in his 1985 book, *Definition of Suicide.*

This debate over terminology is, of course, no mere quibbling over words. At stake is how SMB should be understood, described, diagnosed, and treated. For example, if an individual presents at an emergency unit with superficial wrist cuts, the treatment response is likely to be markedly different, depending on whether this self-mutilative act is viewed as a focal suicide or suicide attempt in which the individual is fending off impulses to end his or her life, or as an attempt at tension reduction and alleviation of a depersonalized state. In the former case, the treatment response might well be protective hospitalization with the prescription of antidepressant medication. In the latter case, the treatment response might well be short-term use of an antianxiety drug in combination with outpatient psychotherapy.

Our position is that the use of terminology that includes the word "suicide" should be avoided in discussing self-mutilation. As time has passed, considerable progress has been made in distinguishing, self-mutilation from suicide in terms of multiple variables. (The specifics regarding these variables are discussed below.) As a result, to continue to describe self-mutilation in terms of suicide serves only to perpetuate an unnecessary conceptual confusion.

Although the position here is that the early writings regarding self-mutilation versus suicide contained a terminological red herring, this is not to say that these early papers did not raise other crucial issues. Menninger's (1935) paper was the seminal one in the field. In his extended study of self-mutilation across cultures, he raised most of the issues that researchers of self-mutilation have since attempted to address. Menninger's paper examined such topics as distinguishing neurotic from psychotic self-mutilation; assessing the problem of intent; and understanding such phenomena as chronic repetition within individuals and self-mutilative epidemics within groups. Similarly, Hendin's (1950) paper was an early attempt at categorization of acts of self-harm in regard to their intent and lethality. Schmidt *et al.* (1954) clarified the distinction between medically serious self-harm and psychiatrically serious intent, and Stengel (1964) made an important attempt to measure intent and dangerousness on multiple-item, standardized scales. These efforts pointed the way for the various key topics and methodological issues that have been focused on since.

A Wrist-Cutting Syndrome?

Perhaps the next significant theme to emerge in the efforts to distinguish self-mutilation from suicide was that of "the syndrome of the wrist cutter." In the 1960s, a number of clinicians working in inpatient psychiatric settings reported an influx of patients who repeatedly slashed their wrists (Offer & Barglow, 1960; Graff & Mallin, 1967; Grunebaum & Klerman, 1967; Pao, 1969). Several of these professionals became convinced not only that this repetitive wrist cutting could be distinguished from suicide, but that it also represented a distinctly different syndrome of self-harm. Thus, in 1967 Graff and Mallin described what they saw as the "typical wrist cutter," based on a study of 21 patients:

> In summary, the cutter is an attractive, intelligent, unmarried young woman, who is either promiscuous or overly afraid of sex, easily addicted, and unable to relate successfully to others. She is an older one in a group of siblings with a cold, domineering mother and a withdrawn, passive, hypercritical father. She slashes her wrists indiscriminately and repeatedly at the slightest provocation, but she does not commit suicide. She feels relief with the commission of her act. (p. 38)

In a paper also published in 1967, Grunebaum and Klerman described what they viewed as the typical wrist slasher. As the following quotation indicates, there were a number of points of agreement between their description and that of Graff and Mallin:

These patients seem to be quite similar. They are generally young, attractive, intelligent, even talented, and on the surface socially adept. . . . Invariably their early lives and family relationships have been unstable. . . . In many cases the father has been seductive and unable to set limits. He is intermittently indulgent, often inadequate at his occupation, and frequently alcoholic. The mother is usually cold, punitive, and unconsciously provocative. . . . Generally it can be said that these patients slash their wrists when they face the loss of a meaningful person or encounter an impasse in their interpersonal relations. . . . Although the patient reports, usually inarticulately, the onset of vague feelings of discomfort . . . she does not relate them to the changes in her interpersonal relations and often does not or cannot verbalize the extent of her tension. (p. 528)

Support for the idea of a separate syndrome of wrist cutting (found among young, single women with a consistent psychological and historical profile) appears to have been considerable through the late 1960s and early 1970s. For example, Pao (1969) discussed psychoanalytically 27 inpatients who had cut themselves, 23 of whom were female. He proposed that such patients comprised a distinct "delicate self-cutting syndrome," the characteristics of which were congruent with those described by Graff and Mallin (1967) and Grunebaum and Klerman (1967). Similarly, Rosenthal, Rinzler, Walsh, and Klausner (1972) studied 23 inpatient wrist cutters in an attempt to identify more specifically the childhood experiences and current psychopathology associated with the wrist-cutting syndrome. Also, in an attempt to determine how wrist cutters fared over time, Nelson and Grunebaum (1971) performed a follow-up study of 19 wrist slashers. They reported that 5–6 years after initial hospital contact, 10 of the patients were improved, 4 were unchanged, 2 were worse, and 3 were dead (all suicides). This latter finding clouded the contention that the wrist-cutting syndrome was separate from suicide.

The first challenge to the idea of a wrist-cutting syndrome came from Clendenin and Murphy in 1971. This study employed an epidemiologically sized sample ($n = 672$) and included a systematic review of St. Louis County police reports regarding "suicide attempts." They compared those who had cut their wrists ($n = 65$) with those who had "attempted suicide" using other methods ($n = 606$) over a 2-year period. A number of their findings contradicted the profile posited by Grunebaum and Klerman (1967), Graff and Mallin (1967), and others. More specifically, 40% of the wrist cutters were men ($n = 26$). Of the female cutters ($n = 39$), only 31% were single; in addition, the age range for both sexes was wide, being confined by no means to the range cited in the previous clinical reports. Clendenin and Murphy concluded that the previous clinical reports were based on unrepresentative samples of patients from private psychiatric hospitals, which tend to have disproportionate numbers of well-educated, single young women.

The Clendenin and Murphy (1971) study was replicated by Weissman (1975), in her epidemiological study of wrist cutting in the New Haven, Connecticut area. Subjects for this study were drawn from a local medical complex. Weissman's findings were nearly identical to the St. Louis County study as to the wrist cutters' sex, marital status, age, and other characteristics. Her conclusions were that wrist cutting was not a separate and distinct clinical syndrome and that the stereotypical profile of the female wrist cutter was unwarranted. Weissman stated that the St. Louis County and New Haven studies had demonstrated "the value of the epidemiologic approach for obtaining base line data on new syndromes, as well as pitfalls of generalizing from selected samples" (1975, p. 1166).

Since the publication of the Weissman study in 1975, there have been no additional papers published on the topic of a wrist-cutting syndrome. It would appear that the epidemiological studies demolished the syndrome as a meaningful idea, particularly since the incidence of wrist-cutting behavior remains relatively high. This is not to say, however, that efforts to define self-mutilation using syndrome terminology have ceased. Recent attempts include Morgan's (1979) and Pattison and Kahan's (1983) discussions of a "deliberate self-harm syndrome" (DSH). These efforts are discussed below.

The Clendenin and Murphy (1971) and Weissman (1975) studies also had a far-reaching methodological impact. Following the publication of their epidemiological studies, clinical researchers using small samples from single settings have tended to be more cautious in claiming generalizability for their findings.

Attempts to Identify Dimensions Useful in Distinguishing Self-Mutilation from Suicide

Since the mid-1970s, researchers interested in self-mutilation have primarily focused on defining specific dimensions that are useful in differentiating self-mutilation from suicidal acts. In general, it can be said that these efforts have identified four related factors as being centrally important and as requiring considerable clarification: (1) the intent of the perpetrator of the acts of self-harm; (2) the physical damage resulting from the self-harm; (3) the frequency or chronicity of the acts; and (4) the methods selected for inflicting self-harm. These factors are reviewed separately.

The Intent of Self-Mutilative Acts

In many ways, the dimension that is the most important in distinguishing self-mutilation from suicide is the matter of intent. If it could be demonstrated that the motivation or intent of self-mutilating acts is markedly different from that of suicidal acts, this would go a long way in supporting the hypothesized distinction. However, assessing the intent of mutilators has been difficult for at least two reasons. First, the intent of self-mutilative acts is inevitably private to its perpetrators. Self-mutilators can never share with us in a direct, immediate way the complex determinants of their acts of self-harm. At best, they can describe after the fact what they remember their intent to have been. This memory, of course, is subject to a variety of distortions. Second, the intent of acts of self-harm is often a mystery to the perpetrators themselves. This intent may be unconscious, preconscious, or just muddled due to a rush of hopelessly confused thoughts and emotions. It is probably not just artifice or reticence that causes many mutilators to "explain" their acts with the words "I don't know." Other mutilators may provide explanations that were originally suggested to them by friends or professionals at previous points in time. Whether these "explanations" resemble their own original intentions is unclear.

Despite these inherent difficulties, researchers have periodically attempted to unravel the complexities of the intent of self-mutilation. One area of discussion has concerned the distinction between conscious and unconscious intent. As noted in Table 2.1, Menninger (1935) emphasized the importance of unconscious intent, inferring from self-mutilative acts the presence of a powerful, although partially neutralized, death instinct. Farberow (1980) stressed the role of unconscious determinants in what he called "indirect self-destructive behavior," which includes such behavior as hyperobesity, smoking, and substance abuse. In contrast, Hendin (1950), Stengel (1964), and Schmidt *et al.* (1954) began the more empirical approach to assessing intent by focusing on its conscious, cognitive, and behavioral correlates. They attempted to measure intent in contradistinction to physical damage performed. Thus, they proposed that individuals may have a serious intent to die, but because of clumsy implementation cause themselves only minor physical trauma. Conversely, they also indicated that individuals may be markedly ambivalent about or even opposed to dying, but (because of miscalculation) cause themselves life-threatening harm. Although these variables were measured on separate scales, these researchers found that the variables nonetheless tended to be highly associated with each other.

Since many researchers have hypothesized that self-mutilating acts are not typically suicidal in intent (e.g., Simpson, 1976; Ross & McKay, 1979; Pattison & Kahan, 1983), the key question has been this: What, then, is the intent of self-mutilation on the part of the perpetrator? Unfortunately, the studies that have attempted to answer this question have yielded highly ambiguous results. For example, in Gardner and Gardner's (1975) study of self-mutilators, 19 of 22 subjects cited relief of tension as a primary reason for self-cutting. Eleven subjects also cited intense anger as a reason for self-harm. That is, they perceived the self-mutilation to be the best method available for reducing uncomfortable affect. However, Gardner and Gardner also reported that 9 of these 22 mutilators cited suicidal thoughts as being associated with their self-mutilating acts. Similarly, Jones, Congin, Stevenson, Strauss, and Frei (1979) found that 85% of their sample of 39 cutters cited tension relief as their motivation for cutting. However, 40% of a subsample of these cutters also reported having a wish to die at the time of their mutilation. In turn, Pattison and Kahan (1983) found that in their review of 56 cases reported in the literature, 69% cited despair, 55% anxiety, and 50% anger/agitation as precipitants to their self-mutilating acts. However, 28% also cited suicidal ideation as related to their self-mutilations.

Thus, the pattern emerging from these studies was that a desire to avoid or reduce the intensity of painful affects was the most frequently cited intent for self-mutilative acts; however, suicidal intent was not uncommonly reported as associated with SMB. It would appear, therefore, that if progress is to be made in distinguishing self-mutilation from suicide, it will not emerge easily from the area of assessing intent.

At the least, intent will have to be assessed differently and more specifically if this dimension is to assist in distinguishing self-mutilation from suicide. This opinion has been endorsed by Morgan (1979): "It . . . seems inappropriate to accord motivation such a key place in case definition [i.e., of suicides vs. self-mutilators] in view of the major difficulties in assessing it in a reliable and objective way" (p. 87). Ross and McKay (1979) reached a similar conclusion:

> After examining the wide literature on self-mutilation, we decided that it would be useful to adopt a behavioral–descriptive rather than an explanatory-based classification scheme. Such an approach makes it possible to at least approximate the classification stage of research. At the point of classification we wish to avoid the complexities and problems in attempting to examine the mutilator's motives or intentions or to determine the environmental or interpersonal conditions which may have preceded the act. (p. 15)

Physical Damage and Related Variables

One dimension that has shown more promise in distinguishing self-mutilation from suicide is that of physical damage inflicted. This dimension has been measured using such variables as risk to life, lethality, medical treatment required, and degree of physical harm. The advantage of using such variables has been their amenability to direct observation and measurement. Thus, the assessment of physical damage has permitted the use of more reliable and valid methods than in the measurement of intent.

There are multiple examples within the literature in which self-mutilators have been found to differ from suicide attempters as to physical damage inflicted. For example, Clendenin and Murphy (1971) found that their sample of wrist cutters was significantly less likely than suicide attempters to be admitted to a hospital for medical treatment, due to "the medically nonserious nature" of their lacerations. Similarly, Weissman (1975) found that the injuries of her sample of wrist cutters (in comparison with those of suicide attempters) presented significantly less risk to life and were significantly less likely to require medical attention. In fact, in Weissman's sample of 32 wrist cutters, none required "medical or surgical hospitalization, reflecting the mildness of their attempts" (p. 1168). Morgan (1979) described a similar phenomenon in discussing his sample of those who performed "DSH." He noted that "only in a small minority is there a serious threat to life . . . in the great majority only simple nursing care was required" (p. 94). Also consistent with these findings is the degree of physical damage reported in Ross and McKay's (1979) study of self-mutilating adolescents. In their study, 86.4% of the 500 self-mutilations that the adolescents inflicted were body carvings of names, initials, various words, and simple scratchings. Although disfiguring, these carvings presented little or no risk to life and generally did not require medical attention.

In addition, Farberow (1980), Worden (1980), and many others have emphasized the importance of "lethality" in classifying acts of self-harm. "Lethality" refers to the risk of dying or possibility of death that is incurred through an act of self-harm. As noted by Simpson (1980), "it is widely agreed that the act of self-cutting is usually of low lethality" (pp. 266–267). Kahan and Pattison (1984) have echoed this statement in saying that "low lethality behavior, like skin carving, poses little direct possibility of death. High lethality behavior, such as shooting oneself in the mouth, has a high probability of death" (p. 25).

Repetition/Chronicity

Another dimension that has been used to differentiate mutilators from suicide attempters is that of repetition. The contention has been that mutilators are far more likely to develop chronic, repetitious patterns of self-harm than are suicide attempters. Many reports have described self-mutilators who are chronic repeaters (Graff & Mallin, 1967; Bach-y-Rita, 1974; Gardner & Gardner, 1975; Ross & McKay, 1979; Morgan, 1979). For self-evident reasons, this pattern has not been reported in suicide attempters, particularly those using highly lethal methods.

Methods of Self-Harm

The fourth dimension that has been useful in distinguishing between self-mutilation and suicide is the method of self-harm employed. This dimension has been examined in terms of two factors: (1) the distinction between direct and indirect forms of self-harm, and (2) the use of multiple methods of self-harm by the same individual.

Farberow (1980) was the first to discuss at length the distinction between direct and indirect methods of self-harm. "Direct" self-destructive behavior refers to actions in which individuals deliberately cause themselves immediate, concrete, physical harm. In contrast, "indirect" self-destructive behavior refers to repetitive forms of behavior that occur over time and cumulatively result in self-harm (e.g., chain smoking, alcoholism, obesity). With these indirect forms of behavior, the individual is generally unaware of or fails to acknowledge the self-destructive elements of the behavior.

Curiously, Farberow classified self-mutilation in the category of *indirect* self-destructive behavior (1980, pp. 18–19). This appears to be inconsistent with Farberow's own definitions, since self-mutilation involves the self-infliction of immediate, direct, concrete, physical harm. Although self-mutilation may also be a repetitive pattern (like chain smoking or alcoholism), the damage inflicted is not cumulative, but is immediate in nature. Moreover, the self-harm is performed with the clear awareness of the perpetrator. Both Morgan (1979) and Pattison and Kahan (1983) have corrected this misconception by referring to self-mutilation as a *direct* form of self-destructive behavior. This would seem to be much more appropriate terminology and classification.

The second topic pertaining to method in self-mutilation concerns the use of multiple forms of self-harm by individual perpetrators. This phenomenon has been reported by Ballinger (1971), Morgan (1979), and Ross and McKay (1979). Most recently, Pattison and Kahan (1983), in reviewing the literature, found that 63% of individuals who had mutilated themselves more than once had used multiple methods. This pattern has not been reported in suicide attempters.

In summary, efforts to identify variables or dimensions that differentiate self-mutilation from suicide have begun to bear fruit. Although the assessment of intent has not been very useful in making this distinction, the dimensions of physical harm/lethality, repetition/chronicity, and use of multiple methods have shown promise. Consistent with the efforts of the various researchers referenced here, the following definition can now be proposed: *Self-mutilation is a direct, physically damaging form of self-harm, generally of low lethality, often repetitive in nature, and commonly employing multiple methods.* This definition incorporates within it the various dimensions discussed above.

Pattison and Kahan (1983) and Kahan and Pattison (1984) have recently presented a very helpful schema that includes most of the elements of this definition (see Figure 2.1). In their schema, self-mutilation is placed in relation to other forms of direct and indirect self-destructive behavior. We have modified their classification scheme somewhat in substituting the term "self-mutilation" for their term, "DSH." The reasons for this substitution are discussed in the next section.

	Direct	Indirect
High lethality	Suicide Single episode	Termination of vital treatment such as dialysis Single episode
Medium lethality	Suicidal repeaters Multiple episodes	High-risk performance (stunts) Multiple episodes
	Atypical self-mutilation Single episode	Acute drunkenness Single episode
Low lethality	Self-mutilation Multiple episodes	Chronic alcoholism, severe obesity, heavy cigarette smoking Multiple episodes

Figure 2.1. Differential classification of self-damaging behaviors. Adapted from "The Deliberate Self-Harm Syndrome" by E. M. Pattison and J. Kahan, 1983, American Journal of Psychiatry, 140, *867–872.* Copyright 1983 by the American Psychiatric Association. Reprinted by permission.

A Deliberate Self-Harm Syndrome?

A new term that has attracted some attention in the study of self-mutilation is "deliberate self-harm", abbreviated as "DSH." This term was first proposed by Morgan *et al.* (1975) and was subsequently discussed at length by Morgan in his book *Death Wishes?* (1979). Morgan defined DSH in the following way:

> Non-fatal episodes of self-harm may be referred to collectively as problems of self-poisoning and self-injury. . . . We have used the term "non-fatal deliberate self-harm" as . . . a way of describing a form of behavior which besides *including failed suicides* embraces many episodes in which actual self-destruction was clearly not intended. *The general meaning of self-harm is also well suited to cover the wide variety of methods used, including drug overdosage, self-poisoning with non-ingestants, the use of other chemicals such as gases, as well as laceration and other forms of physical injury.* (1979, p. 88, emphasis added)

In discussing DSH as a distinct entity, Morgan supported his contentions with data from an epidemiologically sized sample. More specifically, he presented data regarding 1,569 individuals who performed various acts of DSH in the city of Bristol, England, during 1972 and 1973. He also cited several other British epidemiological studies in support of his conclusions (e.g., Smith, 1972; Holding, Buglass, & Kreitman, 1977; Kreitman, 1977). His presentation was consistent with the recommendations of Clendenin and Murphy (1971) and Weissman (1975) regarding the proper method of obtaining baseline data on new syndromes. Using these large samples, Morgan provided statistics regarding the prevalence of DSH and the demographic characteristics of its perpetrators.

The main limitation of Morgan's work on DSH is in the area of categorization or classification. A careful reading of the Morgan quotation provided above indicates that he included a wide variety of behaviors under the rubric of DSH: (1) all failed suicide attempts, including attempts at hanging, drowning, and jumping from a height; (2) drug overdoses; (3) self-poisoning; and (4) self-lacerations. This method of categorizing acts of self-harm seems to be problematic for several reasons. First, including failed suicides and self-lacerations in the same category (DSH) unnecessarily blurs the distinction between genuinely suicidal acts and self-mutilative acts. As this chapter has indicated, suicidal behavior can now be reasonably well distinguished from self-mutilation, using such dimensions as physical damage/lethality, repetition/chronicity, and methods of self-harm. Including truly suicidal behavior and self-mutilation in the same category reintroduces multiple conceptual problems that many researchers have labored to clarify.

Second, it also seems problematic to combine self-poisonings/overdoses with self-laceration, since these behaviors are different in several important ways. In the case of ingesting pills or poison, the harm caused is uncertain, ambiguous, unpredictable, and basically invisible. In the case of self-lacerations, the degree of self-harm is clear, unambiguous, predictable as to course, and highly visible. In addition, the self-laceration often results in sustained or permanent visible disfigurement to the body, which is not the case with overdose. In these various ways, therefore, these two forms of self-harm are quite different; the danger in combining them in a single category is that these important differences (including their clinical implications) are overlooked.

Pattison and Kahan (1983) and Kahan and Pattison (1984) have also employed the category of DSH. In fact, they have proposed that DSH is a distinct syndrome that merits formal inclusion in the future fourth edition of the *Diagnostic and Statistical Manual of Mental Disorders* (DSM-IV). However, it is important to note that their definition of DSH differs substantially from the one proposed by Morgan. In their review of 33 papers containing 56 case histories, they defined DSH as follows:

> [W]e reviewed the available clinical literature and selected index cases according to the following criteria: 1) inclusion of cases of deliberate bodily self-harm of low lethality; 2) inclusion of cases in which there were data on individuals rather than groups; 3) *exclusion of cases with apparently highly lethal intent, such as gunshot, hanging, jumping from heights, and gas inhalation; 4) exclusion of cases of drug or alcohol overdose,* inasmuch as the direct intent of death and the lethality levels are difficult to determine; 5) exclusion of cases of indirect self-harm such as chronic alcoholism, chronic drug use, and compulsive eating; 6) exclusion of all cases involving young children because of possible organic factors. (Pattison & Kahan, 1983, pp. 867–868, emphasis added)

As the italics indicate, highly lethal methods of self-harm such as hanging and jumping were excluded by Pattison and Kahan, as were cases of drug overdose and self-poisoning. We agree with this narrowing of the definition, for the reasons noted above.

However, one problem in nomenclature remains: Is it really feasible to continue to use the term "deliberate self-harm" when it is being defined so differently in Britain and in the United States? The risk, of course, is that clinicians and researchers will continue to employ a term that has little standardization as to definition. For this reason, in this book, we use the behavioral–descriptive term "self-mutilation." We have selected this term in order to indicate, as precisely as possible, which forms of self-damaging behavior are under discussion.

A Recent Empirical Study

In an attempt to learn more about the distinction between self-mutilation and suicide, one of us (B. W. W.) recently conducted a study of self-mutilating adolescents. A total of 52 self-mutilators from four treatment settings in Massachusetts[1] were studied. The study focused on the four dimensions discussed above: physical damage/lethality, repetition/chronicity, methods of self-harm, and intent. (For a detailed discussion of the methods and results of the study, consult Chapter 4 of this book and Walsh, 1987.) The study findings are discussed in what follows.

The sample for the study consisted of 52 adolescents (aged 13–20), of whom 42 were female and 10 male. While in care (for an average of 270 days), the 52 adolescents performed 293 acts of self-mutilation. This represented an average of 5.6 acts per subject. The most common pattern of SMB was the use of two or more methods (e.g., wrist cutting plus cigarette burning, wrist cutting, excoriation, and self-punching). Twenty-six (or 50%) of the subjects used two or more methods. The

1. The four treatment settings were the Community Treatment Complex, Y.O.U. Inc., and the University of Massachusetts inpatient psychiatric unit, all of which are in Worcester, Massachusetts; and the Adolescent and Family Treatment Unit at McLean Hospital in Belmont, Massachusetts.

second most common pattern was the use of wrist cutting exclusively. Fourteen (or 27%) used only this method. The other methods employed included punching walls or breaking glass that resulted in self-harm, cigarette burning, head banging, and inserting toxic fluids into the eyes.

Physical Damage/Lethality

The study found that the SMBs presented by the adolescent subjects were consistently of low lethality. Only 2 of the 52 subjects caused themselves marked physical damage, and none caused severe, life-threatening damage. Only one of the acts (an eye burning) would qualify as a severe form of self-mutilation, and this incident was by no means life-threatening. Conversely, the physical damage caused by subjects was consistently in the superficial to moderate range. Of the subjects, 91% caused themselves no more than moderate physical harm, and of these, 68% caused either superficial or mild damage. These findings lend further support to the idea that self-mutilative acts are typically of low lethality.

Repetition/Chronicity

The study also found that 60% of the subjects were chronic repeaters, in that prior to or during care they had mutilated themselves five times or more. This percentage was less than others have reported (e.g., Pattison & Kahan, 1983). Even so, it was consistent with the idea that the majority of mutilators performed the behavior repeatedly. This is not the case for most suicide attempters.

Methods of Self-Harm

The study also found that 50% of the sample employed multiple methods of SMB, with the favorite being a combination of wrist cutting and self-punching. Since 50% of the sample did *not* use multiple methods, this characteristic was not especially useful in and of itself in distinguishing SMB from suicide.

Intent

In this study, the motivation or intent of mutilators regarding their acts was reasonably useful in making the distinction between SMB and suicide. The study found that only 7 (13%) of the subjects indicated a relationship between a wish to die and their self-mutilating acts. The large majority of subjects cited anger, tension, depression, and interpersonal issues as reasons for causing self-harm. Consistent with this finding were the staff's assessments of the suicidal intent of the study subjects. Staff members judged only 2 (4%) of the 52 self-mutilators to be suicidal at the time of their self-mutilating acts.

In summary, the constellation of low lethality, chronic repetition, multiple methods, and an absence of death-oriented thoughts was generally effective in distinguishing self-mutilation from more serious forms of self-harm. At least for this sample, low lethality and the absence of death-oriented thoughts were the more useful aspects in making the distinction. Chronic repetition and the use of multiple methods, although less frequent in occurrence, nonetheless were present for at least half of the subjects studied.

Self-Mutilators Who Also Perform Suicidal Acts

Although it may be possible to differentiate self-mutilative *behavior* from suicidal *behavior*, it should not be assumed that self-mutilators will never be suicidal. An important finding in the study described above was that 16 (or 31%) of the 52 mutilators had made serious suicide attempts while in care or shortly before. These attempts occurred at times other than when the subjects were actively self-mutilating. The specific suicidal behaviors included 12 incidents of potentially lethal overdose, 3 attempts at hanging, and 1 attempt to jump from a high place. This suggests that while the intent of these adolescents regarding their self-mutilation was not suicidal, their behavior could be suicidal in intent at other times.

In order to learn more about this subgroup of mutilators who had been suicidal, we compared this group (using *t* tests) with the mutilators who had not been suicidal. This statistical comparison used the following variables: (1) the number of self-mutilations while in care,

(2) the reasons cited for self-mutilating, (3) the use of multiple methods, (4) physical damage/lethality, and (5) staff assessment of intent. No significant differences were found between the two groups on any of these variables.

As a second step, we employed a discriminant-analysis procedure to compare the groups. The use of the discriminant-analysis procedure permitted a multivariate statistical comparison of the self-mutilating subjects who had been suicidal with the self-mutilators who had not been suicidal. To effect this comparison, 18 variables were employed that had been used in another portion of the study. (See Chapter 4 for a detailed description of the study and the rationale used in variable selection). These variables concerned traumatic or aversive experiences that had occurred during either childhood or adolescence for the study subjects.

The study found that the mutilators who became suicidal were significantly more likely than the other mutilators to have experienced three types of aversive events. These were (1) having been sexually abused as a child, (2) having suffered a recent loss of a significant other, and (3) experiencing frequent conflict with peers. Of these, a history of sexual abuse was the most useful in discriminating between mutilators who had been suicidal and those who had not. Peer conflict was the least useful in this regard. In combination, the three variables permitted correct classification for 75% of the 52 cases. Thus, the three variables were reasonably effective in discriminating between the two groups.

How are these findings to be interpreted? We developed one possible explanation after informally re-examining the case records of the 16 mutilators who had been suicidal (i.e., examining them without using standardized data collection and statistical analysis). It appeared that after experiencing a loss or peer conflict, these subjects initially responded by self-mutilating. This SMB was intended to reduce anger, tension, or depression, or to effect some interpersonal change (e.g., to renew a boyfriend–girlfriend relationship). When several acts of self-mutilation did not achieve these ends, these individuals became increasingly desperate. As it became clear that their emotional distress and/or interpersonal problems were likely to be sustained in duration, they became suicidal. In contrast to the SMB, the intent of the suicidal acts was not to reduce anger, tension, or depression, or to effect interpersonal change. Rather, the intent was to achieve permanent escape from an intolerable, seemingly insoluble situation that the SMB had failed to alleviate.

In summary, the findings of this recent study, as well as those of Nelson and Grunebaum (1971) and Roy (1978), suggest that there is a subgroup of self-mutilators who at times become seriously suicidal. Although apparently a minority among mutilators, this group presents distinctive challenges for clinicians. These individuals' behaviors escalate over time from acts of low lethality to serious suicide attempts. It is unsafe, therefore, to label an individual as a "self-mutilator" and to assume thereafter that this person's future acts of self-harm will never result in a life-threatening situation. It would appear that those who are particularly at risk for this pattern of escalation are those who have been sexually abused, have had a recent loss, and experience frequent conflict with peers.

Conclusions and Recommendations

This chapter has presented a concise review of efforts to distinguish self-mutilation from suicide. Our conclusion has been that slow but gradual progress has been made over the past 50 years in making this distinction. The dimensions that have proved most helpful in making the distinction thus far have been (1) physical damage/lethality, (2) repetition/chronicity, and (3) use of multiple methods.

Future work in this area might include some of the following features:

1. Investigators should not abandon the difficult, complex area of assessing intent. It remains crucial to understand *why* individuals self-mutilate—that is, what it is they intend through this behavior. Perhaps some of the sophisticated assessment strategies developed by cognitive–behavioral researchers for "tapping" cognitive states could be useful. (See Kendall & Hollon, 1981, and Kendall & Braswell, 1984, for a review of such techniques.)

2. Researchers and clinicians should continue to study the subgroup of mutilators who also present with seriously suicidal behavior. Although apparently a minority among mutilators, this group poses particularly difficult challenges regarding the assessment of intent and risk to life. Since they are particularly at risk, additional information regarding the psychological or life history profiles of these individuals would be especially useful.

3. We also recommend that self-mutilation be defined and studied, at least for the present, as a distinct class of behaviors. Including self-

mutilation in an aggregrate category of self-harm (such as Morgan's "DSH") combines very different forms of behavior into a single grouping. This creates unnecessary confusion.

4. Consistent with item 3, we believe that Pattison and Kahan's proposal regarding a separate and distinct "DSH syndrome" is premature at present. It should be noted that Pattison and Kahan's (1983) sample of 56 cases (from reports in the literature) was hardly epidemiological in scope. As noted by Clendenin and Murphy (1971) and Weissman (1975), proposing new syndromes based on small, nonprobability samples is ill-advised. However, if epidemiological studies were able to confirm the basic features of this DSH syndrome, this would be a major step forward.

5. Perhaps most useful of all would be agreement regarding the basic terminology, definitions, and parameters of the subject area. If nothing else, a moratorium should be declared on the coining of new words, phrases, or terms to describe self-mutilative behavior. We need to agree on the most helpful terms already in use and employ them in clearly defined, consistent ways. Our own preference, of course, is for the term "self-mutilation."

Chapter 3
Distinguishing Self-Mutilation from Suicide: A Definitional Approach

One of the points we stress in the present volume is the importance of distinguishing self-mutilation from suicide. This distinction can be made in multiple ways, including definition, phenomenology, clinical assessment, and treatment response. In this chapter, we focus on the definitional aspects. Edwin Shneidman, the pre-eminent American suicidologist, has indicated the importance of providing a clear and comprehensive definition regarding suicide. He has stated that "meaningful definition is propaedeutic to effective remediation and that what the field . . . most desperately requires is a clarifying discussion of the definitions of suicide—definitions that can usefully be applied to needful persons" (1985, p. 197). We agree with this statement and believe that if the word "self-mutilation" were substituted for "suicide," the statement would apply equally well to the present discussion.

Over the years, Shneidman has proposed several definitions of suicide. Best known is the definition he provided in the *Encyclopaedia Britannica* in 1973: "Suicide is the human act of self-inflicted, self-intentioned cessation" (p. 383). More recently, in *Definition of Suicide* (1985), he has presented a book-length discussion of defining suicidal behavior. The heart of this book is his presentation of 10 "common characteristics" of suicide (i.e., of individuals who have committed suicide or are about to commit suicide). Shneidman has stated, "Taken together, the . . . ten sets of statements about the common characteristics of suicide are what I believe suicide to be, how committed suicide can be understood, what it is like on the inside and, by implication, how individuals who are on the brink of self-inflicted termination can be brought back from the precipice" (1985, p. 197).

The intent of the present chapter is to review these 10 common characteristics of suicidal behavior and to discuss them in counterpoint to 10 basic characteristics of SMB. It should be noted that Shneidman himself has already presented in abbreviated form a comparison between the 10 characteristics of suicide and what he calls "parasuicide" (1985, pp. 214–219). We have chosen to expand on his discussion and, in the process, to identify several points of disagreement. In presenting this comparison, we hope that a comprehensive definition of self-mutilation will emerge, similar to that provided by Shneidman for suicide.

At the outset, a clarification regarding terminology is important. We have chosen not to employ the term "parasuicide" in this book (cf. Kreitman *et al.*, 1969; Shneidman, 1985). As noted by Shneidman, the prefix "para-" means "'similar but not identical with a true condition'" (1985, p. 214). The contention here is that self-mutilation is in many ways distinctly different from and therefore not "similar to" suicide. Ten important points of divergence are reviewed in this chapter. In addition, other ways in which self-mutilation differs from suicide have been discussed in Chapters 1 and 2. As a result, the term "parasuicide" and other similar terms, such as "focal suicide" or "partial suicide" (Menninger, 1938), are not used here. To employ such terms would be confusing or even contradictory. Instead, the term "self-mutilation" is used throughout this book, with the exception of Chapter 8 on "self-injurious behavior" (SIB).

As a further clarification, in discussing the 10 common characteristics of mutilation, we are referring specifically to Type III forms of behavior as described in Chapter 1. Thus, the characteristics presented here are seen as applying to the mild to moderate forms of SMB, such as wrist cutting or excoriation. The characteristics discussed here therefore do not apply to Type IV self-mutilation (i.e., the severe, bizarre forms of the behavior that are generally associated with acute psychotic states).

Definitions of Suicide versus Self-Mutilation: A Comparison

Table 3.1 presents a concise outline of the text that follows. As the table indicates, Shneidman has proposed that suicidal individuals typically share 10 common characteristics. In contradistinction to these 10 items, we have proposed 10 items as characteristic of self-mutilators. Although Shneidman has made a similar comparison in *Definition of Suicide*, the characteristics listed here under "self-mutilation" reflect our own opinions, not Shneidman's. Those interested in the "characteristics of parasuicide" identified by Shneidman should consult his 1985 text.

Common Stimulus

SUICIDE: UNENDURABLE PSYCHOLOGICAL PAIN

For Shneidman, the common stimulus for suicide is unendurable psychological pain. He has stated that "suicide is best understood as a combined movement toward cessation of consciousness and as a movement away from intolerable emotion, unendurable pain, unacceptable anguish" (1985, p. 124). Suicide, therefore, is seen as an attempt to escape from this unendurable pain. Consistent with this idea is the perception of the individual that this pain is long-term and largely unavoidable. Without such pain, there is likely to be no suicide. However, when this pain exceeds the individual's tolerance for a sustained period, the individual loses the belief that life is worth living.

SELF-MUTILATION: ESCALATING,
INTERMITTENT PSYCHOLOGICAL PAIN

Individuals who mutilate themselves describe periods when psychological distress gradually builds until the discomfort is intolerable. This process concludes with an act of self-mutilation. For example, Grunebaum and Klerman (1967) have described a typical sequence of events that leads up to and follows acts of wrist slashing: (1) the loss or threatened loss of a significant relationship; (2) mounting, intolerable tension that the individual is unable to verbalize; (3) a state of dissociation or depersonalization; (4) an irresistible urge to cut; (5) the perfor-

TABLE 3.1
Comparisons of 10 Common Characteristics of Suicidal versus Self-Mutilative Acts

Common characteristic	Suicide	Self-mutilation[a]
Stimulus	Unendurable psychological pain	Intermittent, escalating psychological pain
Stressor	Frustrated psychological needs	Deferred psychological needs
Purpose	Seeking a solution to an overbearing problem	Achieving short-term alleviation
Goal	Cessation of consciousness	Alteration of consciousness
Emotion	Hopelessness–helplessness	Alienation
Internal attitude	Ambivalence	Resignation
Cognitive state	Constriction	Fragmentation
Interpersonal act	Communication of intention	Coercion
Action	Egression	Reintegration
Consistency	Lifelong adjustment patterns	Lifelong adaptive adjustment patterns

Note. Adapted from *Definition of Suicide* (p. 216) by E. S. Shneidman, 1985, New York: Wiley. Copyright 1985 by John Wiley and Sons. Adapted by permission.
[a]Items in this column reflect our own views.

mance of the act, usually without pain; (6) tension relief and a return to normality. This sequence is nearly identical to that described by many others, including Graff and Mallin (1967), Pao (1969), Asch (1971), Rosenthal *et al.* (1972), Friedman *et al.* (1972), Simpson (1975), Carroll *et al.* (1980), and Sweeny and Zamecnik (1981), in regard to self-mutilative acts.

It is important to note that in this sequence the psychological pain or distress is reduced rapidly, usually as a result of the SMB or some other impulsive action. Missing is the chronic, long-term, unendurable pain experienced by suicide victims. Self-mutilators are much more likely to have periods of emotional quiescence that provide relief from their internal distress.

Common Stressor

SUICIDE: FRUSTRATED PSYCHOLOGICAL NEEDS

Shneidman has explained that suicide results from needs that are thwarted or unfulfilled: "Suicides are born negatively, out of needs" (1985, p. 126). The frustrated needs that result in suicide may range from the most basic (e.g., the need to avoid physical pain, injury, or illness) to the most sophisticated (e.g., the need to excel, achieve, provide good works, or understand the world). Prevention of suicide, suggests Shneidman, requires finding relief from the frustration that is (in whatever form) the root cause of the psychological pain.

SELF-MUTILATION: DEFERRED PSYCHOLOGICAL NEEDS

Self-mutilators are also frustrated in their psychological needs, but, as the word "deferred" suggests, their frustration is related to the short-term delay or postponement of needs. In this instance, the difference between self-mutilators and suicides seems to involve the interrelated elements of time and frustration tolerance. Mutilators typically have extremely low frustration tolerance. Very little deprivation or frustration is necessary for a self-mutilator to feel discomfort. Mutilators may become frustrated after a few hours or days of having to defer or delay the meeting of these needs. In contrast, suicidal individuals have often endured months and years of frustration before they become despondent and decide that their pain is intolerable.

Individuals with an impulse disorder are particularly likely to mutilate themselves when they experience a delay in the satisfaction of their needs. They seek immediate satisfaction and rapidly become uncomfortable when this does not happen. For these individuals, self-mutilation provides rapid discharge of frustration, anger, or anxiety.

Common Purpose

SUICIDE: SEEKING A SOLUTION

Suicide is the method selected in order to escape from unendurable pain and intolerable frustration. To the perpetrator, it represents the only way out, the best possible solution to an otherwise insoluble dilemma. As Shneidman has noted, "To understand what a suicide is about, one has to know the problem that it was intended to solve. It is important to view each suicidal act as an urgently felt effort to answer a question, to resolve an issue, to solve a problem" (1985, p. 129).

SELF-MUTILATION: ACHIEVING SHORT-TERM ALLEVIATION

The intent of self-mutilating acts is generally to alleviate distress in the short term. Such acts do not entail a radical, conclusive, or final solution. Rather, the self-mutilation reduces tension for the time being, with little thought or planning given to coping with subsequent experiences of distress or anguish.

Many authors have noted that self-mutilation often becomes a chronic, repetitious pattern (Graff & Mallin, 1967; Bach-y-Rita, 1974; Gardner & Gardner, 1975; Ross & McKay, 1979; Pattison & Kahan, 1983). For chronic repeaters, the self-mutilating acts are clearly not permanent solutions. Their behavior becomes an accepted method to modulate and reduce internal tension. It is a method to which they can return again and again and employ on an as-needed basis.

Common Goal

SUICIDE: CESSATION OF CONSCIOUSNESS

Cessation of consciousness, or death, becomes highly desirable if it is perceived as the only solution to the problem. Death is the escape from a consciousness of pain. For the suicidal individual, the nothingness of cessation emerges as the only logical solution. As Shneidman has dramatically put it, "The moment that the idea of the possibility of stopping consciousness . . . occurs to the anguished mind as the answer or the way out in the presence of the three essential ingredients of suicide (unusual constriction, elevated perturbation, and high lethality), then the igniting spark has been struck and the active suicidal scenario has begun" (1985, p. 130).

SELF-MUTILATION: AN ALTERATION IN CONSCIOUSNESS

Self-mutilators often wish to alter their general state of mind or consciousness, but this does not mean that they wish to terminate consciousness. Their goal in mutilating themselves is to alter radically their present feeling state, cognitive orientation, and relationship to the world. As noted earlier, Ross and McKay (1979) have stated, "There is in the action of the self-mutilator seldom an intent to die and often very little risk of dying" (p. 15).

Interestingly, many authors writing on self-mutilation have cited altered states of consciousness as characterizing the moments before or during acts of self-harm. Grunebaum and Klerman (1967), for example, described states of dissociation as preceding acts of wrist cutting. Podvoll (1969), Asch (1971), Rosenthal *et al.* (1972), Simpson (1975), and Kroll (1978) have all identified states of depersonalization as associated with acts of self-mutilation. In addition, Graff and Mallin (1967), Grunebaum and Klerman (1967), Rosenthal *et al.* (1972), and Bach-y-Rita (1974) have referred to the absence of pain or "anesthesia" reported by mutilators when they cause themselves self-injury. The findings of these studies suggest that a primary goal for self-mutilators may be to alter their present states of mind, to "leap out" of anguish and tension into a revised, reconstituted, less pressured form of consciousness.

Common Emotion

SUICIDE: HOPELESSNESS-HELPLESSNESS

Shneidman (1985) has suggested that the "emotional impotence" of suicide victims prevents them from seeing any solution beyond cessation. Their primary feeling state is described as one of hopelessness-helplessness. This feeling state includes, for Shneidman, the emotions traditionally linked with suicide (e.g., shame, guilt, rage, sadness, loneliness, etc.). Suicides feel helpless because they perceive themselves to have no control over their internal pain and external circumstances. They feel hopeless because they see no end to the unendurable suffering.

SELF-MUTILATION: ALIENATION

During periods of escalating tension, self-mutilators feel increasingly detached from themselves and others. They report feeling emotionally cut off, decentered, and empty (Grunebaum & Klerman, 1967; Podvoll, 1969; Asch, 1971; Rosenthal *et al.*, 1972). They also describe intense feelings of being rejected and isolated from others (e.g., Pao, 1969; Podvoll, 1969; Ross & McKay, 1979). In short, self-mutilators feel both intrapersonally and interpersonally alienated. However, unlike suicides, mutilators do have a method available (their self-mutilating acts) to reduce their discomfort. Moreover, with this method at their disposal, they know that their suffering is time-limited. Thus, they feel neither truly helpless nor hopeless.

The act of self-mutilation rapidly reverses these feelings of alienation. Tension, anger, or anxiety is diminished. In addition, the self-mutilation may reduce isolation, since significant others often react with alarm and intensify their involvement with the mutilator.

Common Internal Attitude

SUICIDE: AMBIVALENCE

Although suicidal individuals are desperate to escape from intolerable pain through cessation, they also wish to be saved from death. Their ambivalence consists of wishing for death as the final solution while simultaneously hoping for rescue and a better life. As Shneidman has stated,

> [T]he prototypical suicidal state is one in which an individual cuts his throat and cries for help at the same time, and is genuine in both of these acts. This non-Aristotelian [i.e., logically contradictory] accommodation to the psychological realities of mental life is called ambivalence. It is the common internal attitude toward suicide: To feel that one has to do it and, simultaneously, to yearn (and even to plan) for rescue and intervention. (1985, p. 135)

SELF-MUTILATION: RESIGNATION

Self-mutilation serves a very useful function: It reduces tension and diminishes alienation, allowing the individual to become reinvolved in life. The resulting wound or scar is a modest price to pay, given the reward. Over time, self-mutilators become resigned to the necessity of occasional self-inflicted wounds. They make such comments as "I've done it for years," "I'm used to it," and "That's just the way I am." Rarely have mutilators been reported to cite ambivalence at the time of inflicting self-harm. Instead, they consistently refer to the painful tension, anger, agitation, or emptiness about which something *must* be done (Grunebaum & Klerman, 1967; Gardner & Gardner, 1975). Thus, they seem driven and resigned to committing these acts.

Ambivalence is inevitable with suicide. Suicide is the ultimate choice: to live or die. For the mutilator, much less is at stake. The price paid consists of momentary physical discomfort, a scar, and some short-term social disapproval.

Like suicides, self-mutilators hope for rescue. However, mutilators can be rescued or salvaged *after* the act. For self-mutilators, the fantasied rescue is from the periodic cycles of escalating tension and social isolation, rather than from the all-or-nothing act of cessation.

Common Cognitive State

SUICIDE: CONSTRICTION

Shneidman (1985) explains that suicidal thought is typically dichotomous. Thought is formulated in all-or-nothing terms; no other rational alternatives are considered to be available by the suicidal mind. He has stated,

> I am not one who believes that suicide is best understood as a psychosis, a neurosis, or a character disorder. I believe that it is much more accurately seen as a more or less transient psychological constriction of affect and intellect. Synonyms for constriction are a tunneling or focusing or narrowing of the range of options usually available to *that* individual's consciousness when the mind is not panicked into dichotomous thinking: either some specific (almost magical) total solution *or* cessation: all or nothing. (1985, p. 138)

Shneidman has also suggested that any intervention with suicidal individuals must begin with this constriction and distorted dichotomization.

SELF-MUTILATION: FRAGMENTATION

The cognitive state of self-mutilators is generally fragmented in several ways. First of all, for those individuals who experience dissociation or depersonalization at the time of self-mutilating, thought processes have become disorganized and diffuse. This form of cognition is characterized not by tunnel vision, but by an unfocused, scattered vision.

In addition, self-mutilators are often fragmented in their decision making as to how to reduce tension. Mutilators often respond to escalating tension by exhibiting an unintegrated (fragmented) range of impulsive acts. As noted in Chapter 4, in the discussion of an empirical study of adolescent self-mutilators, these individuals tend to act impulsively in a variety of ways: self-cutting, violence toward others, aggressive behavior, alcohol and drug abuse, and running away. Each of these behaviors can be viewed as an attempt at tension reduction and release.

"Fragmentation," therefore, refers here to cognition that encompasses several ways of coping with distress. However, each selection or method is limited in its usefulness. As a whole, these methods are unintegrated, random, and fundamentally self-damaging.

Common Interpersonal Act

SUICIDE: COMMUNICATION OF INTENTION

Shneidman (1985) has reported that of completed suicides, 80% have communicated their intent to others prior to the commission of the act. This communication reflects their ambivalence and characteristically includes such behavior as saying goodbye to loved ones, giving away prized possessions, and making final legal or financial arrangements. In addition, an individual's communication may take the less direct form of behaving in ways that are markedly different from his or her usual behavior patterns. "It is a sad and paradoxical thing to note that the common interpersonal act of suicide is not hostility, not rage or destruction, not even the kind of withdrawal that does not have its own intended message, but communication of intention" (Shneidman, 1985, p. 144).

SELF-MUTILATION: COERCION

The commission of self-mutilating acts wields tremendous power within relationships. These acts are generally perceived by others to be so extreme and repugnant that the behaviors cause major shifts and responses within relationships (see Matthews, 1968; Podvoll, 1969; Simpson, 1975; Ross & McKay, 1979). Mutilators become keenly aware of the impact of their acts of self-harm on others. They may then employ these behaviors as a means to elicit or terminate a response from others.

We use the term "coercion" here in the sense defined by Gerald Patterson (1976): that of "control-by-pain" (p. 269). Interpersonal acts of coercion related to self-mutilation probably follow a sequence such as the following: (1) An individual (who is predisposed to self-mutilating) experiences mounting intolerable tension in response to an interpersonal conflict or loss; (2) persons in the immediate environment respond insufficiently to reduce this tension; (3) the self-mutilating act is performed by the individual; (4) persons in the immediate environment become aware of the act; (5) these persons recoil, are alarmed, and "experience pain" due to the self-mutilation; (6) these persons provide a response desired by the mutilator, such as nurturance, protectiveness, reinvolvement, angry condemnation, or the like.

As Shneidman (1985) has indicated, there is danger in using such terms as "coercion" or "manipulation" in that "they seem to add only an emotional, even pejorative, tone to the discussion" (p. 218). We agree that such judgmental connotations are important to avoid. Nonetheless, various authors (Offer & Barglow, 1960; Matthews, 1968; Ross & McKay, 1979) have indicated that the attempt to coerce or control the responses of others is one of the central dynamics in the interpersonal relationships of self-mutilators. To exclude this dimension from the discussion because of its pejorative risks would seem to run another equally important risk: that of omitting a key element in defining the interpersonal field of self-mutilative acts.

Common Action

SUICIDE: EGRESSION

"Egression" means "escape." The common action in suicide is to escape with finality the dilemmas of unendurable pain, frustrated unmet needs, feelings of hopelessness–helplessness, and a constricted view of the future. As Shneidman states,

> Suicide is the ultimate egression, besides which running away from home, quitting a job, deserting an army, leaving a spouse seem to pale. . . we must distinguish between the wish to get away and the need to end it all, to stop it for real. The point of suicide is a radical and permanent change of scene; the action to effect it is to leave. (1985, pp. 144–145)

SELF-MUTILATION: REINTEGRATION

Via acts of self-harm, self-mutilators reintegrate in two ways. First, they effect a psychological reintegration by reducing tension, ventilating intense feelings of anger, anxiety, or sadness, and terminating states of dissociation or depersonalization. The acts of self-mutilation therefore accomplish a reduction in alienated emotions and reintegration of fragmented cognitions. This is what Grunebaum and Klerman (1967) and Rosenthal *et al.* (1972) have described in referring to the cognitive reintegration and return to normalcy that follow self-mutilating acts.

In addition, via the acts of self-harm, self-mutilators are generally successful in reinvolving themselves in a social network from which they have been feeling estranged. Thus, the intended direction of self-mutilating acts is in sharp contrast to that of suicidal acts. Acts of self-mutilation are directed at psychological reintegration, social reinvolvement, and a return to normalcy. In contrast, acts of suicide are directed at psychological disintegration, permanent social disinvolvement, and an escape to cessation never before experienced.

Common Consistency

SUICIDE: LIFELONG COPING PATTERNS

Suicide is consistent with the manner in which a perpetrator has led his or her life. The act is not an anomaly; the suicide is an extension of the person's general coping mechanisms, cognitive and affective styles, and lifelong behavioral patterns. As noted by Shneidman,

> In suicide, we are initially thrown off the scent because suicide is an act which, by definition, that individual has never done before—so there is no precedent. And yet there are deep consistencies with lifelong coping patterns. We must look to previous episodes of disturbance, to capacity to endure psychological pain, and to the penchant for constriction and dichotomous thinking, for earlier paradigms of egression. (1985, p. 148)

SELF-MUTILATION: LIFELONG ADAPTIVE COPING PATTERNS

Self-mutilation, like suicide, is consistent with the patterns of an individual's life. Although the acts may at first seem bizarre, extreme, and incomprehensible, they emerge under scrutiny as congruent with a person's coping style. The acts are chosen because they make sense to the individual, given the person's unique style of thinking, feeling, and reacting to distress. Like suicide, therefore, acts of self-injury are a logical extension of key themes within an individual's existence.

Despite these commonalities, the important distinction here is that self-mutilating acts, however limited as coping mechanisms, are nonetheless ultimately adaptive to sustaining life. In contrast, the coping patterns of the suicide have reached a point of excluding further adaptation. These patterns have shifted to the egression of suicide as the only solution.

Discussion

The similarities between suicide and self-mutilation can appear to be substantial, as evidenced by the frequency with which the two acts are confused. A common example of this confusion occurs when personnel in hospital emergency rooms mislabel or misdiagnose superficial wrist scratchings (intended to reduce tension or to effect interpersonal changes) as "suicide attempts" or "suicide gestures." Such misdiagnoses often lead to unnecessary psychiatric hospitalizations. In turn, inpatient psychiatric treatment that is based on fundamental misunderstandings of the SMB can result in inappropriate and unnecessarily restrictive interventions. In addition, unnecessary stigmatization and financial hardship may result.

Granted, the similarities between suicide and self-mutilation can be deceiving. Both forms of behavior are self-directed, and both result in concrete physical harm. Nonetheless, when the behaviors are analyzed using the framework of Shneidman's 10 commonalities, it is evident that the behaviors are different in many facets, and in several ways are even opposites.

Suicide and self-mutilation are most alike in their most general or global characteristics. Both suicide and self-mutilation are the result of frustrated psychological needs, and both reflect lifelong coping patterns. Yet even in these facets the behaviors are different: (1) The unmet needs of self-mutilators seem to be more short-term, involving deferment, rather than a long-term, continuous frustration of needs; and (2) the lifelong coping patterns of self-mutilators remain on a basic level "adaptive," in that these individuals choose disfigurement over cessation, tension reduction over egression.

In most other areas, the differences between self-mutilators and suicides are more striking. It is in these areas that the potential for clinical utility in distinguishing between these groups is highest. Suicide results from unendurable psychological pain for which there is only one perceived solution: death. The victim is overwhelmed by feelings of hopelessness and feels helpless to change or effect control over quality of life. Death is sought to escape the dreaded pain—to be finished once and for all with the intense, persistent, long-term anguish.

In contrast, the level of distress for self-mutilators is radically different within the dimension of time. The distress of mutilators is periodic and acute; it is not the chronic, unending pain of suicides. Self-mutilators recognize that they can do something to make the pain go away. Much of this pain comes from an internal and/or interpersonal sense of alienation. Mutilators desire reinvolvement; they wish for psychological and interpersonal reintegration. Mutilators also sense that their self-mutilating acts are the means necessary to achieve their goals.

One of the reasons for the helplessness of suicidal persons is their characteristic constriction in thinking. Dichotomous thinking prevents flexibility in finding alternative solutions. The all-or-nothing aspect of this thought fosters, in turn, the intense ambivalence regarding life versus death. The entire being of suicidal persons becomes centered on this fundamental struggle. Everything is at stake pending this decision.

In contrast, self-mutilation is not all-or-nothing; it represents a process within a continuum. Cognition for self-mutilators is not constricted to the same degree that it is for suicidal individuals. Accordingly, mutilators show far less ambivalence toward their acts. Rather, they come to manifest resignation, since they recognize that their self-mutilative acts are the price they must pay for a restored sense of integration and "normalcy."

Another point of distinction that involves the dimension of time is that mutilators are most interested in what happens *after* their acts. They anticipate and experience the outcome of their behavior. Self-mutilators generally report feeling better *after* their acts of self-harm. Their state of mind has been altered, their tension reduced, and their interpersonal field modified.

None of this is true for suicidal individuals. They may speculate or fantasize about the state of cessation or the reactions of others, but they will never experience the results of their behavior *in vivo*. Whatever relief is to be gained is experienced *before* their acts of self-annihilation. Similarly, if others are to react to the suicidal person, they must respond *prior to* the act, when the communication of intention—in whatever form—occurs. Otherwise, the reactions of others are no more than grief responses, which are of absolutely no significance to the suicidal individual after the fact.

Summary and Conclusion

This chapter has been theoretical in orientation. A definition of self-mutilation has been compared and contrasted with a definition of suicide, using a framework provided by Edwin Shneidman. Ten points of divergence between self-mutilation and suicide have been identified. We hope that this discussion, in conjunction with the content of Chapters 1 and 2, has begun to delineate the important differences between SMB and acts of suicide.

II

*Self-Mutilation across
Clinical Populations*

Chapter 4
The Development of Self-Mutilation in Adolescents

As the preceding chapters indicate, the literature on self-mutilation is voluminous. Surprisingly, one population that has not been studied extensively is that of self-mutilating adolescents. This gap in our knowledge base is regrettable for at least two reasons. First, experts beginning with Hall (1904) and including Erikson (1963), Blos (1962), and Masterson (1967) have emphasized that adolescence is a developmental phase distinct from childhood and adulthood. These authors have provided evidence that the physiological, psychological, and social changes characterizing adolescence are distinctive to the phase. They have also stressed that attempts to understand adolescent psychopathology and to change adolescent behavior should be based on specialized knowledge, rather than on formulations pertaining to childhood or adulthood. Second, since SMB typically begins during adolescence (Pattison & Kahan, 1983), it seems important to study the behavior during its period of onset. This should provide information not revealed by studies of adult mutilators, for whom the behavior has already become a sustained habit.

The published reports that focus exclusively on adolescent self-mutilators are as follows: (1) Matthews's (1968) anecdotal report on an inpatient unit for adolescents; (2) Green's (1968) article on self-mutilating youths in a residential school; (3) Crabtree and Grossman's (1974) report on the impact of opening a formerly locked ward on adolescent SMB and other behaviors; and (4) Ross and McKay's (1979) study of adolescent female delinquents in a reform school.

The extent of this literature is problematic, in that the sources are too few in number (only three of the four studies were data-based); each of the reports concerned a small, nonprobability sample (with the exception of Ross & McKay's study); each study sample was drawn from a single setting (precluding adequate generalizability); and each setting was a total institution (again precluding generalizability to other, less restrictive programs, where adolescent self-mutilation also occurs). Finally, none of these reports has proposed a conceptual model that explains adolescent SMB in a reasonably comprehensive way.

Given this dearth of information regarding SMB in adolescents, a basic question that has yet to be addressed is this: How does self-mutilation develop? Clinical experience and the few studies that have been conducted suggest that certain types of childhood and/or adolescent experiences may be related to the development of self-mutilation. Since self-mutilation is such a behavioral aberration, it is likely that significant traumatic or deviant experiences may be the necessary building blocks for the eventual occurrence of SMB. The identification of these childhood and adolescent experiences is potentially quite useful in identifying at-risk adolescents for the purpose of prevention, and also in suggesting specific treatment interventions for those adolescents who are already self-mutilating.

This chapter addresses how self-mutilation develops in disturbed adolescents. This discussion is based on a study conducted by one of us (Walsh, 1987) that was reviewed in Chapter 2. We begin our analysis of the development of SMB in adolescents by briefly describing the research methods that were used to obtain the findings reported in this chapter. We then turn to an examination of the childhood and adolescent conditions that the study predicted would be associated with self-mutilation. We conclude the chapter by presenting a conceptual model for the development of self-mutilation in adolescents, based on the research findings reported here.

Research Methods

The focus of the study presented here was on identifying childhood and adolescent experiences associated with the eventual occurrence of self-mutilation. The initial list of conditions or experiences predicted to be associated with SMB in adolescence consisted of the following:

1. Childhood conditions or experiences
   a. Loss of a parent
   b. Childhood illness and/or surgery
   c. Physical and/or sexual abuse
   d. Marital violence
   e. Familial impulsive self-destructive behavior
2. Adolescent conditions
   a. Recent loss
   b. Peer isolation and conflict
   c. Body alienation
   d. Impulse disorder

The relationship between each of these conditions and SMB was tested by drawing a criterion group of 52 mutilators and a comparison group of 52 nonmutilators from four treatment settings serving adolescents (see Chapter 2, footnote 1). The mutilators and nonmutilators were then compared in regard to the occurrence of the childhood and adolescent conditions, using a variety of statistical procedures.

To be eligible for the criterion group, subjects were required (1) to have self-mutilated while in care and (2) to have been between the ages of 13 and 20 upon admission. These criteria were designed to exclude subjects who had previously mutilated but were no longer actively doing so, and to confine the sample to the developmental phase of adolescence. Thus, the study focused on adolescent self-mutilators who actively presented the behavior while receiving treatment. To be eligible for the comparison group, subjects were required (1) *not* to have mutilated prior to or during care, and (2) to be within the same age range (13–20) as the mutilators. In addition, subjects in the mutilator and nonmutilator groups were matched for sex and treatment program. They were also found not to be significantly different regarding age, psychiatric diagnosis, or length of stay. This suggested that the two groups were reasonably similar *a priori* regarding developmental maturity, sex-role characteristics, and severity of psychopathology. Controlling for the characteristics of age, sex, and diagnosis has been employed in many previous studies of self-mutilation (e.g.,

Gardner & Gardner, 1975; Carroll *et al.*, 1980; Sweeny & Zamecnik, 1981; Schaffer, Carroll, & Abramowitz, 1982).

Results regarding the comparison of the mutilators and nonmutilators are reported liberally throughout the remainder of this chapter. Those interested in more details about the methods of the study should consult Walsh (1987). At this point, we turn to examining the childhood experiences predicted to be associated with the occurrence of self-mutilation. We explain why these conditions were selected for study and what the results were in regard to each condition.

Childhood Conditions and Self-Mutilation

Loss of a Parent

Few experiences, if any, that may occur in a child's life are as profoundly traumatic as the loss of a parent. For those who have been fortunate enough to be spared this trauma, it is difficult to imagine the magnitude of its impact on a child's life. Of course, loss of a parent may occur in a variety of ways that range from temporary to permanent. A temporary separation resulting from a divorce or short-term placement is likely to be experienced differently by a child than is a permanent loss such as the death of a parent. Yet each type of parental loss can leave emotional scars that result in psychological symptoms later in life.

That one of these psychological symptoms is self-mutilation has been indicated by a number of previous authors. For example, a number of psychoanalytic reports have suggested that loss of a parent or a significant other is a key antecedent to self-mutilating acts (e.g., Kafka, 1969; Pao, 1969; Asch, 1979; Friedman *et al.*, 1972). In addition, several empirical studies of adult mutilators have linked loss with SMB, including the findings of Rosenthal *et al.* (1972), Simpson (1975), Carroll *et al.* (1980), and Sweeny and Zamecnik (1981).

As a result, the study described here examined a variety of childhood loss events in relation to the occurrence of self-mutilation. Six different types of interruptions or terminations of parent–child relationships were studied: (1) death of a parent, (2) separation from parents and placement with a relative, (3) placement in foster care, (4) placement in group care, (5) adoptive placement, and (6) separation/divorce.

The study found that three of these childhood loss experiences were significantly more likely to have occurred for the mutilators as opposed to the nonmutilators. These were placement in foster care, placement in group care, and the divorce of parents. (Statistical results for these and the other childhood variables that were significantly related to self-mutilation are presented in Table 4.1). The other types of loss were not significantly different for the mutilators and nonmutilators. A common feature of foster care, group care, and divorce is that each often involves separation from a parent without permanent termination of the relationship. These "lingering" forms of loss may have been more difficult for these children to resolve than the unambiguously permanent terminations of death and adoption. Thus, it appears that a particular manner of losing a parent served as a basic building block for the subsequent psychological vulnerability and deviance of self-mutilators.

Childhood Illness or Surgery

In and of itself, loss of a parent seems unlikely to produce self-mutilation. In a psychoanalytic report, Friedman *et al.* (1972) proposed that a key circumstance in the development of SMB may be that these individuals come to hate their bodies in an intense, self-alienated way. Two questions that were addressed in the present study were these: (1) Is body alienation characteristic of self-mutilators: (2) If so, how does this sense of body alienation develop?

A possible response to these questions comes from the literature on serious, chronic physical illness in childhood. Several previous studies have established a link between childhood illness and body alienation. Hughes (1982), for example, described the drawings of seriously ill children as depicting "ill-defined, distorted creatures with a confusion of body parts, gross injury, or disfigurement" (p. 707). He also indicated that such children commonly refer to themselves as "being ugly, defective and unacceptable" (p. 707). Geist (1979) directly linked childhood illness and body image distortion, noting that "any child or adolescent diagnosed with a chronic illness suffers a loss—of health, body parts, present abilities or future capacities, and, perhaps most importantly, of self and body image" (p. 7). He also found that "chronically ill children frequently discern their bodies as uninte-

TABLE 4.1
Pearson's r Results for Childhood Variables and Self-Mutilation

	Foster care	Group care	Divorce	Physical abuse	Sexual abuse	Surgery	Childhood illness	Family alcoholism	Family violence
Self-mutilation	.29**	.47***	.31***	.44***	.48***	.27**	.48***	.33***	.33***
Foster care	—	.32***	.03	.17	.22*	.20*	-.01	.13	.10
Group care		—	.15	.33***	.26**	.21*	.22*	.31***	.29**
Divorce			—	.14	.18	-.01	.15	.23*	.24*
Physical abuse				—	.33***	.17	.08	.31***	.42***
Sexual abuse					—	.25**	.21*	.10	.41***
Surgery						—	.31***	.10	.33***
Childhood illness							—	.09	.22*
Family alcoholism								—	.33***

*p < .05.
**p < .01.
***p < .001.

grated parts of their psychologically separate selves" (p. 10). This latter comment is strikingly reminiscent of the often-cited lack of body integration (and state of dissociation) reported by self-mutilators (e.g., see Chapter 3 above; see also Graff & Mallin, 1967 and Grunebaum & Klerman, 1967). One possibility, therefore, was that body image problems associated with childhood illness served as a foundation for a profound body alienation in these self-mutilating adolescents.

An additional aspect of experiencing illness during childhood is that sick children are likely to undergo many medical procedures and treatments. Although such procedures are likely to be physically uncomfortable and psychologically disturbing, they may also result in considerable secondary gain. The child who has experienced losses or who has been neglected or abused (a childhood condition discussed below) may find the solicitous attention of medical personnel a unique and gratifying experience. For some, it may be their first experience with having their needs met in an attentive, as opposed to a resentful, manner. These children may come to associate their illness or disability with access to caring and comfort (as well as escape from abuse).

Consistent with this formulation, Rosenthal *et al.* (1972) have suggested that surgery in early life may serve as a prototype for the subsequent self-mutilative "surgeries" of adolescence and adulthood. These children may come to associate the pain, disfigurement, and/or scarring of surgery with obtaining empathic nurturance. When they subsequently become adolescents and encounter the considerable stresses of this developmental phase, it may be that they revert or regress to an old "successful" pattern.

The present study provided empirical confirmation of the role of childhood illness and/or surgery in adolescent self-mutilation. The mutilators were significantly more likely than the nonmutilators to have had serious or chronic illnesses during childhood, such as asthma, eczema, epilepsy, orthopedic diseases, diabetes, and cardiac illness. The mutilators were also more likely to have experienced major surgery during childhood. These surgeries included unusual or disfiguring surgical procedures, and not the more common tonsillectomies and appendectomies (see Table 4.1).

There is, therefore, empirical support for the idea that self-mutilation in adolescents may be related to childhood illness and surgery. Both of these types of experiences may result in a child's coming to view his or her body negatively. The outcome may, therefore, be a distorted body image or profound body alienation. This body alienation may be an important prerequisite in the preparation of one's body as the target of self-harm.

Sexual and Physical Abuse in Children

A third possible source of body alienation in adolescence is suggested by the literature on sexual abuse. Both Grunebaum and Klerman (1967) and Carroll *et al.* (1980) have found overt sexuality in the home to be associated with SMB. Rist (1969) and Goodwin, Simms, and Bergman (1979) have noted that a sense of body alienation is characteristic of sexually abused children. Sgroi (1982) has found that children who have been molested or raped often come to view their bodies as contaminated and dirty. Like chronically ill children, they may also experience their bodies as somehow separate from their real selves—as alien and even disloyal or traitorous. This again may set the stage for eventual states of dissociation and nonintegration of self and body.

Browning and Boatman (1977) reported that the majority of the subjects in their study of incest victims had physical abnormalities. Thus, these individuals experienced two different potential sources of body alienation. In addition, Goodwin *et al.* (1979) and Gross (1979) have found high incidences of self-destructive behavior in incest victims.

In a similar vein, the literature regarding the physical abuse of children has identified connections between victimization and body image problems (Gelles, 1980). The literature on physical abuse has also reported associations among abuse, marital violence, and family alcohol abuse, all of which were examined in the study described here. This triad of impulsive behaviors has been found repeatedly to be reciprocally related (Lystad, 1975; Straus, 1979; Gelles, 1980; Steinmetz, 1980; Rosenbaum & O'Leary, 1981).

The present study provided empirical support for the relationship between sexual and physical abuse in childhood and the later development of self-mutilation in adolescence. Self-mutilating teens were significantly more likely to have suffered these traumatic experiences than the comparison group of nonmutilators. Indeed, these abuse variables yielded among the highest correlations of the five childhood conditions examined in the study (see Table 4.1). It would appear, therefore, that physical and sexual abuse are especially important contributors in the subsequent development of self-mutilation during adolescence.

Self-Destructive Behavior within the Family

The study also examined a range of self-damaging behaviors within the families of the study subjects, including acts of self-mutilation, suicide, alcohol abuse, and drug abuse. It seemed inherently logical that the mutilators might have learned to mutilate themselves through direct observation of family members committing self-destructive acts. In a similar way, it seemed possible that the mutilators had been influenced by the self-destructive substance abuse of family members.

The study found that only one of these four self-destructive family patterns was associated with self-mutilation: family alcohol abuse (see Table 4.1). This was a particularly interesting finding, since it indicated that straightforward parental modeling of self-mutilative or suicidal behaviors was not sufficient to account for SMB in offspring. This indirectly lends support to the need for a more complex conceptual model, such as the one presented below.

Family Violence

The last childhood variable studied here was family violence. This was defined as recurrent aggression in the family that did not directly involve the child. In these situations, the child may have observed violence but was not a victim of it in a concrete, physical way. As predicted, the mutilating adolescents were found to be significantly more likely to have experienced family violence in their childhoods than the comparison group of nonmutilators. This finding added to the overall dismal picture of the childhood experiences that these mutilators had endured.

Summary of Childhood Experiences
Associated with Self-Mutilation

The profile that emerged was that the childhood experiences of the self-mutilators were replete with dysfunction and psychopathology. The study found that the mutilators were significantly more likely to have experienced losses during childhood through placements outside the family and through divorce. They were found to have suffered from poor health during childhood, culminating in serious or chronic illness and/or surgery. They were also found to have been victimized both physically and sexually, and to have repeatedly witnessed violence, impulsivity, and alcohol abuse. The combined impact of these experiences may have included the following: (1) the establishment of a vulnerability to loss, due to traumatic separations from parents; (2) the establishment of the role of victim, due to the recurrent episodes of abuse (which, in most cases, were inflicted by significant others); (3) the establishment of a distorted and alienated body image, based on their experiences of physical illness and abuse; and, finally, (4) the establishment of a predilection toward impulsive, self-destructive behavior, based on their exposure to violence, alcohol abuse, and victimization. The result was therefore the establishment of a loss-vulnerable individual trained to be violent, impulsive, and substance-abusing, with a strong tendency toward self-abuse or self-victimization.

This being said, it is nonetheless important to note that not all children who have endured such experiences become self-mutilators. It is likely that certain other experiences or "ingredients" must be added during adolescence in order to trigger the eventual implosive act of self-mutilation. These experiences are discussed in the next section.

Adolescent Conditions and Self-Mutilation

As noted above, very little research has been conducted on adolescent self-mutilators. This lack of data makes it quite difficult to identify conditions that might trigger self-mutilation during adolescence. General knowledge regarding adolescent development and clinical experience with mutilators are the best sources of conjecture regarding adolescent SMB. This section describes the adolescent conditions that were predicted to be associated with self-mutilation, and also the findings that were obtained in the study. (Statistical results for the latter are presented in Table 4.2).

Recent Loss

Given the traumatic histories of these self-mutilators as children, it seemed likely that they would be subject to additional losses as adolescents. Having experienced separations from parents during childhood, including high rates of foster care placement, group care placement, and divorce, these children were predicted to reach adolescence in a precarious state. Additional losses during adolescence were seen as likely to precipitate psychological crises and perhaps self-mutilation.

The study found that loss during adolescence was significantly more common for the group of mutilators than for the nonmutilators. These losses were generally due to breakup of important peer relationships, relocation of the family home, or separation from family due to placement in residential treatment. Thus, it appeared that these types of losses did serve to precipitate self-mutilation during adolescence if other predisposing events from childhood had also occurred.

Peer Conflict and Intimacy Problems

Given their histories of loss and abuse, it would be expected that these adolescents would have difficulty achieving stable and intimate relationships with peers. Mutilators were seen as likely to be distrustful and skeptical regarding human relationships and to experience considerable conflict when interacting with peers. Their backgrounds of violence and abuse were predicted to provide poor training in basic techniques of conflict resolution.

These expectations were confirmed in the study: The adolescent mutilators proved to be significantly more likely than the nonmutilators to have conflict with peers while in care. Contrary to what had been predicted, however, these mutilators also proved to be more socially active than their nonmutilating peers at the treatment programs. These results were interesting, in that they revealed that the

TABLE 4.2
Pearson's r Results for Adolescent Variables and Self-Mutilation

	Recent loss	Alcohol abuse	Drug abuse	Eating disorder	Illness	Inattentive to appearance	Sexual identity distress	Inactive with friends	Peer conflict
Self-mutilation	.33***	.25**	.26**	.58***	.55***	.34***	.50***	−.23*	.27**
Recent loss	—	.04	.03	.31***	.31***	−.06	.19	−.10	−.14
Alcohol abuse		—	.43***	.09	−.08	.19	.13	.02	.23
Drug abuse			—	.17	−.03	.18	.21*	−.07	.26**
Eating disorder				—	.42***	.22*	.30***	−.01	.02
Illness					—	.15	.30***	−.02	.07
Inattentive to appearance						—	.22*	.13	.17
Sexual identity distress							—	−.05	.30***
Inactive with friends								—	−.08

*p < .05.
**p < .01.
***p < .001.

68

mutilating adolescents were not withdrawn or asocial. Rather, they seemed especially active in relationships within the deviant peer group. Within the treatment settings, they tended to have many short-term, conflictual, combative relationships. However, they tended to avoid interactions with less disturbed peers outside the treatment settings. Thus, another activating factor in adolescent self-mutilation was found to consist of relationship losses due to peer conflict and relationship instability within their treatment programs.

Body Alienation

Another major developmental challenge for disturbed adolescents is coping with the physical changes of puberty. Even normal adolescents experience considerable distress over these bodily changes. As Malmquist (1978) has noted, "Changes in the body-image of the adolescent, for whatever reason, can be expected to lead to anxiety. A change in the body is experienced as an alteration of part of the self" (p. 815). A normal acceptance of pubertal changes requires a foundation of physical mastery experiences and positive body image. Individuals who have experienced considerable body alienation during childhood (due to illness, surgery, and/or abuse) are also likely to experience the changes of puberty as highly alarming and aversive. For those who have been physically abused, their increased body size and physical strength may initiate stimulating but frightening thoughts of retaliation and revenge. For those who have experienced sexual abuse, the development of primary and secondary sex characteristics may intensify feelings of shame, guilt, and sexual abhorrence. For those who have been or are still seriously ill, the changes of puberty may amplify their feelings of physical imperfection and disfigurement. The cumulative impact of these pubertal changes is likely to intensify a sense of body alienation that has begun in childhood.

The present study found that these adolescents experienced this sense of body alienation in a variety of highly dysfunctional ways. The mutilating teenagers were significantly more likely than the non-mutilators (1) to have eating disorders, such as anorexia, bulimia, or obesity; (2) to be inattentive to their physical appearance; (3) to express distress over sexual identity; and (4) to have current serious and/or chronic illness. In fact, of these variables, the relationship between eating disorders and SMB yielded the highest correlational results in the study, followed by adolescent illness and sexual identify distress (see Table 4.2). Thus, the body alienation variables emerged—as a group—as the strongest predictors of adolescent SMB.

It is clear that self-mutilation was only one way in which these adolescents expressed their body alienation. For most, there was a pervasive pattern of disrespect, discomfort, and debasement of their physical selves. Self-mutilation was simply the most dramatic form of expression of this bodily disaffection.

Impulse Disorder

As noted above, the self-mutilators in the study had typically witnessed their parents coping with stress in highly impulsive ways (e.g., through child abuse, violence, and alcohol abuse). Given these histories, it is not surprising that the mutilators developed similar impulsive patterns of their own during adolescence. The present study found that mutilating teenagers were significantly more likely than non-mutilators to abuse alcohol and drugs. They also exhibited high rates of other impulsive behaviors. For example, 73% of the mutilators were violent while in care, and 46% had run away at least once from their treatment programs. However, since the nonmutilators also showed high frequencies of violence and running away, these variables did not serve to differentiate between the two groups.

In most instances, self-mutilation is an impulsive act. As such, it is one component of the overall impulsive style of these adolescents. When they are stressed by loss, peer conflict, body alienation, or other factors, they are likely to select an impulsive means of responding.

A Predictive Model of Adolescent Self-Mutilation

Although difficult to achieve, the accurate prediction of self-destructive behavior is a goal for many clinicians. Toward this end, we have identified in this chapter a number of childhood and adolescent conditions associated with the occurrence of self-mutilation. These results were employed in devising a predictive model of adolescent SMB.

The first statistical procedure used in this portion of the study was a stepwise multiple-regression analysis. For this analysis, all of the variables that had previously been found to be significantly associated with SMB were employed. Accordingly, four childhood indices (placement/divorce, physical/sexual abuse, illness/surgery, and family violence/alcohol abuse) and four adolescent indices (recent loss, body alienation, peer conflict/activity, and substance abuse) were entered into the regression analysis (see Table 4.3 for specific results). In the resulting, final regression equation, these eight indices accounted for 67% of the variance in the occurrence or nonoccurrence of self-mutilation. Stated more simply, this analysis indicated that the four childhood conditions and the four adolescent conditions were quite effective in predicting the subsequent occurrence of self-mutilation in the adolescent subjects. The analysis also indicated that the most powerful predictor of SMB was body alienation, followed by childhood loss and physical/sexual abuse. Thus, these results indicated that both childhood *and* adolescent conditions were necessary to adequately explain the occurrence of SMB. As a result, a complex, interactive model that is developmental in nature is presented.

In order to be more specific regarding the characteristics of this model, we present a pictorial representation of the model in Figure 4.1. The arrows in the figure indicate the *intercorrelational* relationships identified in the study between the various childhood and adolescent conditions. The r values indicate the specific Pearson correlation results between items. The R^2 value is from the regression analysis just discussed. It indicates the percentage of variance explained by the eight childhood and adolescent conditions.

The model represented in Figure 4.1 permits several interpretations. It is clear that the early life experiences of these youngsters were exceptionally problematic. As discussed above, parental loss was common for these children, either through placement or through divorce. Thus, losing a parent in these ways served as a basic building block for the psychological vulnerability and deviance of self-mutilators. That these children experienced divorce and/or placement is not surprising, given the severity of deviance that their families manifested. For example, as one of the arrows in Figure 4.1 indicates, placement or divorce

TABLE 4.3
Summary Table for Stepwise Multiple-Regression Analysis of Predictors of Self-Mutilation

Variable	Multiple R	R^2	R^2 change	Simple R	β	F ratio $(df = 1, 95)$
Body alienation index	0.73929	0.54654	0.54654	0.73929	0.49010	35.936***
Childhood loss index	0.78480	0.61591	0.06936	0.53294	0.20911	9.215**
Abuse index	0.80028	0.64044	0.02454	0.56674	0.14682	3.680*
Prior illness index	0.80753	0.65210	0.01166	0.48135	0.10135	2.011
Substance abuse index	0.81265	0.66040	0.00829	0.30055	0.11258	3.223
Peer relationship index	0.81691	0.66734	0.00695	0.04467	0.07537	1.434
Recent loss index	0.81887	0.67055	0.00321	0.33764	0.05597	0.703
Family impulse disorder index	0.81957	0.67169	0.00113	0.40430	0.04095	0.328

*$p < .01$.
**$p < .001$.
***$p < .0001$.

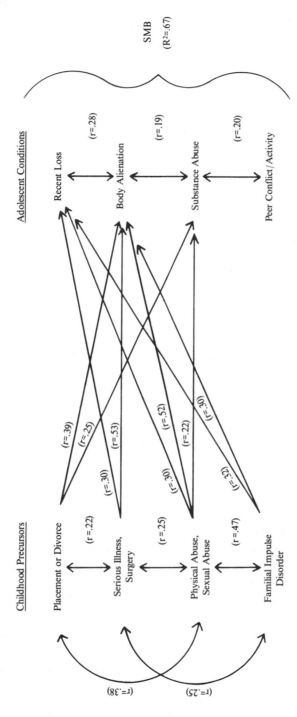

Figure 4.1. A model of the development of adolescent self-mutilation.

73

was found to be associated with physical and sexual abuse ($r = .25$). The occurrence of physical and sexual abuse is important in attempting to explain SMB: The experience of abuse may have established the role of being victimized for these children.

Especially important in the present model is the relationship that these children experienced with their bodies. The physical and sexual abuse that they had endured caused them to have complex, dysfunctional relationships with their physical selves. They came to experience their bodies as somehow separate from their real selves—as contaminated, alien, and grotesque. That these experiences of abuse were related to subsequent body alienation is reflected by the strong correlational relationship ($r = .52$) shown between these two items.

An additional source of the body alienation for these children was their experience with serious illness and surgery. The correlational results confirmed that the mutilators were significantly more likely than nonmutilators to experience serious physical problems and related surgeries during childhood. Also, the association revealed between illness/surgery and body alienation ($r = .53$) suggests that these childhood health problems substantially contributed to the eventual body disaffection of these mutilators.

The fourth childhood condition associated with SMB was that of family violence and alcohol abuse. These events appeared to contribute to the general climate of aversiveness that these children endured. Also, it is not surprising that the combination of violence and alcoholism, along with abuse, eventually culminated in the dismantling of many of the family units via the placement of children and/or the divorce of the parents.

What is particularly striking is that all four of these childhood conditions were found to be significantly associated with adolescent body alienation (as noted in Figure 4.1). Thus, body alienation not only emerged as the single strongest predictor of self-mutilation; it was also the only condition associated with each of the predisposing childhood conditions. As a result, in turning to discussing the adolescent conditions related to SMB, we assign body alienation the central role.

The specific body alienation variables that were associated with SMB were eating disorders, adolescent illness, distress over sexual identity, and inattention to physical appearance. It is clear that by the time they reached adolescence, the mutilators had serious problems regarding their physical selves. The substantial literature regarding adolescent eating disorders suggests a number of ways in which such body alienation becomes manifest. For example, adolescents suffering from eating disorders have been shown consistently to misperceive and distort their body size and weight (McCrea, Summerfield, & Rosen, 1982). They have proved to be exceptionally negative and self-denigrating in regard to their personal attractiveness (Noles, Cash, & Winstead, 1985), and to be dysfunctionally uncomfortable with normal pubertal development (Strober, 1981). These characteristics also apply to the self-mutilators in the present study, who were consistently inattentive to their physical appearance. They also expressed considerable distress over sexual identity, as well as complaints about many physical ailments (some clearly physical, other appearing to be psychosomatic).

This body alienation was, therefore, experienced on several levels. Physically, these self-mutilators were beset with long-term illness and short-term ailments. Psychosomatically, they suffered from eating disorders ranging from bulimia/anorexia to obesity. Psychologically, they expressed their internal conflicts via negative, distorted cognitions and feelings regarding their body shape, size, and sexuality. Behaviorally, they manifested diverse forms of bodily disaffection through inattention to appearance.

Related to this body alienation were the other adolescent conditions indicated in Figure 4.1. Recent loss was a significant problem for the mutilators. Generally, this occurred through separation from family due to placements or through breakups with peers due to conflict. Also associated with this chain of events were alcohol and drug abuse. Like their parents, these adolescents abused substances repeatedly.

Why, then, was the specific behavior of self-mutilation selected by these adolescents? One possible interpretation is that the SMB was selected because it expressed within a single act the collective impact of the various childhood and adolescent conditions. Via the act of self-mutilation, these individuals acted out all of the familiar roles from childhood: the abandoned child, the physically damaged patient, the abused victim, the (dissociated) witness to violence and self-destructiveness, and finally, the aggressive attacker.

These individuals chose SMB because it also met all of their *current* psychic requirements. It discharged tension in a concrete, abrupt, dramatic, impulsive fashion. It was directed against their bodies in a deliberate, self-defacing, self-disfiguring way, derived from their sense of body alienation. And it was one of the few ways in which they were able to attract solicitous attention from peers and adults. Finally, the act expressed their cumulative despair and rage at having experienced profound losses in the past and at experiencing additional painful losses in the present.

Implications of Treatment

The present study has lent support to the findings of other authors who have indicated that self-mutilation is especially difficult to treat (e.g., Offer & Barglow, 1960; Grunebaum & Klerman, 1967; Ross & McKay, 1979). The findings reported here suggest that SMB is difficult to treat for at least three reasons. First, it is difficult to treat in and of itself, because the behavior often fulfills multiple, complex functions for its adolescent perpetrators. These functions include both the modification of intensely uncomfortable internal affective states (e.g., anger, anxiety) and the manipulation of interpersonal relationships and other contingencies in the environment. Thus, if treatment is to be successful, it needs to assist the self-mutilators in developing adaptive alternative methods for reducing internal discomfort and effecting interpersonal and environmental changes. Acquiring skills such as the assertive venting of emotions and the resolution of conflicts is not easy for disturbed adolescents.

A second reason why SMB is difficult to treat is that it often occurs in combination with other forms of highly dysfunctional behavior that hinder treatment. For example, the study found that the mutilating adolescents showed a high incidence of alcohol abuse (42.3%), drug abuse (50%), and violence (73.1%). These behaviors tend to impede stable, consistent participation in treatment services. In addition, the mutilator group was found to suffer from high rates of chronic or serious physical illness (67.3%) and eating disorders (84.6%). These problems also hinder consistent participation in treatment. Thus, when these problems of impulsivity, illness, and eating disorders occur in combination, it is not surprising that mutilators prove to be resistant to treatment.

A third reason that contributes to this difficulty is related to the childhood backgrounds of the mutilators. In this study, it was found that the mutilators were significantly more likely than the nonmutila-tors to have experienced loss of a parent during childhood and to have been abused. Moreover, they were found to be significantly more likely to have encountered recent loss. These experiences of loss and abuse may well have rendered these adolescents skeptical of relationships in general and of helping professionals in particular. Thus, clinical interventions that are based primarily on the achievement of a thera-peutic relationship may be very difficult to implement.

Consistent with these findings, a treatment approach designed to deal with challenging, interrelated problems such as SMB, eating disorders, substance abuse, and peer relationship difficulties will need to be complex and multimodal. Interventions will require a broad spectrum of techniques. We have employed a combination of residen-tial care; remedial schooling; vocational training; highly structured contingency management; and the clinical services of individual ther-apy, family therapy, group therapy, and psychopharmacology in treat-ing this configuration of dysfunctional behaviors. Particular emphasis has been placed on dealing with the body alienation of these clients. This emphasis has included training in such basic areas as personal grooming, clothes selection, and use of makeup. In addition, individ-ual psychotherapy sessions have frequently targeted issues related to body image distortion and bodily self-hatred. Such an approach has shown preliminary promise in reducing significantly the incidence of SMB (Walsh & Rosen, 1985) and other problem behaviors (Rosen, Walsh, & Lucas, 1988). Part III of this book presents a range of treatment options for clinicians who treat self-mutilators. Those inter-ested in how these various modalities are integrated into a cohesive package should read Chapter 13 with particular attention.

Chapter 5

The Problem of Contagion

In a small, private, coeducational high school, five girls were close friends and members of the school gymnastics team. They lived on the same corridor of a school dormitory, trained together for gymnastics, studied together, and socialized within the same peer network. As a group, they were average to above-average students. They had what one of them described as "intense friendships" with each other.

Although there was a camaraderie and closeness among the five gymnasts, there was also an underlying sense of alienation from other students at the school and a competition for affection and warmth within the group. Each claimed to be heterosexual (although several expressed typical adolescent confusion and ambivalence about their sexuality), yet they had no close relationships with boys.

There were many similarities among these five teenagers. They were all athletic, attractive, and personable. They also cut themselves. They cut their wrists, stomachs, backs, and legs. They used razor blades, knives, glass, and other sharp objects capable of breaking the skin. Their cuts ranged from minor scratches that did not bleed to major incisions that required stitches.

Perhaps most remarkable was the fact that these incidents of self-harm occurred in distinct episodes. One girl, as the result of a personal, family, or academic problem, would trigger an episode by cutting herself. The group would rapidly coalesce around the wounded member, providing support and nurturance. They would also be most inquisitive about what triggered the cutting. Within several days, one or more additional members of the group would cut themselves. Each of them would then receive the same outreach from the others, including sympathy from the original member who had triggered the episode.

Within a few weeks, the string of self-mutilative acts would end. A more normal routine would resume. The girls would return to their studying and training, and a period of relative calm would ensue for a few weeks or months. During these quiet periods, no self-mutilation would occur. However, at times, the gymnastics training would become intense, resulting in pain and sometimes injuries. These injuries sometimes seemed to serve the same function as the acts of cutting.

During the course of an academic year, there were four distinct periods of self-mutilation involving three or more members of the group. These adolescents saw themselves as quite similar, yet they denied that the cutting of one group member influenced the others. They saw themselves as a group that had come together because they shared similar problems and had similar needs. They did not believe that they "caused" each other to cut.

Overview

Self-mutilation has an intriguing and troublesome characteristic that sets it apart from many other serious psychiatric problems: It occurs in contagious or epidemic fashion. The phenomenon of contagion has generally been defined as a sequence in which one individual inflicts self-injury and then others in the immediate environment imitate the behavior. The earliest reference to contagion in the modern psychiatric literature is that of Holdin-Davis (1914), who described an epidemic of self-defacing hair removal (trichotillomania) in an orphanage. In 1935, Menninger referred to another hair-pulling epidemic, and also cited outbreaks of self-mutilative facial scarring with sabers among 19th-century Prussian military students.

Since the 1960s, references to contagious SMB have almost exclusively described epidemics of wrist and forearm cutting (Graff & Mallin, 1967; McKerracher *et al.*, 1968; Lester, 1972; Gardner & Gardner, 1975; Kroll, 1978). Offer and Barglow (1960), for example, described a 3-day period on an inpatient unit when eight adolescents lacerated their arms. They cited individual psychopathology, staff anxiety, and peer group competition as contributing to the epidemic. Matthews (1968) described a more extended contagion experience involving 11 adolescent inpatients over a 7-month period. He emphasized the role of high-status instigators who influenced an entire peer group to self-mutilate. He also recommended "pruning" the high-status instigators from treatment programs to prevent extended epidemics.

Crabtree and Grossman (1974) have discussed the institutional contributors to contagion. They noted a marked reduction in SMB when a change in administrative policy transformed a locked inpatient ward into an open-door unit. They felt that opening the unit "enhanced staff and patient morale, enhanced . . . patient dignity, and lessened regressive trends [such as SMB]" (p. 350).

The most extreme example of self-mutilative contagion has been described by Ross and McKay (1979). Their study of a Canadian training school for delinquent girls revealed that 86% of the inmates (117 out of 136) had carved their bodies at least once. Ross and McKay stated that this astonishingly high rate of occurrence was due to (1) elaborate peer group customs through which girls demonstrated ties of affection by mutual cutting; (2) exacerbation of the frequency of the SMB in direct proportion to staff attempts to eliminate it; and (3) the expression of frustration and anger by the girls in response to the understimulating, restrictive environment of the total institution.

Ironically, Ross and McKay were also the first to question the existence of a contagion phenomenon. They stated, "[I]n spite of the frequency of references in the literature to epidemics of self-mutilation, there is really very little concrete evidence of such phenomena . . . it may be that the epidemic is more metaphorical than actual" (pp. 62–63). Their conclusion was that many anecdotal reports do not constitute hard evidence of an epidemic or contagion phenomenon.

Self-Mutilative Contagion: An Empirical Test

The implicit conflict between the idea of self-mutilative epidemics and the skeptical position assumed by Ross and McKay (1979) resulted in our devising an empirical test (Walsh & Rosen, 1985). The study was devised to address the research question: Is there empirical support for the concept of self-mutilative contagion?

The study was conducted at the Community Treatment Complex (CTC) in Worcester, Massachusetts. CTC is a community-based network of services for disturbed adolescents, consisting of a private school, a day treatment program, and three residential treatment programs.

The sample for the study was comprised of 25 adolescent subjects; 16 were male and 9 were female, and the mean age was 16.1 years. Their diagnoses included schizophrenia, borderline personality, depression, and a variety of impulse disorders. The subjects were in long-term treatment ranging from 1 to 3 years. At any one time, half of the subjects lived in CTC residences, with the others residing at home or in foster care. Subjects were under the direct supervision of CTC from 12 to 24 hours per day; this presented excellent opportunities for data collection.

Data for the study were collected daily for a 1-year period. Records were kept prospectively as to the occurrence or nonoccurrence of nine categories of events: self-mutilation, physical aggression, suicidal talk or threats, substance abuse, inappropriate sexual behavior, fire setting, running away, encounters with police, and psychiatric hospitalization. Eight categories were selected in addition to self-mutilation, in order to test whether contagion occurred for multiple behaviors or was specific to self-mutilation. These particular categories were selected because they were generally of high visibility and therefore likely to be recorded reliably (subsequent interrater reliability checks found 92% agreement).

When the 1-year data collection period was completed, the patterns of occurrence for the nine categories were analyzed. Our prediction was that self-mutilation would occur in clusters or bursts across subjects, suggesting contagion. Conversely, we expected the occurrence of most, if not all, of the other categories to be scattered randomly throughout the year. To test these predictions, one-sample runs tests were performed for each of the nine categories. The runs test was selected because it is an appropriate statistical procedure for discriminating whether events over time occur in random fluctuations or in distinct clusters. As Siegel (1956) has noted, "the total number of runs in a sample is random. If very few runs occur, a time trend or some bunching due to a lack of independence is suggested" (p. 52).

Table 5.1 indicates the frequencies of occurrence and runs tests results for five of the nine categories. Four categories were eliminated

TABLE 5.1
Frequencies of Behavior Occurrence and z Values for Runs Tests

Category	Number of incidents	z
Self-mutilation $(n = 10)$	73	2.64*
Aggression $(n = 15)$	39	0.08
Suicidal talk $(n = 11)$	78	0.88
Substance abuse $(n = 8)$	42	1.03
Hospitalization $(n = 14)$	31	0.35

Note. Total $n = 25$.
*$p < .01$.

because rates of occurrence were low during the year (i.e., fewer than 20 incidents). As the table indicates, only one of the categories yielded significant results: self-mutilation. The clustering or bunching of runs of self-mutilation was found to be significant at the .01 level.

The results of this study begin to answer Ross and McKay's (1979) skepticism regarding self-mutilative contagion. The statistical analysis confirmed that self-mutilative acts were bunched or clustered in time across subjects, suggesting that the adolescents were triggering the behavior in each other. Several times during the year, a high incidence of the behavior occurred; at others, the group was quiescent. (For example, by month, the lowest frequency of SMB during the year was 0. The highest was 13, involving eight different adolescents.)

It is striking that among the categories, only self-mutilation proved to be significantly clustered. This suggests (consistent with the findings of Offer & Barglow, 1960, and Matthews, 1968) that social or group factors were especially influential in producing the self-mutilation. Thus, an adequate understanding of self-mutilation occurring in epidemics should in all likelihood emphasize group process variables. This emphasis is reflected in the next section.

Understanding Self-Mutilative Contagion

Explaining why groups of people deliberately and repeatedly disfigure their bodies requires complex theory and multiple speculations. As the previous discussion of the contagion literature suggests, a comprehensive explanation must include the dimensions of individual psychopathology, peer group interaction, and (where appropriate) institutional milieu. The role of individual psychopathology is discussed in other chapters of this section (see Chapters 4, 6, and 7). The role of peer group influences and institutional factors is presented here. To give this discussion a clinical context, we begin with a case example.

Case Example of a Contagion Episode

Of the 10 adolescent subjects who self-mutilated during our study described above, 7 were the most active, accounting for 69 of the total number of 73 incidents (95%). A brief description of each of these adolescents is provided, followed by the sequence of events of a contagion episode.

THE CLIENTS

Rhea was an overweight 17-year-old from a primitively disorganized family. Prior to entering a CTC group home, she had been sexually abused for years by her father, uncle, and older brother. Highly visible on the backs of both of her hands were a cross and the word "MOM." She had inflicted these scars with lit cigarettes. In demeanor she was quiet, girlish, and ingratiating. She formed strong attachments to staff members and was strongly reactive to the absence of favorite staffers for even a holiday or weekend. Rhea generally elicited sympathetic responses from staff and clients alike.

Peg was a stocky, mannish-looking 18-year-old. Prior to entering the group residence, she was reported to have cut her body over 100 times. She was abandoned at birth and raised in a succession of foster homes. Several of the homes were described in records as neglectful or abusive. In the program, Peg was generally sullen and withdrawn. When severely stressed, she became transiently psychotic. During such periods, she would isolate herself in a remote place and inflict multiple, small, deep incisions on her arms and thighs with pieces of shattered glass.

Angela was a plump, physically precocious 14-year-old. She was adopted at birth and was still living with her adoptive family during her care at CTC. Earlier in her life, her self-mutilation had occurred after family arguments. Once she became sexually active, however, her wrist scratching generally occurred after a fight or breakup with one of her short-term boyfriends. Within the program's peer group, she was extremely provocative with boys. This behavior produced resentment in the more passive, withdrawn girls.

Joanna was a tall, masculine 20-year-old. She came from a family with a multigenerational history of sexual abuse. Her own adult sexual activity tended to be impulsive and was bisexual. She presented rapid mood swings, alternating between periods of social, age-appropriate behavior and regressed temper tantrums. She frequently abused alcohol and drugs. When she self-mutilated, she favored long, parallel scratches on her arms and breasts. Her mutilating tended to occur shortly after sexual contacts and during drinking bouts.

Bob was a skinny, gawky, borderline-retarded boy of 18. His hygiene was generally poor, and he made little eye contact while in conversation. He came from a family of borderline retardates and incarcerated offenders who abused him when they were at home. He preferred to spend much of his time alone, listening to music through earphones. His rather infrequent attempts at SMB were seemingly half-hearted, superficial scratches on one wrist.

Darlene was a tall, gaunt-looking 15-year-old, also with borderline retardation. Her history of extreme abuse included being locked in a closet for hours and being chained to her bed. Her desperate and incessant attempts to gain staff or peer attention often took the form of asking repetitive, inappropriate questions. She also would focus on the mannerisms and habits of other clients and imitate them for a day or two. When these peers became irritated, Darlene would move on to someone else. Her self-mutilation was varied, ranging from eye poking to wrist scratching to primitive tattooing.

Gino was a bright, attractive 16-year-old, popular with the female clients. Unlike the other mutilators, he was socially very skilled and had a history of delinquent offenses. He came from an upper-class home, and both of his parents were professionals. His self-mutilation consisted of superficial scratches and was interpreted to be generally manipulative in intent. He seemed to enjoy inciting more primitive clients to mutilate themselves.

THE CONTAGION SEQUENCE

Professionals working in inpatient and residential treatment settings know how reactive clients can be to staff turnover and terminations.

Many self-mutilators, like the clients described above, are especially "loss-vulnerable" because of their histories of abandonment and abuse. The contagion sequence to be described here began with the announcement of two staff terminations. After 3 years of employment, married houseparents from one of the CTC group homes announced that they were leaving for another position. This announcement initiated a 3-week chain of self-mutilating events. Not surprisingly, Rhea, the most noticeably dependent and sensitive of the seven clients, was the first to mutilate herself. Within hours of the announcement, she withdrew to a bathroom and cut her hands with a razor she had kept hidden (and unused) for several months. Staff and clients alike were dismayed at Rhea's cutting, because she had been able to stop mutilating for the previous 5 months. In response to her cutting, she was given considerable staff support and was urged to work through her feelings of loss and sadness with her therapist and the houseparents themselves.

Darlene, the retarded 15-year-old, was the second to inflict self-injury. This occurred the day after Rhea's cutting. She emerged from a bathroom exhibiting her forearms, which she had cut with a shard of glass. To several people, she repeated the words, "I'm upset too." The solicitous attention of a nurse seemed to calm her down. A contract was devised to reward her for no further cutting.

The evening after the resignation was announced, Joanna failed to report back to the residence after work. She eventually called the houseparents at 11 P.M. Obviously intoxicated, she said in a defiant tone that she had cut her scalp and breasts and had had sex with a man she did not know. When she resumed drinking later the same day, she was suspended from the residence and transferred to a local detoxification unit.

The suspension and transfer of Joanna seemed to quiet the peer group temporarily. No subsequent incidents of SMB ensued over the next 4 days. However, during the 4-day period, Gino began making unsettling remarks to the peer group about the unfairness of Joanna's suspension. He argued vociferously (and rather eloquently) that the houseparents' leaving and the suspending of Joanna proved how little staff members cared. He expressed disgust that the staff was "only in it for the money." He also attempted to bring Joanna alcohol while she was in the detoxification unit.

On the fifth day, a burst of SMB occurred. Darlene began the incident by removing the bandages from her forearm and scratching her cuts again. She stated she "couldn't stand being in a place where nobody cared." As the group became increasingly stressed, Peg began to show evidence of one of her psychotic decompensations. She said she heard voices calling her "slut" and telling her to cut herself. On hearing that Peg had cut herself, and observing Peg's psychotic distress, Rhea "couldn't control herself any longer" and reburned the "MOM" scar on her hand with a match.

By the end of the fifth day, staff members were understandably agitated, expressing a mixture of anxiety, frustration, abhorrence, and helplessness. In an attempt to quiet the client group and interrupt the contagion, staffers met individually with each client with a history of SMB, urging each to discuss any impulse to mutilate. For some clients (especially the psychotic Peg), medication increases were ordered. Individual behavioral contracts were devised. A special meal was prepared to try to distract the group from the climate of self-mutilation and to provide a message of nurturance.

No further incidents ensued for 3 days. However, on day 10, another burst occurred. This time, Angela began the mutilating after becoming furious at a slight from Gino, whom she had hoped to begin dating. She scratched an obscenity on her calf and said to Gino, "This is what I think of you!" Bob, the retarded 18-year-old, observed the interaction and subsequently made random scratches on his calf. When asked why he did it, Bob gave a sheepish grin and said, "It looked like fun; I thought I'd try it." Later in the day, Joanna, by now out of the detoxification unit, repeatedly picked the scabs on her scalp. Gino concluded the day by scratching his wrist several times. He said with sarcastic laughter that he had decided "to join the club," but he also became furious that his "suicide attempt" was not taken more seriously by the staff. He demanded that staff members "suspend him home," saying that he "needed a break from this place."

The pattern of events described above continued for 2 additional weeks. At the conclusion of the 3-week period, nine clients had self-mutilated on 20 different occasions. The number of lacerations, excoriations, and self-inflicted burns totaled over 50. Many additional attempts were prevented through staff intervention.

Discussion

As this case example suggests, self-mutilative contagion is a complex phenomenon involving multiple, interacting components. The remainder of this chapter focuses on four types of factors that contribute to contagion episodes: (1) primitive communication patterns, (2) attempts to change the behavior of others, (3) peer group influences, and (4) responses to staff and treatment. Each of these factors should be considered in attempting to identify contributors to an episode of contagion, and each should be targeted for intervention in attempting to alleviate or prevent contagion.

PRIMITIVE COMMUNICATION PATTERNS

Desire for Acknowledgment. Individuals who mutilate themselves generally have limited ability to use verbal communication for dealing with emotions. They are not adept at expressing feelings for the purpose of ventilation. Even when they are able to find the words to say how they feel, they do not seem to experience emotional relief.

In contrast to verbal communication, self-mutilation serves as a concrete, physical, dramatic, and highly visible form of expression. It conveys feelings of anguish, rage, loneliness, and other intense emotions with graphic clarity. In fact, a more striking way of communicating intense inner discomfort is difficult to imagine. One "advantage" of SMB, therefore, is that it delivers a message in a powerful fashion for individuals deficient in skills of verbal expression.

Desire to Punish. Primitive communication can be used to affiliate with others and express emotions. It can also be employed to retaliate and seek revenge. A self-mutilating peer group can meet some of the interpersonal needs of its members for extended periods of time. However, since the members have generally experienced histories of neglect, abuse, and abandonment, they are not generally capable of stable, long-term intimate relationships. Small slights and insensitivities are experienced as major narcissistic injuries. When alliances shift even slightly or subtly within the peer group, jealousies quickly emerge, and panic may result. At these times, self-mutilation as a communication ceases to be an attempt at affiliating and obtaining interpersonal acknowledgment. Instead, it becomes an attack and an accusation.

An example of this form of SMB occurred in the gymnast peer group described at the beginning of this chapter. On one occasion, one of the girls failed to fold her roommate's laundry, as had been her habit. Her roommate reacted intensely to this oversight, perceiving it to be an indication that her friend no longer liked her. Later in the day, the roommate cut herself and informed her friend that she had done it because "you upset me."

One incident of self-mutilation of this sort may then lead to retaliatory strikes. Other members of the group attempt to hurt the initiator who used the self-mutilation as a weapon. They then harm themselves in revengeful reciprocation.

ATTEMPTS TO CHANGE THE BEHAVIOR OF OTHERS

Desire to Shock and Offend. Studies of sexual deviants such as exhibitionists have identified that one of the reinforcers of the behavior is the shock expressed by the victim. Thus, the individual who exhibits his or her genitals is excited and imbued with a sense of power by the shock and recoil of the surprised observer. A similar process may contribute to the occurrence of self-mutilative acts. Some mutilators harbor a secret delight at provoking disgust in others by exhibiting their wounds. This shock can be sought *within* the mutilating peer group when one member outdoes the others with a more severe or especially unusual form of SMB. It can also occur outside the group as members enjoy their power to offend and drive away nonmembers. In either case, the incentive for the self-mutilating acts is the desire to be labeled as outrageous, notorious, and frightening. In order for an entire peer group to assume notoriety as its goal, the group must feel largely alienated from the others in the immediate environment. This alienation is not unusual for adolescent and young adult peer groups, especially those in institutional settings.

Self-Mutilation as Manipulation. SMB generally has a powerful impact on people. In some cases, the intent of the act is to demand that others change their behavior. Perhaps the most common example is SMB designed to restore a terminated relationship or to gain dominance in an interpersonal conflict. Also common are individuals with a history of SMB who threaten to mutilate themselves unless their demands are met. Graphic examples of this strategy come from the behavior of Angela, one of the CTC clients described above. She frequently manipulated her parents with the threat to injure herself. These threats were employed for a whole series of demands, ranging from mundane requests for special desserts to entreaties for expensive vacation trips. Because the parents were terrified of Angela's SMB, they frequently acceded to her demands. Angela later used this same strategy in her relationships with boyfriends.

This strategy can also be used within a peer group and can contribute to contagion. However, within a peer group of mutilators, mere threats are generally ineffective as a manipulative device. These individuals are less reactive to strategies they themselves have used. Generally, only *acts* of self-mutilating, not threats, are effective in manipulating other mutilators.

PEER GROUP INFLUENCES

Intense Group Dynamics. Individuals who are part of a self-mutilating peer group sometimes describe a phenomenon similar to one reported by Vietnam veterans. These veterans have referred to the "realer-than-life" experiences of being in combat. Highly emotionally charged combat situations induce maximally intense emotions, ranging from terror and despair to excitement and exhilaration. Although most veterans would not describe combat as enjoyable, they frequently say that the experience is so vivid and engrossing that the return to civilian life represents a letdown. Everyday experiences become understimulating and painfully mundane in contrast to the life-and-death experience of war. Thus, combat is seen as "more real" than civilian life, and postwar adjustment problems may result.

These veterans also talk about the relationships they form with fellow soldiers. They view these relationships as being deeper and more significant than any other type of friendship. A tight bond forms between soldiers as they fight side by side and literally save each others' lives. Here again, the contrast to civilian life is marked. Civilian friendships are not based on a common need for survival; as a result, a deep bond does not develop.

When groups of friends self-mutilate, similar experiences can occur. Periods of contagion within the group produce extreme stress. The series of self-mutilative acts are so salient and frightening that these episodes take on the same "realer-than-life" quality. In contrast, everyday life may be experienced as dull, unreal, or pale in comparison to the high-intensity contagion period. Like the soldiers, these self-mutilating clients would not say they enjoy these episodes, yet they may have difficulty adjusting to life without them.

The relationships between friends who mutilate themselves also parallels the bond that forms between soldiers. Self-mutilative episodes are often perceived as "life-or-death" situations by the individuals involved. Although their behavior is rarely life-threatening, they may see themselves as at risk of dying or being seriously injured. They also see themselves as potential saviors within a "life-threatening" crisis.

Friendships within these groups are often experienced as more intense and meaningful than other friendships because of the mutually shared problem. Their bond is strengthened because they have a previous history of difficulty forming close friendships. Their isolation from others magnifies the significance of the relationships solidified by self-mutilation.

Modeling Influences Such as Disinhibition. Albert Bandura (1969, 1973, 1977) has written extensively about the influence of modeling on human behavior. "Modeling" is defined as learning that occurs (or responses that are acquired) through the observation of others. Bandura has shown that an exceptionally broad repertoire of behaviors can be acquired simply through the observation of others. Behaviors acquired through modeling range from responses that are highly socially desirable to those that are extremely deviant (e.g., violent aggression, airplane hijackings). Modeling influences that have been shown to be conducive to aggressive acts undoubtedly play a role in the acquisition, instigation, and maintenance of SMB as well.

One dimension of modeling that is important in understanding self-mutilative contagion is disinhibition. "Disinhibition" refers to modeling influences that lower an individual's usual resistance to performing a behavior. For example, individuals are generally disinclined to mutilate themselves. They think of it as painful, disfiguring, socially embarrassing, stigmatizing, indicative of mental illness, and so on. However, in settings where others self-mutilate, the normal inhibitions against such behavior may be substantially reduced. This disinhibition occurs because others who self-mutilate may receive a great deal of solicitous attention. This may make the behavior more attractive. Also, others may manifest reduced levels of distress following the "release" of the SMB (Grunebaum & Klerman, 1967; Rosenthal *et al.*, 1972; Simpson, 1975). This may encourage the nonmutilator to reduce his or her level of stress as well via SMB. In addition, self-mutilators frequently report anesthesia or an absence of pain to others; this too may serve as a disinhibition. Clearly, if one can gain a number of positive rewards from SMB without the unpleasant experience of pain, one may be more inclined to attempt the behavior.

During a contagion episode of SMB, disinhibition plays an important role. Normal tendencies not to inflict self-injury are reduced as a group momentum in support of SMB mounts. During peak contagion periods, a failure to self-mutilate may seem more deviant (to peers) than the decision to mutilate. An example of this disinhibiting influence was provided by the CTC client Bob in the case episode described above. He explained his incident of SMB by saying, "I thought I'd try it."

The Role of Peer Hierarchies. Humans, like other social animals, form hierarchies within groups. A hierarchy may be based on any one of many variables, depending upon the group. Aggression, attractiveness, intelligence, wealth, and notoriety are some common characteristics that may be critical in the ordering of a hierarchy.

Within groups of individuals who mutilate themselves, hierarchies also form. The characteristics that decide the "pecking order" include the severity of the self-mutilation. That is, who cuts the most often? Who cuts the deepest? Who has the most serious problem with SMB? Who is the most troubled? The hierarchy also forms according to who is most capable of providing support and nurturance to other members who are in crisis.

Members who cut themselves most frequently and severely tend to have the most prominence within the group. They are the center of attention and are seen as most at risk and most in need of protection. Members who are most adept at responding to the crises of others also achieve high status.

Given that high status is important to group members, there is pressure to self-mutilate and pressure to be a savior. These pressures facilitate the contagion phenomenon. When one member self-mutilates, other members need to reassert their place within the hierarchy. They need to demonstrate that they also still self-mutilate and that they are still available to provide empathy and assistance to other members who are in crisis.

Competition for Staff Resources. Clients in treatment programs compete for finite resources. Among the most important resources in such settings are staff time, attention, and conversation. Staff persons can assume many symbolic meanings for clients. They can be viewed as nurturing figures and parental surrogates. They can be seen as links to the outside world or as gatekeepers between the worlds of sanity and mental illness. They can also be viewed as withholding, punitive, and uncaring, or as charismatic, wise, and estimable. All these meanings—and there are many others—result in staff attention's assuming important significance in most client groups. Clients who are adept at obtaining staff attention are likely to have high status with their peers. Those who are inept at attracting staff concern are likely to feel ignored and insignificant.

One effective means for engaging staff members in intense involvement is SMB. It is a behavior that is hard to ignore or put on extinction. It generates powerful staff reactions, such as sympathy, solicitous concern, frustration, and anger (Offer & Barglow, 1960; Matthews, 1968). Regardless of the emotional tone of these reactions, the responses are forms of attention.

SMB presents staff members in treatment programs with a difficult dilemma. To attend to the behavior in a solicitous, supportive fashion runs the risk of reinforcing it and thereby increasing its incidence. To ignore it is ethically questionable and has been found to escalate the severity of self-mutilating acts (Offer & Barglow, 1960; Lester, 1972).

Clients are generally aware of the dilemma facing staff members. Some choose or feel compelled to exploit the dilemma by relying on SMB as a primary means of initiating contact with the staff. Within a milieu of contagion, clients are especially influenced to mutilate themselves. Nonmutilating clients observe that mutilators receive medical attention, medication adjustments, extra therapy hours, and staff scrutiny. Clients may even be aware of researchers studying self-mutilation. The temptation becomes considerable to follow suit and obtain the substantial benefits of SMB. One dynamic that occurs during contagion episodes is that clients mutilate themselves with increasing frequency as they perceive staff resources to be rapidly dwindling.

Anticipation of Programmatic Consequences. Individuals who are in residential or inpatient treatment facilities quickly become aware of the programmatic rules of such settings. They discover which behaviors are punished, which are ignored, and which are rewarded. They discern which staff members are aloof, which are empathic, and which are strict. They also decide which contingencies they wish to avoid and which rewards they value most.

In the contagion episode described above, clients were clearly aware of the rules of the CTC program. They knew that acts of extreme violence, fire setting, or sexual deviance would result in immediate dismissal from the program. They also knew that serious suicide attempts and psychotic decompensations would result in psychiatric hospitalizations. These were contingencies that clients generally wished to avoid. The uncertainty of a new program placement or the total institutional environment of an inpatient unit were felt to be unpleasant.

Seriously disturbed clients sometimes report a need to "explode." Their internal levels of discomfort become so intolerable that some form of outlet is necessary. Generally, staff members attempt to defuse these states of discomfort via individual and group therapy and structured activities. However, sometimes these interventions are not enough to alleviate the stress. The clients instead act out, become disruptive, and break rules.

Astute clients know which rules to break. They discriminate which contingencies are tolerable and which are to be avoided if at all possible. For example, clients at CTC were aware that self-mutilation did not generally result in untoward consequences. SMB would almost never result in dismissal from the program or psychiatric hospitalization. Thus, one reason why clients may have self-mutilated was their ability to anticipate consequences. SMB was "selected" because it was an intense, deviant behavior that nonetheless resulted in consequences that clients felt they could tolerate. Other behaviors were not selected by the group because their consequences were undesirable.

Conclusion

This chapter has approached the topic of self-mutilative contagion from three perspectives: anecdotal, empirical, and theoretical. Two anecdotal examples have been presented in order to describe the phenomenology of contagion episodes. An empirical test providing evidence that SMB does occur in epidemic fashion has been reviewed. Finally, a number of theoretical statements have been proposed as explanations for the contagion phenomenon. Those interested in treatment approaches for reducing or preventing contagion should consult Chapter 12.

Chapter 6
Self-Mutilation
in Borderline Personalities

In the minds of most clinicians, the diagnostic category most closely associated with the occurrence of SMB is borderline personality disorder (BPD). In actuality, this clinical impression or intuition has the support of several research findings. For example, Gunderson, Kolb, and Austin (1981) have found that impulsive, self-destructive acts such as SMB are a useful variable in discriminating borderlines from other seriously disturbed individuals. Gardner and Cowdry (1985) reached a similar conclusion in delineating four types of self-destructive behavior characteristic of BPD, one of which is self-mutilation. Schaffer *et al.* (1982) explored the association from an opposite or complementary direction: They studied a sample of self-mutilators in order to discover the prevalence of the diagnosis of BPD. Using Gunderson's Diagnostic Interview for Borderlines, they found that the sample of mutilators was significantly more likely to be diagnosed as having BPD than a sample of matched controls. Thus, it can be said that there is empirical support regarding the association between SMB and the BPD diagnosis in both directions: Borderlines have been found to be frequently self-mutilative and self-mutilators have been found to be frequently diagnosed as borderlines.

Given this degree of interaction, we felt that it was important to include in this book a discussion of self-mutilation occurring in borderline personalities. In so doing, we decided to take the straightforward approach of examining the criteria presented in the revised third edition of the *Diagnostic and Statistical Manual of Mental Disorders* (DSM-III-R; American Psychiatric Association, 1987) for the diagnosis of BPD. What follows is by no means an attempt to review the complex subject of borderline personalities. Nor does this discussion focus on the complex distinction between BPD and narcissistic personality disorder in relation to SMB. Attending to such topics would clearly require volumes. The present discussion focuses exclusively on self-mutilation as it relates to the characteristics or components of the DSM-III-R BPD diagnosis.

The DSM-III-R diagnostic criteria for BPD consist of eight characteristics (American Psychiatric Association, 1987, pp. 346–347). These pertain to the current and long-term functioning of the individual. For an individual to be diagnosed as having BPD, at least five of these characteristics must be present. One of these characteristics is engaging in physically self-damaging acts such as self-mutilation. Since SMB is only one of eight criteria for BPD, it can be seen as composing only a modest proportion of the total symptom configuration. However, a careful examination of the other criteria indicates that SMB relates to each of them in a direct fashion. This chapter looks at each of the DSM-III-R criteria for the diagnosis of BPD and shows how SMB is associated with these other areas of borderline dysfunction. Treatment goals and the therapist's responses are also discussed for each of the diagnostic criteria. It should be noted that the order of presentation of the diagnostic criteria has been altered from the order given in DSM-III-R.

Characteristics of the DSM-III-R Diagnosis of Borderline Personality Disorder

In beginning our analysis of the relationship between DSM-III-R characteristics of borderline personality and self-mutilation, we turn to that characteristic of BPD that is specific to the issue of self-damaging behaviors.

"Recurrent Suicidal Threats, Gestures, or Behavior, or Self-Mutilating Behavior"

Gunderson (1984) has stated that suicide attempts and SMBs that are designed to exact a "saving response" from others are the most problematic expression of the manipulativeness of borderline patients (p. 5). These individuals have a true sophistication in their ability to use self-destructive behavior to achieve a desired outcome. Even experienced clinicians have considerable difficulty in choosing an appropriate response to these self-destructive acts.

Borderline personalities who injure themselves generally do not wish to die. Often, if any risk is posed by the self-inflicted injuries of borderlines, it is through some form of miscalculation. Borderlines employ self-mutilation or other forms of self-harm to evoke a reaction in others and to create an altered, more desirable emotional state within themselves. Although they generally do not wish to die, they can be extremely convincing that their intent is suicidal. They may take great risks, such as climbing on roofs, ingesting pills, or preparing to hang themselves, in order to convince others of their suicidal intent. Their acts are frightening and potentially dangerous, and as such it is difficult for clinicians to discriminate threat from reality. Real injury can occur through miscalculation if the person actually falls, overdoses, or hangs himself or herself by accident.

In the treatment of individuals with BPD, there is usually an evolution over time in the response of clinicians to the self-mutilative acts. At the beginning of treatment, when a clinician has not had time to adequately assess an individual, a reasonable degree of caution necessitates taking the self-destructive threats and acts very seriously. When the clinician does not know an individual well enough to determine whether a behavior is manipulative, then there is little choice but to assume that such behavior represents genuine risk. As time passes, however, it becomes clear that the numerous threats, gestures, and self-mutilations have been manipulative. At this point, the clinician can begin to respond more therapeutically and strategically.

A case in point is that of a 22-year-old woman who contacted her therapist the night after her first therapy appointment. In a very distraught voice, she expressed her intention to kill herself. Not knowing the patient well, the therapist spent an hour on the phone "talking her down" and coaxing her to make a commitment that she would not harm herself until he could see her the next day. Subsequent therapy sessions were characterized by the young woman's acting distant and somewhat mysterious. Following each session, she would phone the therapist's answering service in the middle of the night and express suicidal intent. The service in turn would contact the therapist, who

would return the client's call. The frequency of the phone calls escalated; by the fifth week of treatment, the therapist was being called
three or four nights a week. Each phone call had a new twist: She
would reveal very personal material or describe an act of self-mutilation as it was being performed. The client also gradually escalated the
severity of her threats and acts of self-harm. This served to keep the
therapist responding, and the client always allowed the therapist to
"talk her down" successfully by the end of the conversation.

Gunderson (1984) points out that many clinicians are pushed to
polar extremes in responding to individuals with BPD. Either a clinician responds in a very conservative manner to make sure an individual is protected, or the clinican treats all the dangerous behavior as
manipulative and is uniformly unresponsive to these acts. Gunderson
suggests that neither of these extremes is advisable. He believes that an
individual with BPD is asking the clinician for a response, and that
the clinician's job is to help the individual to express his or her needs
more directly. Once the need is communicated directly, it is no longer
manipulative. The clinician and client can discuss the request and
make reasonable decisions together. The therapist neither ignores nor
overreacts. The therapist responds in a supportive fashion, yet not as if
the situation were a matter of life or death.

Gunderson also points out that a borderline personality is desperate to believe that the therapist truly cares about him or her. The
borderline interprets saving responses as a sign of the therapist's concern, and believes that the therapist would not have gone to the trouble
of reacting if the therapist did not feel something for him or her.
Gunderson suggests that a therapist should indicate to the borderline
individual that a saving response is a poor way to gauge how much a
therapist cares. Saving responses are dictated by law and have little to
do with how a clinician feels about a client. The clinician must
respond to a risk of self-harm, no matter who the individual may be.
Revealing this reality to borderline individuals can serve to remove
much of the emotional satisfaction derived from this type of manipulation.

Since so many of the responses of borderline personalities are manipulative, it is important to view these self-destructive acts as within
their control. These self-destructive acts should not be viewed as invol-
untary responses of mentally incompetent people. Rather, these acts
should be viewed as having been selected for their effect and used in a

deliberate way. Successful treatment of self-destructive behavior in borderline individuals rests on this assumption. Clinicians must help borderline individuals to accept the responsibility of their actions. Eventually, the individuals must learn alternative ways to meet their own needs. These alternatives are discussed in the following pages.

"Chronic Feelings of Emptiness and Boredom"

It is very common for borderline individuals to report that they feel empty and bored. These individuals have a very low tolerance for these feelings, and they search for ways to feel more alive and engaged. Self-mutilation is one way to overcome this unpleasant state of emotional emptiness. Self-destructive behavior may be uncomfortable and even traumatic, but it is far from boring. The process leading up to an act of self-harm, including the threats, the preparations, and the anticipation, is often invigorating. Also, many borderline individuals report dissociative states leading up to their self-mutilative acts. They describe feeling anesthetized or even partly dead. These fears about being emotionally dead are quelled by self-mutilation. The experience of pain and the sight of blood provide concrete reassurance that they are indeed alive.

Acts of self-mutilation also result in a flurry of activity and an outpouring of reaction from others. In this way, the self-mutilation satisfies both an intrapsychic and an interpersonal need: An internal sense of deadness is alleviated, and an interpersonal state of disengagement is altered as well.

In treating this characteristic of borderline individuals, therapists need to focus on two basic tasks. First, there is a need to increase the individuals' tolerance for feelings of boredom. These feelings are experienced by all people at some time. Normalizing these feelings through the use of desensitization approaches (see Chapter 9 on behavioral treatment) is helpful in reducing the need for self-stimulating acts such as SMB. The second task is to help the patients develop relationships, activities, and values that give life sufficient interest, challenge, and meaning. These are the most basic antidotes to feelings of emptiness and boredom. Learning to tolerate boredom and to develop meaningful relationships and activities will be very difficult for borderline individuals, but this must be accomplished if maladaptive responses such as self-mutilation are to be eliminated.

"Frantic Efforts to Avoid Real
or Imagined Abandonment"

As noted in DSM-III-R, borderline personalities have great difficulty being alone. This intolerance is directly related to the feelings of boredom and emptiness. Most individuals with BPD feel empty, afraid, and desperate of being abandoned. Many have experienced profound losses as children. They fear the return of the feelings of hollowness and deprivation that they experienced at that time; these feelings then lead to frantic efforts to engage others. An escalating pattern often develops. As friends and family members become weary of these incessant demands, they distance themselves emotionally. In response to this isolation, borderline individuals initiate more drastic strategies, such as inflicting self-harm. Acts such as self-mutilation have such powerful demand characteristics that these acts are very likely to be successful in bringing others to the rescue. Few human beings can ignore what is perceived as a life-or-death threat.

For the clinician, the same imperative exists to save another person. Yet, as already discussed, there is a need to modify this saving response. For example, the therapist should not respond to the self-mutilation by providing extra sessions or extended meetings. Nonetheless, the therapist must be active and empathic in treating a borderline personality. Considerable notice needs to be given to such a patient regarding vacation schedules and canceled sessions; otherwise, the borderline will fear abandonment and will be unable to sustain treatment. A successful therapeutic relationship results when the individual sees the therapist as dependably available and generally responsive, but as nonreactive to or controlled by the self-mutilation.

"A Pattern of Unstable and Intense Interpersonal
Relationships Characterized by Alternating
between Extremes of Overidealization
and Devaluation"

Individuals with BPD are uncomfortable with stable, consistent relationships; rather, they seek the intensity of exciting, dramatic, and unusual relationships. If a relationship is too casual, distant, or predictable, then borderline individuals feel uneasy. They begin to experience the uncomfortable feelings of boredom, emptiness, and fears of abandonment discussed above. They will then attempt to make changes in a coercive fashion to bring about intensity, excitement, conflict, and intrigue.

One method that borderline individuals use to control the emotional valences in relationships is SMB. If relationships have become distant and tedious, self-mutilative acts will quickly change the status quo. The resulting solicitous responses of others create just the intensity and nurturance that borderlines seek. At these points, the mutilators are likely to characterize the relationships as ideal, as perfect, and as meeting their needs totally. However, as the relationships return to "normal," with a diminution of solicitous, protective concern, borderlines are likely to attack their partners—to characterize them as selfish, uncaring, hateful, and so on.

Since borderlines are most comfortable in these variable, intense relationships, they also attempt to create this type of relationship with their therapists. They use a variety of manipulative ploys, including SMB, to intensify and control the relationship with their therapists. A major task in therapy is to help these individuals learn to tolerate and appreciate stable, consistent, dependable relationships. As such, it is very important that therapists develop a consistency in responding to borderline individuals, no matter how the individuals are acting. In addition, it is important for therapists to present themselves as fellow human beings with strengths and flaws, thereby undermining the cycles of idealization and devaluation.

For example, a 27-year-old borderline woman presented extremely different types of problems from one session to the next when meeting with her therapist. One week she complained of suicidal ideation and depression, and reported that she had self-mutilated. The next week she complained of confused thinking and depersonalization. Another week she was emotionally expansive and impulsive. These changes went on week after week in therapy. During each session, the therapist was alarmed and would try to intervene intensively on the "problem of the week"; however, by the next session the patient had moved on to an even more pressing problem. The therapist became frustrated in trying to work on this woman's constantly shifting symptomatology. His interventions seemed to be consistently obsolete as the client revealed a new crisis situation. The client then began to attack the therapist's competence, saying he had not helped her with *any* of her problems.

This pattern of being unstable and unrealistic in relationships must be labeled and changed over the course of treatment. The therapist needs to identify these issues for the client and must become relatively nonreactive to the "problem of the week" or the attacks on competence. The therapist must emphasize that the value of the treatment relationship is based on its consistency and predictability; the therapy thereby becomes the prototype for safe, dependable, stable relationships.

Initially, this is very different from the kind of relationship that the borderline will be willing to accept. The borderline will prefer to create a stormy, chaotic milieu within the therapy. He or she will use SMB and other dramatic behaviors or symptoms to provoke anguish in the therapist. The therapist needs to ride out this storm by responding in a supportive, stable, and nonpunitive way. Gradually the borderline individual will learn new, more stable forms of responding within the relationship. With a modest degree of success in the therapy, the borderline individual will begin to learn that intensity, closeness, and dependability can be experienced in a relationship without the occurrence of frequent crises. Over time, these positive developments within the therapeutic relationship can be generalized to relationships in the outside world.

"Affective Instability: Marked Shifts from Baseline Mood to Depression, Irritability, or Anxiety, Usually Lasting a Few Hours and Only Rarely More Than a Few Days"

Rapid shifts in affect have a negative impact on relationships. People are forced to respond differently to a borderline individual, depending upon his or her prevailing mood state. Depression requires one form of response (e.g., solicitous concern), elation another (e.g., excited endorsement), and so on. These marked changes in mood allow the borderline individual to achieve many of the dysfunctional goals outlined above. The borderline also learns that mood swings allow for escape from unpleasant feelings that cannot be tolerated. If a borderline individual is feeling anxious, depressed, empty, or alone, he or she will want to end these feelings as quickly as possible. The borderline is likely to use a deviant method to alter his or her mood. Substance abuse, aggression, or self-harm will alleviate or alter most mood states, since these acts provide for rapid discharge of unpleasant feelings. These problematic behaviors become important tools in the modulation and change of affective states.

Borderline individuals may learn through therapy how to modulate their moods without using SMB or other maladaptive behaviors. Many of these techniques are covered in Part III of this book. Borderlines, however, may be highly resistant to learning these new skills. If they learn how to control their moods, they fear that they will be bored or boring and that their relationships will be less intense. These fears prevent many borderlines from choosing to learn new methods of stabilization. These fears must be overcome for treatment to be successful.

"Inappropriate, Intense Anger or Lack of Control of Anger: e.g., Frequent Displays of Temper, Constant Anger, Recurrent Physical Fights"

Displays of anger are a specific example of the affective instability of borderlines. Individuals with BPD have very little tolerance for inhibiting the expression of anger. They dislike how anger feels and believe that others should always be aware of how angry they are feeling. To control and slowly dissipate the anger is perceived to be impossible; the anger must be discharged immediately. Anger may be expressed in a multitude of inappropriate ways, including verbal abuse or violence. But anger may also be expressed through self-injury. Manipulative borderlines recognize that attacks against their own bodies may be used to hurt others, especially parents or loved ones.

Anger that is vented via self-inflicted wounds has a distinct advantage over other forms of anger expression. Verbal abuse or aggression toward others is likely to generate retaliation. Self-mutilation is much less likely to generate retaliatory anger; it is also more likely to generate caring and empathy from others. This is why SMB is often chosen as the weapon for anger expression.

Therapists are often the target of this self-mutilative expression of anger. The borderline individual may be afraid to show anger directly to a therapist, out of concern that the anger may lead to rejection. By forcing the therapist to respond to a self-mutilative act, the borderline may feel relief from the anger. The self-mutilation may be used to protest a perceived lack of responsiveness or even a critical comment made by the therapist. This process needs to be revealed by the therapist and presented to the individual. The therapist must help the borderline individual to see that the anger is being expressed through SMB and to learn that direct assertive communication is more effective and adaptive in learning to control anger.

"Marked and Persistent Identity Disturbance Manifested by Uncertainty about at Least Two of the Following: Self-Image, Sexual Orientation, Long-Term Goals or Career Choice, Type of Friends Desired, Preferred Values"

The identity disturbance that occurs in individuals with BPD leads to feelings of low self-esteem. Their profound sense of self-doubt is one cause of their drastic changes in behavior. Their changing moods and actions reflect their shifting, unstable self-concept. It is not surprising that borderline individuals ask, "Who Am I?" They act and feel in such dramatically different ways that confusion is inevitable.

Self-mutilation may result from these identity disturbances for several reasons. In the first place, being a self-mutilator is itself an identity. It is one answer to the question "Who am I?" Although this is an identity based on deviance, it still serves many of the purposes of other healthier identities. Being a self-mutilator helps in obtaining group membership, affects friendship patterns, and establishes certain limits and expectations for a lifestyle.

Self-mutilation also helps resolve guilt or tension related to identity confusion. The SMB may act as punishment that the individual believes is deserved, due to gender confusion or other ego-dystonic thoughts or actions. Once meted out, the self-inflicted punishment reduces guilt and allows the individual to shift away from concerns about identity.

In addition, the SMB is a statement to others. It informs others how the mutilator feels about himself or herself. This communication usually results in reassurance and positive feedback, which temporarily improve the mutilator's self-esteem. The saving response itself is taken as a sign that others see the mutilator as worthy and deserving to be saved and loved. A borderline individual therefore has many reasons relating to identity problems to use self-mutilation: The SMB establishes an identity, punishes the "bad" self, and elicits positive feedback from others.

The therapist can be very helpful in demonstrating the relationship between identity issues and self-mutilation. The therapist is able to show the individual that SMB usually occurs when self-esteem is low. Thus, one goal of therapy is the enhancement of self-esteem, since the risk of self-destructive behavior decreases as self-esteem improves. Most people, typically during adolescence, experiment with various identities in search of one that is best suited to their needs. Therapy is an excellent medium to assist a borderline individual in defining a more satisfying and socially acceptable identity.

These identity issues were quite salient in the case of a young woman whom we will call Christa. When Christa was 18 years old, she began to self-mutilate. She was a college freshman, away from home for the first time and confused about a variety of identity issues. She did not feel comfortable with the high-achieving and socially adept students at her university. She felt isolated and alone. Eventually she began to gravitate toward fringe members of the university environment. These individuals were similarly alienated. Many had histories of deviance, including drug abuse, self-destructive behavior, and other antisocial habits.

Christa's self-mutilation was easily tolerated within this peer group, and Christa was more comfortable with these individuals. However, she was still ambivalent about being a member of this deviant group. Christa had expectations of finishing her undergraduate degree and establishing a good career. She recognized that affiliation with this group was inconsistent with some of her values and lifestyle choices.

In her junior year in college, Christa became involved in a homosexual relationship with another student. Although the relationship was satisfying in some ways, Christa experienced tremendous anguish over the sexual contact. The tension and guilt she experienced were overwhelming, and Christa increased the frequency and intensity of her self-mutilation to cope with these feelings.

At about this time, Christa entered therapy. Over the course of treatment, which lasted until 2 years after Christa's graduation from college, much of the therapy centered on identity issues. The therapist assisted Christa in clarifying her identity confusion in several areas. In time, but with great difficulty, Christa pulled away from the deviant peer group. She got a job in a hospital as a lab technician, and she began to associate with her coworkers, who were a much healthier peer group. She ended her first homosexual relationship and began a new relationship with another, healthier woman. Christa decided she was comfortable being in a homosexual relationship, but was still unsure whether she was "a lesbian." She still wished for marriage and a family, but believed she could choose those options in the future. As Christa's conflict over these identity issues decreased, her level of self-mutilation lessened and eventually stopped altogether.

"Impulsiveness in at Least Two Areas That Are Potentially Self-Damaging: e.g., Spending, Sex, Substance Use, Shoplifting, Reckless Driving, Binge Eating"

Much of what a borderline individual does seems to be done on the spur of the moment or spontaneously. Borderlines themselves report that they are often surprised by the self-damaging acts that they perpetrate. Since the acts are impulsive and unplanned, other people are invariably caught off guard and surprised as well.

This impulsivity is yet another factor that relates to the occurrence of self-mutilation. Self-inflicted injuries are virtually always available as a response. Unlike some other forms of impulsive behavior, such as substance use or binge eating, self-mutilation can be performed immediately, without preparation, and with no material cost. With other forms of self-damaging acts, the individual may have to take steps before the act can be accomplished (e.g., obtaining money and arranging to buy drugs or large amounts of food). A self-mutilative act can be performed simply by punching the nearest wall or by finding any available sharp object to inflict a scratch or cut. Thus, when the need arises to do something impulsive, self-mutilation is easier and faster than most other choices.

Treating the self-damaging acts requires that the individual be motivated to stop being impulsive. Since the impulsive mode is so intricately connected with the borderline lifestyle, many borderlines have great difficulty in altering this approach. They lack the ability to delay gratification, to dissipate unwanted feelings, and to tolerate frustrations. Until these deficits are corrected, the impulsive style is likely to continue.

Since the urge to self-mutilate may emerge with little warning, the individual may have very little time to inhibit and prevent the self-inflicted injury. One treatment technique that may be effective is to help the individual identify situations that are likely to produce SMB. This helps the mutilator to become aware of times that he or she is at increased risk. For example, if the borderline is feeling bored and alone and his or her self-esteem is low, this is a time for careful self-monitoring, as there is an increase in the danger of performing impulsive acts.

Learning cognitive–behavioral strategies for reflective thinking is also useful. The individual learns to think before acting and to decide whether the behavior he or she is about to perform is really a wise choice. Thinking about the importance of self-protection counteracts impulses for self-damaging acts. These strategies are discussed in greater detail in Chapter 9.

General Comments and Summary

The eight characteristics of BPD listed in DSM-III-R are all associated with acts of self-mutilation. Because of the interconnection between SMB and the overall psychopathology, it is usually necessary to address most of the components of BPD before an impact can be made on the SMB.

More so than in many other forms of psychopathology, the relationship between the client and therapist is a critical yet highly difficult part of treatment. Self-mutilation is often used in a manipulative attempt to achieve a special, intense, overinvolved relationship with the therapist. The challenge for the therapist is in maintaining appropriate boundaries, resisting manipulation by insisting on direct communication, and providing time and attention that are independent of acts of self-harm. All are necessary components of successful treatment of SMB within the broader symptom configuration of BPD.

These elements are reflected in the case example that serves to conclude this chapter. The individual described here was seen in twice-weekly therapy for over 4 years. As an indication of how demanding therapy with borderlines can be, this client only began to improve in a general way and to curtail her self-mutilative acts after 3 years of work.

Case Example of a Borderline Personality

Artha entered outpatient treatment at the age of 18. She was referred to the therapist by a social worker from an inpatient psychiatric unit. At the time of the referral, Artha was about to be discharged from the unit after a 6-week stay. She had been admitted to the unit because of self-destructiveness and drug abuse. As noted in her discharge summary, she lived "an erratic lifestyle, including frequent suicide attempts of wrist cutting and pill ingestion, promiscuity, polydrug use, frequent battles with her mother, school failure, and stormy peer relations."

After discharge, Artha began her individual treatment. (At the same time she entered family treatment. This family work is summarized in Chapter 11 on family therapy.) At her first interview, she presented as a bright, plump, attractive, punkishly dressed young woman. She wore her hair in jagged bangs across her face, which partially obscured her eyes. Her ears bore an astonishing number of small, multicolored pierced earrings; on the therapist's count, there were 15 in one ear and 12 in the other. As a result, when Artha sat in direct sunlight, she became a kaleidoscope of reflected, colored images. This came to symbolize for the therapist the rather dramatic, fascinating, but also essentially fragmented lifestyle that Artha began to describe.

At the time of the first interview, Artha lived at home with her mother and older brother (aged 24). She was repeating her senior year in high school. She described herself as a talented artist and an "academic chameleon." She stated that when a teacher inspired her and noticed her special talents, she would do superior work; however, when an instructor was dull or pedestrian, she would quickly tune out and flunk almost on principle. She said she frequently experimented with drugs in order "to intensify her senses." She also acknowledged that she used drugs to escape her problems and to forget for a time that "life sucks." The problems that she identified early on consisted of the following.

Artha's father had died of a heart attack when she was 14 years old. She described her father as "a short, cuddly, warm, and loving man" who treated her as his favorite. She said her father was like the "hub of a wheel and the rest of the family were the spokes." She stated that she had never been the same since his death. Shortly after he died, she began to smoke marijuana. This served to relax her and to help her forget that she would never see her father again. She stated that she had never been able to cry about her father and had not talked about his death with her mother or brother. She described her mother as "holed up in her room for years" after the loss of her husband.

Artha's drug use resulted in a major shift in her choice of friends. She began to hang out with other "druggies," who were also involved in petty theft and vandalism. She said she decided to adopt a lifestyle of "party till you drop" and felt that "finally she was having some fun." Her mother became aware of these activities but seemed powerless to prevent them. She would occasionally confront and slap Artha, demanding that she "settle down and not add to our problems." However, Artha openly defied her mother, and the depressed woman would become exasperated and withdraw.

Eventually, even the partying began to bore Artha. She referred to her "druggie" friends as "legally dead." However, her straight friends would no longer have anything to do with her. Artha was left with a choice between remaining with her drug-involved friends or spending time alone. She said she tended to get jumpy and fearful when she spent too much time in her room by herself; this allowed her too much time to think. As a result, she would seek out her familiar peer group and take what it had to offer.

By her sophomore and junior years in high school, Artha had become a major management problem for school authorities. She was defiant and rude to teachers. She was suspected of providing drugs to younger students, and she frequently skipped classes. Only by periodically "turning on the charm" was she able to avoid suspensions. However, she was not able to avoid academic problems, resulting in her repeating her senior year.

Her life outside of school was also problematic. Prior to her father's death, she had begun to date boys. After the death, she began a series of short-lived sexual encounters with boys she scarcely knew. She seemed intentionally to seek out boys whom her mother would find objectionable. These relationships tended to last a week or two and were dominated by drinking and drug use, staying out all night, and having sex without concern for birth control.

These relationships tended to conclude with explosive conflict. Artha would complain that "the guy was treating me like shit" and that "he wasn't smart enough to dress himself." During the periods when she was without a boyfriend, she was morose and irritable at home. These were also the periods when she cut herself. Generally, the cutting consisted of multiple parallel cuts on her arms that did not require medical attention. In addition, from time to time, she ingested pills from the household medicine cabinet without regard for what she was taking. Generally, she kept these ingestions secret; she either vomited what she had swallowed or "slept it off." Asked why she took pills in this manner, she replied, "I don't know. It was like playing with suicide, but different."

In outpatient treatment, Artha initially responded very positively. She complimented the therapist on how understanding and intelligent he was, and ridiculed the "mercenaries" at the inpatient unit. She seemed comfortable in the sessions and revealed the material presented above. However, after 2 months or so, she became increasingly demanding and devaluing. She objected to the therapist's ending the hour on time when she was "in the middle of something important." She criticized his interpretations when they were inaccurate, saying that this indicated his relative inexperience. She also wondered out loud whether she shouldn't see a more senior person. If the therapist forgot a detail that she had previously mentioned, she would become furious and accuse the therapist of not really caring. On several occasions, she stormed out of the office in midsession, stating dramatically that she would never return. This was generally followed by an apologetic and contrite phone call in which she requested another appointment.

This type of stormy behavior was common during the first 2 years of treatment. During this time, Artha was able to graduate from high school. She continued to live at home and to battle frequently with her mother. Artha worked sporadically at a series of menial jobs that she considered beneath her. She did not require a subsequent hospital admission, but she gave the therapist many anxious moments with late-night phone calls (relayed through an answering service), during which she reported taking pills and lacerating her body.

Eventually, the therapist set limits on Artha's phone calls. He stated that as an outpatient therapist he could not serve as a one-person emergency mental health clinic. He indicated that he would no longer accept phone calls between sessions, and provided her with the phone numbers of a crisis hotline and the local emergency mental health evaluation unit. This intervention was, of course, received with rage. Artha initially tested the therapist's resolve regarding the phone calls, but within several months she came to accept the restriction. The therapist had to explain many times that his intent was not to punish, but to provide clear and consistent boundaries on what he could and could not do. As treatment progressed, this definition of boundaries also entailed indicating that Artha and the therapist would not have a social relationship and that they would not become sexually involved.

In the third year of treatment, Artha began to make progress. By now she was able to discuss events from her childhood that had been formative, painful, and traumatic. She came to recognize that her problems dated to before her father's death; in fact, she articulated that her father's need to be at the center of everything had stunted the growth of everyone else in the family. During the third and fourth years of treatment, she rarely needed to test the resolve and concern of the therapist. She stated that he was the first man who had not exploited her and who had not allowed himself to be exploited. At this time she settled into a job at an art supply and framing store, which was much more satisfying for her.

Artha continued to struggle with self-destructive urges. As before, when a relationship ended or became too intense, she tended to cut her arms in a superficial manner. She was able to eliminate this pattern only during the final year of treatment. This change involved two important steps. The first was that she decided that she had to forego smoking marijuana altogether; she became convinced, and the therapist agreed, that marijuana reduced her self-control and made her depressed and paranoid. The second step entailed discussing at great length in therapy her thoughts and feelings regarding her body. She described her family's lifelong preoccupation with diets and thinness. She recalled frequently being teased about being the plumpest in the family. She also focused on her problems with eczema as a child. Although the eczema had long since disappeared, she was able to link this childhood condition with her present distorted body image and her conviction that she was ugly and undesirable.

Eventually, Artha came to view herself as reasonably attractive. She discarded her punk look as fashions changed, and she felt better about herself. Toward the end of treatment, she became involved in an interesting new hobby that led to some income: She began to make ceramic and porcelain earrings in bright, multiple colors. As she refined her craft, she began to wear the earrings, but only one in each ear. Noticing the change, the therapist commented that the effect was as bright and colorful as before, but now the earrings were of her own making and were all of one piece.

At her final session, Artha presented the therapist with a gift of a single earring that she had made. She suggested playfully that he should consider piercing one of his ears; she said, "You could stand to loosen up a little." The therapist made no promises about ear piercing, but agreed that her present would make a fine lapel button or tie tack.

Chapter 7

Self-Mutilation in Psychotics

Self-mutilation performed by psychotic individuals is a very different phenomenon from other types of self-mutilation. The etiology, dynamics, assessment, and treatment of this problem are distinct from those for other forms of self-harm. These mutilators are best understood within the broader context of their psychotic thinking. Just as psychosis is at the extreme end of the continuum of psychopathology, the self-mutilation of these individuals is at the extreme end of the spectrum of self-destructiveness.

The actual injuries resulting from self-mutilation in psychotic populations range from small wounds to grotesque and bizarre disfigurement. In the most severe and dangerous cases, this SMB can produce risk to life for the perpetrators and disbelief and revulsion in others. In these cases, it is difficult for even the most experienced professionals to remain composed and disciplined when responding to the behavior. Indeed, just the reading of this chapter may be unsettling to some, since graphic descriptions of such acts as self-blinding and self-castration are included in the following pages.

Clinical Population and Symptom Pattern

The population described in this chapter falls within several diagnostic categories, including acute psychotic states, schizophrenia, psychotic depression, and manic–depressive illness. What is common among these various diagnostic groups is the occurrence of thought disorder. The thought disorder may be the primary diagnostic symptom or may be secondary to a mood disorder.

Because of the severe nature of their psychopathology, individuals with these diagnoses are often institutionalized for significant portions of their lives. Some of them are "revolving-door" patients in state psychiatric hospitals. Although self-mutilation also occurs in acute psychotic disorders, it is more typically found among the chronically disturbed.

The frequency of self-mutilation in psychotic individuals varies markedly. Many psychotic self-mutilators engage in only one episode of self-inflicted harm; others are chronic repeaters. For this psychiatric population, there is generally an inverse relationship between the severity of the injury and the frequency of the self-mutilative acts. The more severe the injury, the less often the occurrence. This relationship is due to a combination of intrapsychic dynamics and environmental factors. Some individuals who have committed extreme self-mutilative acts express a profound sense of relief following the act. They describe a fundamental alteration of the self that precludes the need for any additional SMB. For example, individuals who perform a self-enucleation or self-castration may experience a complete and final expiation of "sinfulness" or "evil." This precludes the need for further acts of self-harm. In addition, when extreme forms of SMB occur, the perpetrators often require sustained medical treatment following the injury. Some individuals are physically incapable of committing additional self-mutilative acts until they have recuperated. Another factor in the low rate of extreme forms of SMB is the reaction of treatment staff. After a severe act of self-mutilation, strict measures are taken to prevent recurrence. As a result, patients may have all sharp objects confiscated; they may be put on "special" status or placed in isolation or restraint; and, they may be medicated to the extent where further acts of self-harm are unlikely. In contrast, milder forms of SMB within this population do not result in such intense forms of supervision or intervention. As a result, superficial cutting or scratching may occur at much higher rates—up to several times a day during periods of acute psychiatric distress.

Distinction from Other Clinical Populations

Although the severity of the SMB is often more severe in psychotic individuals, it is the relationship between the psychotic process and the self-mutilation that most clearly separates this population from other groups. The break from reality experienced by these individuals is the precondition that distinguishes this form of SMB. This break with reality can take several forms.

Delusional thinking is found in significant percentages of psychotic self-mutilators (Sweeny & Zamecnik, 1981). The content of this delusional thinking is highly variable. Generally, the basis for the delusion includes a rationale or justification for the self-mutilation itself. Although this rationale is illogical (as is the case with all delusional thinking), for the patient the delusion is the compelling *reason* for self-mutilating. For everyone else, the justification for the self-mutilation is nonsensical and absurd; for the patient, the self-mutilation represents a natural, inescapable conclusion based on his or her idiosyncratic thought process.

The impact of the delusional system may be exacerbated by other features of the psychotic thought process, such as concrete thinking. A case in point is that of a 25-year-old schizophrenic woman who had recently given birth to a child. The woman was judged to be legally incompetent, and the child was removed by state authorities in order to place it for adoption at birth. Due to her psychosis, the patient believed the child was taken away from her because she had been unable to breast-feed the baby. Furthermore, she felt she had not been able to breast-feed the baby because her nipples were "blocked up" (i.e., clogged with some substance that prevented the flow of milk). Consistent with this delusional belief, she conceived a concrete solution to her problem of blocked-up breast milk. Her "cure" was to stick needles or pins into her breasts repeatedly over several months, as a way to unclog her nipples and allow the flow of milk. Through this method, the individual believed she would be able to have her child returned to her. This woman's thought process, therefore, showed evidence of both delusion and concretization in regard to her SMB.

Examples of the delusions that lead to SMB include removing a rotten appendage, exorcising unwanted demons, and demonstrating loyalty to God. Whatever the content of the delusions, these individuals believe that their bizarre thinking is valid and that the resulting self-mutilation is a necessary or highly desirable act.

A closely related phenomenon is seen in individuals with "command" hallucinations. These individuals hear a compelling message that orders them to commit the self-mutilation. Such persons often feel powerless to disobey these hallucinated commands. Often the command hallucination is perceived as coming from the voice of God, the Devil, or some mythic, powerful entity. The powerful status of the "speaker" makes it extremely difficult for these persons to ignore or defy the commands. Thus, it is important to note that an especially dangerous symptom pattern is one in which the patient is both deluded and receiving command hallucinations to self-mutilate. Later in this chapter, we discuss how to assess patients for the presence of these command hallucinations and delusions. Suggestions for management and treatment of these conditions are also presented.

Psychotic self-mutilation can also emerge as part of a psychotic transference. The self-mutilation in these situations is a primitive attempt to establish closeness with the person toward whom the patient has developed the transference. The psychotic transference results in a persistent need for the psychotic to have contact with this significant other, typically a member of a ward staff or a therapist. The medical needs of the patient often require this staff member to respond to the patient, even when this contact may not be therapeutic.

Two brief case examples will help to illustrate this clinical dilemma. The first case was that of a schizophrenic woman in her early 30s who developed a psychotic transference toward a doctor who worked occasional night shifts at a state hospital. This woman would go to extreme lengths to insure contact with this physician whenever he reported to work. When the patient became aware that this doctor was on site (usually when she heard his name paged on the intercom), she would severely lacerate her arms, often to such an extent that she required multiple sutures. Since the doctor was often the only physician available, he was compelled to respond to her medical needs, even though it reinforced the psychotic transference. Eventually, in an attempt to prevent the patient from knowing his whereabouts, the doctor requested that he no longer be paged over the intercom. Even this procedure was not totally successful in preventing the patient from detecting the doctor's presence. It was subsequently decided that whenever this doctor was working, the patient would be brought to the emergency room of a nearby general hospital if she injured herself. This resulted in a reduction in the frequency of her acts of self-harm.

The second case was that of a 40-year-old man who had received a variety of diagnoses over time, including schizophrenia, manic-depressive illness, and sexual deviance. This patient developed a psychotic transference toward a nurse who worked on his ward in a state hospital. When she was on duty, he frequently exposed himself to her. In addition, on several occasions, he cut his penis so severely as to require medical attention. The wounds on his genitals required cleaning and dressing by nursing staff. In several instances, the patient was able to manipulate this nurse into providing him with medical attention.

The manipulative use of SMB to gain medical attention is seen in many nonpsychotic individuals as well, especially in borderline personalities (see Chapter 6). However, as the examples above indicate, the manipulations of psychotic mutilators are often based on delusional beliefs. These beliefs form the basis for a psychotic transference, which in turn results in the manipulative use of the SMB.

Another distinguishing characteristic of psychotic self-mutilation concerns the location on the body of the inflicted wounds. Psychotics frequently mutilate parts of the body not harmed by less disturbed individuals. Whereas less disturbed individuals tend to cut, burn, or disfigure an arm, leg, or stomach, psychotics not uncommonly injure especially vulnerable and symbolic parts of their bodies, including their eyes, nipples, and genitals.

Self-mutilative acts by psychotic individuals may also be accompanied by rituals. These rituals can be highly elaborate ceremonies that have a delusional basis. The actual cut or wound made by these patients is frequently symbolic. While nonpsychotic individuals usually make incisions in random patterns, the psychotic mutilator may make deliberate patterns or designs with their self-mutilations. Triangles, crosses, and other self-inflicted symbols and rituals have meaning within the conceptual framework of their delusional systems. In summary, location, type of wound, and rituals surrounding the act all have meaning and significance beyond what is found in nonpsychotic populations.

Review of the Literature

Now that we have discussed a number of differences between psychotic self-mutilators and other clinical populations, it is important to review the literature regarding SMB within this very disturbed group. In an examination of this literature, it is striking that many of the case descriptions of psychotic self-mutilators concern acts of self-enucleation (for review, see Krauss, Yee, & Foos, 1984) or self-castration (for review, see Greilsheimer & Groves, 1979). Other types of psychotic self-mutilation reported in the literature include autocannibalism (Mintz, 1960; Betts, 1964), female genital self-mutilation (French & Nelson, 1972; Goldney & Simpson, 1975), and self-inflicted penis removal (Greilsheimer & Groves, 1979). This list should not be misinterpreted to mean that these are the only forms of self-mutilation within psychotic populations. It may be that self-enucleation and mutilation of the genitals generate more than their share of professional interest because these acts are so profoundly pathological and bizarre.

The incidence of self-mutilation of the eyes or genitals is actually quite low. For example, in their review of male genital SMB, Greilsheimer and Groves (1979) found 40 cases reported in the literature dating back to 1901. They reported that 87% of these genital mutilators were psychotic at the time of the act. There was a history of previous self-mutilative acts in 20% of these cases. In 25% of the cases reviewed, alcohol was consumed in connection with the mutilation. They also found that the wish to be or fear of being female was the most commonly cited reason for mutilation of the genitals. Of course, the fact that Greilsheimer and Groves discovered only 40 cases of genital self-mutilation does not mean that these were the only instances. There may have been a number of other incidents that have gone unreported. In our own experience, such acts are not extremely rare in state hospital settings.

Religious delusions have often been noted as being associated with extreme forms of SMB. Clark (1981) reviewed 26 cases of psychotic self-mutilation in the literature and found 13 patients who quoted Biblical texts as influencing their self-mutilation:

> The texts are all in the words of Jesus himself. They are as follows: Matthew 5:29: "And if thy right eye offend thee, pluck it out . . . 30: And if thy right hand offend thee, cut it off." In Mark, Chapter 9, verses 43, 45,

and 47, nearly the same words are used. The verse suggesting self-castration is in Matthew 19:11; "For there are some eunuchs . . . which have made themselves eunuchs for the kingdom of heaven's sake." . . . These quotations are from the King James translation: the one most available to fundamentalist Protestants. (p. 244)

Six of the nine subjects in a study by Sweeny and Zamecnik (1981) were assessed as having delusions that prompted their self-mutilation. All of the subjects were delusional for several weeks prior to the SMB, and it was concluded that the self-mutilation was not an impulsive act. This study also reported that a self-imposed change in physical appearance, such as shaving one's head or removing one's eyebrows, was a key variable in predicting self-mutilation in schizophrenic patients. A highly visible change in physical appearance was seen as a warning sign worthy of clinical precaution. The results of this study also suggested that experiencing a loss of a significant other was a common precipitant to SMB.

Shore (1979) concluded that virtually all reported cases of self-enucleation or genital mutilation were of individuals who were psychotic—typically, paranoid schizophrenics. In assessing the command hallucinations experienced by these individuals, Shore recommended determining whether the individual is suspicious of the motives of the voices or feels absolute trust in or controlled by the voices. If a patient is suspicious of the hallucinations, he or she will usually appear agitated and will be less likely to cooperate with a command from an untrusted source. On the other hand, if the patient perceives the voice as emanating from a heavenly or trusted source, then the patient will appear outwardly calm and will be more likely to obey a command to sacrifice a part of his or her body as a spiritual show of faith.

Sweeny and Zamecnik (1981) noted a difference in the content of auditory hallucinations and delusions between schizophrenic self-mutilators and a schizophrenic control group. The hallucinations of the self-mutilators included such statements as "Cut your throat," "Shoot yourself, you will not die," and "You're no good." The mutilator group also experienced religious delusions and beliefs of being controlled and requiring purification. The hallucinations for the control patients were more benign, such as "Get out and run and do good." The delusions of control patients were also less ominous, such as the belief that people were making fun of them and whistling at them.

Case Example of a Self-Enucleation

Given the relatively few examples of self-enucleation reported in the literature, and the extreme severity of the act, there remains a need to explore these incidents on a case-by-case basis. The following case description is provided as a source of anecdotal data for clinicians working with psychotic patients at risk for self-mutilation. This is one of the few cases of self-enucleation with whom we have had direct contact.

At the time of his self-enucleation, Mr. M was a single, 31-year-old white male well known to the local mental health system. He had an extended history of mental illness and had had several admissions to the state hospital. Mr. M's first psychiatric hospitalization had occurred at age 18. Since that time, Mr. M had generally lived at home with his mother when he was not hospitalized. Mr. M had been diagnosed variously as having bipolar affective disorder and schizophrenia, chronic undifferentiated type. There was no doubt that Mr. M had suffered from chronic mental illness for at least 13 years. During this period he had presented a pattern of periodic decompensations, erratic employment history, poor compliance with treatment programs and medication regimens, rather limited social relationships, and vacillating self-care skills and personal hygiene. His strengths included good intelligence, a sense of humor, and a generally pleasant demeanor. Caregivers who had known Mr. M over the years stated that he had no prior history of self-destructive behavior.

During his most recent state hospital stay, plans had been made to place Mr. M upon discharge in a setting other than his home. The reason for this change was that he was becoming increasingly difficult at home, refusing to do chores, smoking in a dangerous fashion, failing to practice reasonable hygiene, and isolating himself in his room. Thus, at the time of Mr. M's act of self-mutilation, he was living in a supervised community residential program. Despite his participation in the program, his mental status had deteriorated over the previous several months. He had periodically stopped taking his antipsychotic medication.

Two days before the self-enucleation, he was perceived by his outreach worker as quieter and more paranoid than usual. However, he did not present any self-destructive ideation or behavior. Staff members at his residence were alerted to be attentive to his medication ingestion, since it seemed possible that his deterioration was due to his "cheeking" his medications. Record material indicated that Mr. M seemed depressed and required reassurance that he was safe in his residence and that no wanted to harm him.

On the morning before his self-enucleation, an overnight counselor at the residence found notes written by Mr. M that were ominous in content. The notes read: (1) "Julie forgive me," (2) "Good Bye Julie," (3) "Perhaps it was a good home. . . . It was the best," and (4) "Always try to live in a good home. . . . I'm a coward." ("Julie" was a high school friend Mr. M had not seen in over 10 years.)

Mr. M left the residence unaccompanied that morning and went to the local emergency mental health center. When he arrived, he asked that he be given a "lethal dose of poison." At this point, Mr. M was readmitted to the state hospital. He arrived on the hospital ward during a 3 P.M.–11 P.M. shift and was noted to be agitated and restless. In a nursing assessment note, Mr. M was described as saying, "I want something lethal—a lethal injection," and "I'm a dirty bastard." Due to his restlessness and preoccupation with death-oriented thoughts, a 5-mg dose of Prolixin was provided to Mr. M at 7:15 P.M. This produced no improvement. He was described as agitated and restless on the 11 P.M.–7 A.M. shift as well. At 1:15 A.M. the next day, he was given an additional 5 mg of Prolixin, again with poor effect. He was reported to be up all night and at one point ran screaming down the hall of the ward and knocked over a table. Mr. M had to be physically restrained and removed to an observation room because of this behavior.

Throughout the night, Mr. M talked in a rambling, deluded fashion. He talked repeatedly about "crucifying a girlfriend," and said that he was a murderer of several young girls and that he would soon die and return "as a Jewish black prince." He also referred to himself as a "dirty bastard" and was self-deprecating in other ways. However, when asked whether he planned to hurt himself, Mr. M emphatically said, "No."

Mr. M remained psychotic and bizarre over the next 12 hours. He was being watched very closely by the staff. However, at one point he managed to briefly slip away from the staff and to enter a bathroom unescorted. The staff then heard Mr. M scream. Upon opening the door to the bathroom, the staff found Mr. M standing with one hand covering his right eye, which was bleeding profusely. Mr. M was then seized by the hands and led to the nursing station. He was asked where his eyeball was, and Mr. M replied that he had flushed it down the toilet.

Case Analysis

How can Mr. M's self-enucleation be understood? One place to begin is with the previous reports on the subject. Self-enucleation is known to be a rare event in the history of modern psychology. In their review article, "Autoenucleation," Krauss *et al.* (1984) identified 19 cases of bilateral enucleation and 31 cases of unilateral enucleation in the literature, dating back to 1846. Since the number of self-enucleators has been so small, attempting to define a pattern or profile for these individuals must be done with caution. Nonetheless, in reviewing the modern psychological literature on the topic (e.g., Menninger, 1935; Rosen & Hoffman, 1972; Maclean & Robertson, 1976; Crowder, Gross, Heiser, & Crowder, 1979; Krauss *et al.*, 1984; Eisenhauer, 1985), certain commonalities do emerge across the cases reported. Briefly, these are as follows:

1. Self-enucleators have tended to be psychotic; often they have been diagnosed as chronically psychotic or more specifically as paranoid schizophrenic.
2. At the time of their self-mutilating acts, many of these individuals have been preoccupied with religious delusions of grandeur and/or persecution. Command hallucinations have also been frequently present.
3. Related to these religious preoccupations have been feelings of intense guilt, unworthiness, and sinfulness.
4. Not uncommonly, these individuals have endured a forcible sexual encounter or are preoccupied with homosexual fears and/or desires.
5. Often, these individuals appear to have struck a "psychic bargain" (Menninger, 1935), in which they expunge their guilt and avoid suicide at the expense of sacrificing the eye.
6. It is not uncommon for these individuals to have little or no previous history of suicidal behavior or SMB.
7. The act of self-enucleation is in some cases performed in an intoxicated state, generally after the use of alcohol or LSD.

8. Finally, a key precipitant for the acts has often been the loss or significant disruption of an important interpersonal relationship.

Many of the items in this profile pertain to Mr. M. He had clearly been episodically psychotic for at least a 13-year period. In addition, he presented what was for him an unusual amount of religious preoccupation at the time of the act. He referred to "crucifying a girlfriend," and "confessed" to a litany of imaginary sins such as murders and rapes. He predicted his resurrection as a "Jewish black prince." Also, like many other self-enucleators described in the literature, Mr. M quoted the Biblical passage from the gospel of Matthew that has been cited above: "And if thine right eye offend thee, pluck it out."

Like other enucleators, Mr. M also seemed preoccupied with sexual matters at the time of his eye removal. He frequently referred to children he imagined he had fathered and rapes he believed he had committed. More importantly, Mr. M implied on several occasions that homosexual contact had recently occurred between himself and his roommate at his residence. Whether this homosexual contact was real or imagined is unclear. Nonetheless, what is important is that during the week prior to the act, Mr. M was apparently experiencing intense anguish regarding homosexuality.

There is also some evidence that the self-enucleation was a "psychic bargain" for Mr. M. Prior to his readmission to the state hospital, he initially expressed fears of being *given* a lethal dose of poison. Later, this fear was transformed into a *request* for a lethal dose of poison. His verbalizations became preoccupied with death. Thus, the self-enucleation may have been a bargain he struck—one that permitted him to avoid suicide and expunge his various "sins" of murder, rape, and homosexuality, at the very serious cost of removing his right eye.

Mr. M's situation is also consistent with the profile as to the issue of loss. The move from his home to residential care was a major change for Mr. M. This residential placement must have entailed a significant loss. His note "Perhaps it was a good home. . . . It was the best" may have been a grieving statement about no longer living with his mother.

The final key determinant in Mr. M's eye removal is that he had once again discontinued his psychotropic medication. From his previous history, it is clear that this decision consistently led to rapid and profound intensification of his psychosis. This deterioration occurred once again in this case; it set the stage for his rage, fears, anguish, and delusions to overwhelm him, culminating in the self-enucleation.

Assessment of Self-Mutilative Potential in Psychotic Patients

Preventing extreme acts such as the one Mr. M performed is highly desirable. The ability to predict and prevent such acts is expected by courts, families, and staff workers in psychiatric facilities. Clinicians are supposed to be able to foretell which people are at risk of committing serious harm, and then to take precautions that prevent the behavior.

The ability to successfully predict self-mutilation in psychotic individuals would be highly advantageous in several ways. Of primary importance, of course, is the safety of the individual. Accurate predictions of self-mutilation would allow for treatment and management procedures to prevent serious self-harm. Successful prediction would also permit a reduction in restrictive interventions for psychotic patients who are *not* at risk. The fact that psychotic patients are so hard to assess allows for a small number of false-positive predictions of the occurrence of self-mutilation. However, too many false-positive predictions result in overly restrictive treatment and an inefficient use of clinical resources. If a patient is believed to be at risk of self-injury, the patient must be watched carefully, have his or her freedom curtailed, and even be locked up or physically restrained.

Unfortunately, the current "state of the art" in the prediction of self-mutilation in psychotic patients is in the realm of good clinical hunches rather than scientific precision. Clinicians can maximize the quality of their clinical opinions, however, by conducting a thorough clinical assessment that identifies key risk variables. The protocol presented in Figure 7.1 is based on our own experience and on the references in the literature regarding self-mutilation in psychotic individuals.

This assessment protocol is designed to discuss and explore directly the underlying psychotic thought process that might trigger an incident of self-mutilation. This direct approach allows for rapid analysis of an individual's condition. Some psychodynamically oriented clinicians may object that direct exploration of psychotic material may lead to a weakening of the patient's defenses and an exacerbation of the psychotic state. Other, more behaviorally oriented clinicians may be concerned about reinforcing the psychotic thinking by paying attention to and asking repeated questions regarding psychotic material. Although these concerns are sometimes valid, the risks of exacerbating psychosis by talking directly about the psychotic material are less than the risks of being uninformed about highly dangerous psychotic beliefs.

Treatment of Psychotic Self-Mutilators

Psychotropic Medication

It is obvious at this point in our discussion that self-mutilation in psychotic patients is almost always the result of thought disorder. The best treatment of the SMB, therefore, is the reduction or elimination of the psychotic thought process. The most effective (indeed, arguably the only) effective means of altering thought disorder is through the use of psychotropic medication. Antipsychotic drugs that reduce delusions will have a simultaneous, beneficial impact on the prevention of self-mutilation.

The specific choice of an antipsychotic agent is made according to the same guidelines for medicating any psychotic individual. Tolerance of the various dosage levels, side effects, and existing medical condition of the patient frequently dictate the selection of a particular medication. There is no indication that any one drug is more effective than any other in the treatment of self-mutilation.

In some cases, the use of lithium carbonate, antidepressants, or antianxiety agents may be indicated by the symptom picture. However, these drugs are usually indicated in populations where thought disorder is not the main diagnostic symptom.

Psychotherapy

Many clinicians have become frustrated and disillusioned with the use of psychotherapy with schizophrenic patients. Psychotic individuals have limited ability to achieve insight or use logic—skills that would allow them to benefit from psychotherapy. The delusional systems of

Figure 7.1. Protocol for assessing risk

Part 1. Observation and Historical Information
I. Review history to determine whether previous self-mutilation or suicide attempts have occurred.
II. Determine whether any self-imposed changes in physical appearance have been made (e.g., shaving one's head).
III. Note a sudden calmness following a period of agitation.
IV. Assess whether any recent interpersonal loss has occurred.

Part 2. Assessment of Mental Status Relevant to SMB
I. Auditory hallucinations
   A. Determine if auditory hallucinations are present and, if so, determine their content and source:
      1. Do you hear a voice telling you to hurt yourself?
      2. Whose voice is it?
      3. What does the voice tell you to do to yourself?
      4. What does the voice say after you have hurt yourself?
   B. Evaluate the level of trust and coercion relating to the hallucinations:
      1. Why does the voice want you to hurt yourself?
      2. Do you trust the voice? Is the voice trying to help you or hurt you?
      3. What would happen if you resisted hurting yourself when the voice tells you to hurt yourself?
      4. Do you have control over your own actions when the voice tells you to hurt yourself?
         (If no:) Why does the voice have control over you?
         What would happen if you tried to take control from the voice?
      5. Do you feel the voice is trying to get you to punish yourself?
         (If yes:) Why?
         Do you believe you deserve this punishment?
      6. Does hurting yourself protect you or anyone else from harm?
II. Delusional beliefs
   A. Religious delusions:
      1. What are your religious beliefs?
      2. Do you believe you have a special relationship with God?
      3. Are you able to communicate with God?
         (If yes:) How?
      4. Have you been thinking about any particular passage in the Bible?
         (If yes:) Which ones?
      5. Do you have a relationship with the Devil?
         (If yes:) Why is the Devil interested in you?
      6. Do you think God (the Devil) wants you to hurt yourself?
         (If yes:) Why?
      7. Do you believe hurting yourself will protect you or your family from God (the Devil)?
   B. Persecutory delusions:
      1. How do other people generally treat you?
      2. Is there anyone who is against you or out to get you?
      3. Why are they out to get you?

    4. Do any of these people want you to hurt yourself?
       (If yes:) Why?
    5. Do you trust their motives in their wanting you to hurt yourself?
    6. How able are you to resist their pressure for you to hurt yourself?
  C. Somatic delusions:
    1. Do you think there is anything wrong with your body?
    2. Do you think your body is rotten or diseased?
       (If yes:) Why?
    3. What caused this to happen to you?
    4. What can you do to make yourself well?
    5. Does this disease make you want to hurt yourself?
  D. Delusions of grandiosity:
    1. What special qualities do you have?
    2. How powerful are you?
    3. How knowledgeable are you?
    4. Does feeling special ever lead you to hurt yourself?
    5. Does injuring yourself prove you are special (strong, knowledgeable, etc.)?

III. Forms of SMB
  A. Identify the part of the body that the individual says he or she is most likely to injure, and the way in which this injury would be accomplished:
    1. When you have hurt yourself in the past, what part of your body have you injured?
    2. If you ever hurt yourself again, what part of your body will you injure?
    3. Why have you chosen this part of your body to injure?
    4. How will you injure yourself (e.g., with a knife, etc.)?
    5. Is there a body part that you find particularly unacceptable or troublesome?
  B. Determine whether any rituals are part of the SMB:
    1. Do you always injure yourself in the same way?
    2. How important is it to hurt yourself in a very exact way?
    3. Are there any habits or rituals you follow when you hurt yourself?
  C. Discuss level of pain:
    1. Have you experienced pain when you hurt yourself?
    2. What is the effect of this level of pain on whether you will hurt yourself or not?

IV. Genital self-mutilation
  A. Do you experience any sexual thoughts or feelings that bother you?
  B. Do you believe it is wrong or sinful to have these thoughts or feelings?
  C. Are you comfortable with your sexual or gender identity?
    1. Do you feel that your dissatisfaction with being a male (female) may cause you to injure yourself?
    2. How will this injury help you with your feeling about being a male (female)?

these patients are often so entrenched that psychotherapy is rendered futile. The utility of psychotherapy for psychotic self-mutilators is inversely related to the degree of thought disorder: The greater the thought disorder, the less effective the psychotherapy.

When psychotherapy is employed, a problem-oriented focus on symptom reduction is probably the most realistic and helpful approach. This form of treatment assists clients in monitoring their psychotic thinking and recognizing the hallucinations or delusions that are likely to lead to acts of self-harm. If an individual is capable of this type of self-monitoring, then he or she may be able to use a cognitive–behavioral strategy either to reduce the influence of the psychotic thinking or to give self-instructions to seek staff support.

To use this type of cognitive–behavioral approach, the individual must be capable of the following:

1. Recognizing and labeling psychotic thinking versus reality-based thinking.
2. Identifying which psychotic thoughts are most likely to lead to self-mutilation.
3. Generating new thoughts that block or compete with the psychotic thoughts (e.g., "I don't want to hurt myself," "I'm going to ignore the voices that tell me to hurt myself," "I'm going to tell the staff about these voices," etc.).

As mentioned above, the more severe the psychosis, the less likely it is that the individual will be able to benefit from this type of approach.

We do not consider other forms of psychotherapy, especially long-term, insight-oriented therapy, to be worthwhile clinical endeavors with this population. Although many of the formulations and insights gleaned by the therapist may be valid, the patient's ability to benefit from these insights is seriously limited. The use of operant behavioral techniques, however, can have some beneficial applications. These techniques are covered in the next section.

Clinical Management

Most psychotic self-mutilators are placed in psychiatric hospitals, either for long-term institutional care or for short-term acute management of their psychosis and related problems, including self-mutilation. As such, this section on clinical management focuses on clinical management issues within an inpatient psychiatric setting.

The degree of physical risk a patient poses is the overriding management issue with self-mutilators. As indicated in the case example presented above, permanent, severe self-injury can occur in a matter of seconds. Since many patients give few overt cues as to impending self-mutilative acts, staff members face a very difficult challenge. The first and most obvious question in developing a management plan for this population is whether a patient is at risk. If the answer to this question is "yes," then a series of other questions must be answered in order to decide on the level of restrictiveness that is necessary:

1. How much physical injury is likely if the self-mutilation occurs?
2. How much advance warning (if any) will be available to the staff about an impending self-mutilative act?
3. When the patient has an impulse to self-mutilate, how long does the patient remain at risk?

The most dangerous situation exists when (1) the potential for serious physical injury is great, (2) the degree of advance warning available to staff is minimal, and (3) the patient's urge to injure himself or herself is intense and long-lasting.

The dilemma for inpatient clinical management is to balance the risk to the patient with the rights of the patient to the least restrictive form of treatment. The proper balance is always open to interpretation and ultimately rests on the clinical assessment of the team and careful adherence to existing regulations. In conjunction with these considerations, several guidelines are provided for the use of management procedures:

1. A *formal* assessment of risk should be conducted as a basis for implementation of any restrictive management procedures.

2. The established treatment plan should specify a sequence of gradually lessening restrictions. For example, an individual formally evaluated and considered to be at high risk for self-mutilation may initially be placed on "suicide precautions" in a locked unit. From this point, the individual may progress through a set, predetermined sequence of lessening restrictions, such as moving to close-observation

status; to off-unit privileges with other individuals for a set period of time; to off-grounds privileges; and, finally, to day or overnight passes.

3. The staff and individual should negotiate the exact sequence of the behavioral expectations required, as well as the length of time required to advance to the next step.

4. Any return of symptoms involving the SMB should result in specified re-establishment of an earlier point of the sequence.

In addition to providing a system of management, these guidelines also represent a behavior modification plan in which the individual is reinforced with increased independence as he or she demonstrates sufficient self-control. Other rewards can be used that further strengthen noninjurious behavior. For example, individuals may earn extra time with staff, a special outing, or additional cigarettes when they are able to prevent any SMB for an agreed length of time. (A more detailed discussion of operant behavioral techniques is found in Chapter 9.)

Another key aspect to management of SMB on an inpatient unit is the response by medical and psychiatric staff. Medical and psychiatric staff members are trained to be empathic to patients experiencing psychiatric or medical problems. However, as described in some of the anecdotal accounts at the beginning of this chapter, this solicitous care may perpetuate the self-mutilation. If the self-mutilative act is the result of a psychotic transference or a primitive need for nurturance, then the care and attention provided to wounds will constitute a powerful reinforcer for continued self-injury. If the self-mutilative act is motivated by a psychotic need to be cared for by a staff member, steps should be taken to reduce the manipulative use of self-mutilation to gain access to this kind of solicitous care.

Chapter 8
Self-Injury in Retarded and Autistic Populations

Throughout the first seven chapters of this book, we have consistently employed the term "self-mutilative behavior" (SMB). In this chapter regarding self-harm among retarded and autistic individuals, we employ a different term, "self-injurious behavior" (SIB). We substitute this term here because a substantial literature has consistently used this terminology for self-destructive behavior occurring in organically deficient individuals.

Although the terminology is different, there are similarities between SMB and SIB. Both terms refer to self-inflicted injuries that may be performed either as a method of communication or as a means of discharging emotions. However, in general, the SIB of the developmentally disabled and autistic can be distinguished from the SMB of psychiatric populations in the following ways:

1. Retarded clients often display more "primitive" forms of self-injury. For example, common types of SIB include head banging, biting, scratching, slapping, and punching. Although some emotionally disturbed individuals who are neither retarded nor autistic also show these behaviors, it is more common for these individuals to employ more complex forms of behavior (e.g., to use a tool such as a knife, piece of glass, cigarette, etc.) and to employ behaviors that require more fine motor coordination (e.g., to inflict cuts, scratches, or burns).

2. The frequency or rate of SIB in developmentally disabled clients tends to be much higher than that of SMB in psychiatric populations. It is not uncommon to find clients who abuse themselves scores of times per day via hitting, biting, or head banging. In contrast, the frequency of SMB in psychiatric populations tends to be much less. Typically, these individuals do not abuse themselves every day; rather, the SMB occurs at intervals ranging from every few days to every few months. When the SMB does occur, a relatively small number of injuries are made.

3. The occurrence of SIB is most influenced by the immediate, existing environmental influences, such as the availability of reinforcement or level of stimulation. SMB on the other hand, while affected by situational influences, is largely mediated by more complex psychological determinants.

4. It is also more common for SIB to be caused by or related to clearly identifiable organic problems than is the case with SMB.

SIB is discussed here as a subcategory of SMB. This chapter discusses SIB as it occurs in both retarded and autistic individuals; for purposes of simplification, retardation and autism are discussed together. It is, of course, recognized that these two classes of disorders are not synonymous. However, the forms and frequency of occurrence of SIB in these populations are extremely similar.

Background

Until recently, the methods of treatment devised to deal with SIB were nearly as primitive as the behavior itself. For example, a common intervention for retarded and autistic clients who bit themselves was to remove the teeth of these individuals. This procedure was obviously effective in reducing injuries; as a "treatment" technique, however, it indicates the extreme measures that have often been used to prevent these individuals from harming themselves. Indeed, there is a disturbing list of such extreme measures that have been used and are still being used for this purpose. The list includes handcuffing individuals who punch themselves; imposing full or "four-point" restraint on individuals who run into walls; secluding individuals in padded rooms; medicating individuals to the point of sedation; and securing protective helmets on individuals to prevent injuries from head banging. Not surprisingly, these measures have frequently raised ethical concerns. The rationale for employing such procedures has usually been as follows: "Nothing else has worked. Everything has been tried to stop the behavior, but the individual continues to inflict serious injury. Therefore, radical procedures must be used to prevent continued self-harm."

The people who employ extreme measures to control SIB include well-intentioned professionals and family members. A case in point is that of a 24-year-old moderately retarded woman who was the only child of an upper-middle-class family. This woman, whom we will call Sally, exhibited multiple forms of SIB. She banged her head against hard objects, resulting in lacerations to her scalp; on two occasions, this head banging resulted in loss of consciousness. She also frequently slapped her face so hard that she produced red welts, and scratched herself on her arms and legs. When Sally reached age 19, her behavior was no longer tolerable to her parents. She was then placed for the first time out of her home in a private psychiatric hospital. There, her treatment initially consisted of administration of a variety of drugs, none of which made an appreciable impact on the SIB. As a result, restraint was then used to prevent serious injury, and Sally was required to wear a helmet at all times.

After 8 months of treatment in this facility, the parents were dissatisfied with the slowness of their daughter's progress, and so they transferred her to a group home. A behavior modification procedure was then implemented, resulting in some modest changes in Sally's behavior. The frequency of SIB decreased; however, she still abused herself several times daily.

A year later, the parents were exasperated at the inability of the professionals to extinguish the SIB, so they decided to take Sally back home. Because they were desperate and wanted to prevent long-term institutionalization, they secretly implemented their own radical strategy. They cleared out a closet in their home and put padding on its walls. They also attached handcuffs to the closet walls. Thereafter, whenever Sally abused herself, she was brought to the closet, handcuffed, and left alone in the dark for several hours.

Within 2 months, the frequency of Sally's SIB had decreased from several times a day to once a month. After 1 year, the parents very rarely needed to use the closet as a consequence; the threat of the closet was sufficient to control the behavior. Sally's parents eventually revealed this strategy to professionals 2 years after they had initially employed the procedure. Sally's parents were very committed to and concerned about their daughter. It was with feelings of guilt and anxiety that they developed their plan to isolate and restrain her for SIB; they retained these feelings of shame and revulsion, despite the success of the plan.

Review of Literature and Theories
on the Causes of Self-Injurious Behavior

As in the case example of Sally, a review of the literature concerning SIB reveals some drastic treatment approaches (e.g., see Smolev, 1971; Frankel & Simmons, 1976). The earliest reports of success in treating SIB are found in studies that used electric shock as a punishment for the behavior. These studies demonstrated that an aversive stimulus would suppress the problem behavior (Tate & Baroff, 1966; Lovaas & Simmons, 1969); they were instructive in showing that SIB could be altered by using a punishment paradigm exclusively. This was an important step, as these findings were the first to reveal conclusively that it was possible to change this troublesome problem behavior at all. However, despite the empirical reports regarding the efficacy of punishment techniques, a generalized acceptance of the use of electric shock for SIB (outside of laboratory or academic settings) was not forthcoming because of widespread ethical concerns and objections.

Once it was discovered that the incidence and intensity of SIB could be reduced, additional behavioral interventions were devised that were not based on a punishment paradigm. These techniques included the use of extinction (Hamilton, Stephens, & Allen, 1967; Tate & Baroff, 1966; Ferster, 1961), time-out procedures (Wolf, Risley, & Mees, 1964; Hamilton *et al.*, 1967), positive reinforcement of incompatible behaviors (Corte, Wolf, & Locke, 1971; Repp, Deitz, & Deitz, 1976), and reinforcement of low rates of SIB (Deitz & Repp, 1973; Schaefer, 1970).

The success of these techniques in reducing SIB, in combination with advances in understanding psychophysiology, led to several theories about the etiology of SIB. In an excellent, comprehensive review article, Carr (1977) identified the four most commonly accepted hypotheses regarding this etiology: (1) Organic impairment results in the SIB; (2) a lack of sensory stimulation in the environment leads to the development of stereotypic behaviors such as SIB; (3) positive reinforcement is provided that gradually shapes and maintains the behavior; and (4) negative reinforcement supports the SIB, since the individual may avoid or escape from unpleasant situations by performing the behavior.

None of these hypotheses has achieved dominance in explaining SIB. Each perspective has its strong points; each is unable to explain the phenomenon fully. Fortunately, these theoretical views are not mutually exclusive. In some cases, SIB may be determined by multiple related factors; in others, there may be several independent factors that result in its development. It is worthwhile, therefore, to examine each of these hypotheses regarding etiology. In combination, these hypotheses provide a reasonably comprehensive model for explaining the occurrence of SIB. For a more detailed discussion of these issues, the reader should consult Carr (1977).

Hypothesis 1: Organic Factors

Many forms of mental retardation have an identifiable organic cause. These causes range from trauma and head injuries to genetically linked abnormalities. The organic hypothesis regarding the etiology of SIB states that the SIB results from the same organic disorder that has caused the mental retardation. Thus, the SIB is viewed as one symptom within an organic brain syndrome.

The strongest support for this position has come from studies of Lesch–Nyhan syndrome. Lesch–Nyhan syndrome is an X-linked genetic disorder found only in males (Lesch & Nyhan, 1964; Dizmang & Cheatham, 1970). It is a form of cerebral palsy that includes mental retardation and a variety of motor movement and physiological abnormalities. One characteristic set of symptoms found in these individuals is the repeated biting of the fingers, tongue, and lips. There has been considerable speculation that the consistency of the occurrence of self-injurious biting in these individuals is due to the biochemical imbalance that produces the disease. The SIB is seen as a manifestation of the biological condition of the individual and as unrelated to any environment or learned phenomena.

Evaluation of an organic origin of SIB is difficult, due to the present limitations of physiological assessment. When a particular individual is found to have an organic problem, establishing organic determinants of the SIB is usually possible. However, when no organic cause can be determined (as is usually the case), it remains unclear whether there is a functional cause of the SIB, or whether the organic problem has simply not been diagnosed. As the sophistication of physiological assessment improves, a better evaluation of this hypothesis will be possible.

Hypothesis 2: Insufficient Sensory Stimulation

Several authors have suggested that SIB is the result of insufficient sensory stimulation (e.g., Dennis & Majarian, 1957; Green, 1967). Animal studies have demonstrated that extreme deprivation will lead to gross disturbances in development (Cross & Harlow, 1965; Harlow & Harlow, 1971). A deficiency in sensory stimulation can lead to unusual behavioral patterns and marked impairment of functioning.

In humans, insufficient sensory stimulation may occur in one of two ways: Either the environment may be devoid of stimulating situations, or the person may have an inability to process or receive sensory input. According to this hypothesis, if insufficient sensory stimulation is available, an individual may begin to engage in stereotypic behaviors. These behaviors will recur if they provide sensory stimulation. All forms of SIB provide some form of intense sensory experience. In a deprived or physically handicapped individual, such behaviors as head banging or self-scratching may have a profound impact. The SIB may serve an important purpose if it provides relief from the deprivation of sensation.

Many large institutions for the retarded and autistic have chronic understaffing and overcrowding problems. This can result in an institutional milieu lacking in basic interpersonal attention and in normal, appropriate environmental stimulation. According to the sensory stimulation hypothesis, these conditions may lead to the occurrence of SIB. It may be that the only time these individuals get relief from the boredom or monotony of institutional life is when they injure themselves.

Hypothesis 3: Positive Reinforcement

Many studies have now shown that SIB can be markedly reduced and even eliminated by using positive reinforcement of behaviors incompatible with SIB (Lovaas, Freitag, Gold, & Kassorla, 1965; Peterson & Peterson, 1968). It has also been shown empirically that social reinforcement, such as attention from others, can maintain or support SIB once it has been established (Lovaas *et al.*, 1965; Lovaas & Simmons, 1969). These findings are, of course, important for designing treatment interventions. They also raise the question as to whether the etiology of SIB is related to positive reinforcement of the SIB itself.

Developmentally disabled people frequently lack the appropriate social skills to obtain reinforcement from their environment. Problem behaviors, especially dangerous ones, are usually immediately noticed by significant others. SIB in particular tends to elicit a caring response from family or staff members. It is easy to see how a shaping situation may occur through which the retarded or autistic person learns that certain self-injurious acts will lead to attentive reactions from those in the environment.

The family members of self-abusing retardates will frequently "do almost anything" to prevent loved ones from harming themselves. "Almost anything" can include talking, providing favorite foods, and taking the retardates for a walk or drive in order to distract them from self-injurious impulses. For most people, these types of responses are, in effect, forms of positive reinforcement. Thus, developmentally disabled or autistic individuals are likely to repeat the SIB because it has resulted in obtaining significant rewards. Studies have found that SIB can be changed even in clients with an organic disorder such as Lesch–Nyhan syndrome (e.g., Duker, 1975) using positive reinforcement strategies.

In addition, it has been found that positive reinforcement of other, noninjurious behaviors is effective in lowering and eliminating the SIB in these organically impaired people. These results raise challenging questions regarding the hypothesis that SIB in these individuals is organic in origin. If the SIB is the result of an organic problem, how can it be significantly reduced by positive reinforcement that in no way alters the physiological state of an individual? It is conceivable that positive reinforcement could be powerful enough to inhibit the occurrence of an organically based SIB. However, it is also possible that positive reinforcement plays a formative role in the development and continuance of SIB, even in organic disorders like Lesch–Nyhan syndrome.

Hypothesis 4: Negative Reinforcement

The negative reinforcement hypothesis also contends that SIB is learned response. According to this position, however, the learning occurs when the person is able to avoid or escape something unpleasant by engaging in SIB. Like the positive reinforcement hypothesis, this theory recognizes that a caretaker will do "almost anything" to stop a person from self-injury. Thus, for example, if a disabled person does not want to take a bath, he or she may not have the ability to negotiate this effectively with a caretaker. If the person then begins to bang his or her head and the caretaker decides to postpone the bath, then the SIB has been negatively reinforced. The disabled person thereby avoids the unwanted bath, and the SIB is strengthened. The caretaker is also negatively reinforced; the SIB stops when the caretaker allows the person to avoid the bath. A reciprocal pattern may therefore be established.

Several studies have shown that negative reinforcement maintains SIB (Wolf, Risley, Johnston, Harris, & Allen, 1967; Jones, Simmons, & Frankel, 1974; Carr, Newsom, & Binkoff, 1976). In addition, many retarded or autistic people who engage in SIB receive intermittent negative reinforcement. This intermittent reinforcement makes subsequent attempts at extinction especially difficult. To return to the example of the avoidance of the bath, it is highly unlikely that a disabled person will be able to avoid *every* bath; rather, he or she will avoid some of the baths. Thus, an intermittent schedule of negative reinforcement develops.

COMBINED PERSPECTIVES

Empirical and logical support exists for each of these four perspectives regarding the etiology of SIB in retarded and autistic clients. Research to date has failed to declare a clear winner among the four positions. Taken collectively, however, they provide a useful model for a broad-based understanding of the causes of SIB. From a practical point of view, the four hypotheses are useful in combination to screen and assess for the development and instigation of SIB.

Clients can be assessed on a case-by-case basis for each possible source of SIB. That is, each case can first be examined for possible organic causes leading to SIB. The level of sensory stimulation provided by the environment should then be measured as to its adequacy. Positive reinforcement that may be shaping and maintaining the behavior should be identified. Finally, avoidance or escape situations that provide negative reinforcement for the SIB should be noted. If any of these causes appear to be contributing to the SIB, treatment should be provided to alleviate the cause. The treatment may be medical and/ or environmental. Although the treatment section at the conclusion of this chapter focuses primarily on behavioral interventions for SIB, one should not ignore medical treatment or environmental changes when creating treatment plans.

Self-Injurious Behavior as Communication

In addition to the positive and negative reinforcement conditions already described, SIB has an additional component that can be rewarding for retarded or autistic clients. These individuals are often tremendously impaired in their ability to communicate their needs and feelings to others. These deficits in communication are, of course, most directly related to limitations in expressive language. The frustration that these individuals endure is undoubtedly considerable. They lack a normal range of verbal articulation and emotional expression. What options are available to them to express the range of emotions they feel? Family and professionals exert pressure on these people to be calm and cooperative and to refrain from excessive behavioral displays of emotions. Yet behavioral displays such as tantrums, aggression, or SIB often provide relief from accumulated frustration. SIB or other behavioral excesses send a message to significant others that something is wrong. Without this behavioral expression, caretakers would be unaware of the individuals' discomfort or frustration.

Generally, the communication expressed via SIB is a global message that "something is bothering me." The message does not specify what the "something" is that is causing the distress. However, even this global communication can be highly effective. After the message is communicated, people in the environment usually attempt to decipher the message. A family member or professional searches to find the cause of the discomfort. Guesses or predictions as to the source of the discomfort are then generated.

A common example of this type of interaction is found in group homes for the retarded and autistic. In these settings, staff members often expend considerable effort in attempting to determine the precipitants of the SIB. These staff members strive to understand what a self-injurious client is attempting to express. They then hope to change the precipitant of the SIB and to provide relief to the individual. The following are some common examples of hypotheses or guesses generated by staff at a group home in an attempt to decipher the message "expressed" via a self-injurious act: The individual was (1) angry over some incident that occurred; (2) lonely and missing family and friends; (3) frustrated by an inability to meet certain demands or expectations; (4) sad about a staff member's departure; (5) frightened by a perceived threat from another client; (6) physically not feeling well; (7) upset about a limit that was set. The list of such guesses can be endless. Staff or family members often attempt to identify which guess is correct. They will inquire, "Are you sad that John R doesn't work here any more? I bet you miss him." Or, "Are you angry that you didn't go home to visit your family this weekend?"

Often, an individual who cannot express these complex feelings is able to acknowledge by saying "yes" or "no" whether the caretaker has tapped the right feeling. In other cases, the individual may not be aware of the source of feelings that have caused the SIB. When staff or family members provides a reason to explain the behavioral outburst, the retarded or autistic person may experience some relief from a sense of vague discomfort. Either way, the disabled person has succeeded in communicating a message that, when decoded, leads to increased understanding. When viewed from this perspective, SIB serves a useful function. Unfortunately, the level of communication is primitive, and self-harm is a by-product of this dangerous form of expression.

The appropriate treatment for SIB employed as communication is to assist the individual in developing alternative forms of communication. Some retarded and autistic people have enough rudimentary language skills and sufficient cognitive ability to learn to articulate their feelings and needs more effectively. Others can be taught to use sign language for some expressive purposes.

For seriously regressed individuals, caretakers need to develop considerable familiarity with the individuals' demeanor so that frustration can be discerned before the SIB occurs. An example of this technique can be seen in the case of Holly, a 44-year-old moderately retarded woman living in a group home. Holly's pattern was to punch and slap herself whenever she became upset. This behavior resulted in painful welts and contusions for Holly, and was quite upsetting to family and staff. After careful observation, the staff determined that Holly most frequently became upset and engaged in SIB when she did not receive a weekly phone call from her sister. Once the staff members recognized that the absence of the phone call was the precipitant of the SIB, they took several steps to alter the chain of events. First, they explained to Holly's sister that her forgetting to call made Holly very agitated. This explanation made the sister considerably more diligent about calling when promised. In addition, the staff arranged for other phone calls to be made to Holly by other individuals within the agency. Holly enjoyed phone calls, despite her limited expressive language. Until the staff arranged for additional calls, Holly was being called exclusively by her sister. The staff hoped that these additional calls would lessen Holly's intense dependence on phone calls from her sister. Holly was also encouraged, with staff assistance, to initiate calls to her friends.

The intent of these environmental changes was to assist Holly in changing a part of her life that was unsatisfactory. The staff discovered Holly's dissatisfaction by attending to her SIB as a form of communication. Although the missed phone call was not the only precipitant of Holly's SIB, these changes regarding calls did result in a marked decrease in the frequency of the SIB. Further steps were taken to alleviate other precipitants.

Assessment and Treatment of Self-Injurious Behavior

With careful assessment and treatment, most SIB can be sharply reduced or eliminated. As discussed earlier, the initial assessment of the problem should include an examination of possible organic or physiological disorders that may be causing the self-injurious actions. A physician who specializes in the problems of the organically impaired should perform this evaluation. Once these causes have been investigated, the SIB should be examined to determine whether some environmental stressor is eliciting the behavior. If a stressor is found, attempts should be made to alter the environmental conditions that produce the stress. If none of these steps are successful in changing or eliminating the SIB, a behavior modification plan should be developed to reduce the occurrence of SIB and to strengthen alternative adaptive behaviors. The following steps are suggested as a method for implementing this type of plan.

Step 1: Data Collection

As noted, the rates of SIB in retarded clients may be quite high. Once treatment begins, a slow gradual decrease in the frequency and/or intensity of the behavior may be difficult to observe, since the rate of SIB may remain high for some time. For example, a decrease in head banging from 100 times per day to 80 times per day may indicate that a treatment is working; however, caretakers may have a hard time discriminating this change.

Collecting behavioral data is therefore a very helpful technique in demonstrating the effectiveness of a treatment plan. Frequency counts of occurrences of the SIB are usually sufficient to document changes in these behaviors. Figure 8.1 shows a baseline frequency count (using a 2-hour time sample) for a 23-year-old male who bit himself.

Step 2: Removing Reinforcement
that Maintains Self-Injury

In developing a treatment plan for SIB, the next step following assessment is to remove any positive or negative reinforcement that may be maintaining the behavior. Typically, positive reinforcement is provided in many ways, including trying to comfort the person, providing physical contact (including restraint), and providing a positive activity

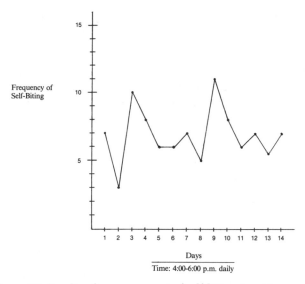

Frequency of Self-Biting

Days

Time: 4:00-6:00 p.m. daily

Figure 8.1. Baseline frequency count of self-biting in a 23-year-old retarded male.

to distract the person from continuing the SIB. Negative reinforcement is provided whenever the SIB results in escape or avoidance of unpleasant tasks. With retarded and autistic individuals, the "unpleasant tasks" may be things that most people find enjoyable. For example, these individuals may experience socializing, athletics, or family contact as aversive if they lack the skills to succeed or if the task is overstimulating. If SIB results in avoidance of or escape from these activities, then the SIB is negatively reinforced. Other common examples of aversive situations that may be avoided through SIB include chores, personal hygiene, or work.

In establishing a treatment plan, it is imperative that as much of this reinforcement as possible be eliminated. Two general rules should be followed in this regard:

1. The occurrence of SIB should be ignored whenever possible.
2. SIB should not result in an individual's being excused from some unwanted activity or situation. Whenever possible, the individual should be required to participate in or perform a specified activity that has been presented.

Step 3: Selecting Target Behaviors

The most critical component in developing a behavioral treatment plan for SIB is the creation of a reinforcement procedure for adaptive social behaviors that are incompatible with the SIB. In establishing this part of the treatment plan, careful selection of one or more appropriate positive target behaviors is important.

The target behaviors that may be selected will vary, depending upon the type of SIB and the skill level of the individual. For example, the simplest and broadest category of incompatible behaviors is "all noninjurious behaviors." That is, the individual earns the selected reinforcement whenever he or she is *not* engaging in SIB for a specified period of time. If the SIB occurs, the reward is not earned. The advantage of selecting this option for target behaviors is that it is a relatively easy discrimination for low-functioning people to make. It is an all-or-nothing discrimination—SIB versus non-SIB. As part of a shaping approach to decrease SIB, this is often a good starting point. The disadvantage of this strategy is that since it is a shaping procedure, some behaviors that are not particularly adaptive may be reinforced. As an example, consider a man who bangs his head severely. When the simple all-or-nothing strategy is used, the individual may be reinforced whenever the head banging does not occur for a specified time period (e.g., 10 minutes). If the individual does not bang his head but is incontinent during the reinforcement period, he will still earn the reward for not banging his head. However, with this approach, the incontinence is inadvertently reinforced.

Some of the problems inherent in reinforcing a person for not engaging in SIB can be overcome by having other behavioral plans in place for commonly presented problems. In the example above, if the individual were on a separate behavioral program for incontinence, then differential reinforcement could be provided for that problem behavior. With a broad-based behavioral plan, reinforcing an individual for not engaging in SIB can be effective with less risk of "side effects."

The choice of target behaviors can also be more specific. For example, the individual may be required to be calm and cooperative before receiving positive reinforcement. These behaviors are incompatible with SIB. Since SIB is a form of agitation and noncompliance, its occurrence does not result in reinforcement. In addition to

SIB, other inappropriate behaviors are incompatible with calm and cooperative actions. If the person does not show SIB but does have an aggressive outburst, he or she will not receive the reinforcement. The advantage of this definition of target behaviors over the first example is that a narrower range of inappropriate behavior will be reinforced. The disadvantage is that it entails a more difficult discrimination —one that may be too complex for some individuals. As a result, behavior change for these individuals may occur somewhat more slowly.

Many other choices of positive target behaviors can be made. Some highly specific target behaviors are appropriate in cases where the SIB is very circumscribed and predictable. For example, if a person's only form of SIB is biting his or her fingers, the target behavior may be "keeping one's hands out of one's mouth." When the individual is reinforced for this incompatible behavior, the SIB should be lessened as the individual associates rewards with altering his or her behavior.

Another example of a specific target behavior in a higher-functioning individual would be to reinforce the appropriate expression of feelings. The target behavior in this instance might be learning to say "I'm angry" instead of using SIB as a form of communication. If the SIB does not occur and the anger is expressed appropriately, the individual is reinforced.

Step 4: Selecting a Reinforcement

Once the target behavior has been identified, a reinforcement needs to be selected. Finding an available and potent reinforcer for mentally retarded or autistic individuals can be a challenging task. Unfortunately, the SIB is often more reinforcing to these individuals than most reinforcers that can be used by parents or staff members. Changing the SIB requires finding a reinforcement that is sufficiently rewarding to compete successfully with the reinforcing aspects of the SIB.

The most readily available reinforcement is typically social reinforcement. Praise, attention, and physical contact can be dispensed contingently to reinforce the positive target behaviors. Initially, however, these social rewards may not be sufficiently powerful to change the individual's behavior. Additional reinforcements are usually necessary with these populations.

The choice of these additional reinforcements is often linked to the frequency of the SIB. If the SIB occurs at a low rate (i.e., once a day or once a week), then "expensive" or not readily available reinforcements may be used. For example, going out to eat or buying an article of clothing may be highly rewarding for the individual, but rather "expensive" in terms of money and use of time. For low rates of SIB, however, these expensive rewards can be used, since they do not need to be employed frequently.

In altering high rates of SIB (e.g., 20 times a day or more), the use of very frequent rewards is necessary. Indeed, for extremely high rates of SIB, rewards may be necessary as frequently as every few minutes during the initial phases of treatment. In these instances, readily available, inexpensive reinforcements are required. Common examples of these kinds of rewards include food, drinks, objects (paper, pencils, trinkets, etc.), and tokens that can be exchanged for other rewards. Other possible reinforcements include listening to music, going for walks, having quiet time, watching TV, doing enjoyable activities, and taking pictures. Careful observation and experimentation are often necessary to find the best available reinforcement.

Satiation with a reinforcement may become a problem if the same reward is provided repeatedly. It is helpful to have more than one reinforcer available and to provide the individual with a choice of reinforcements whenever possible. "Bonus rewards," or rewards given for extended periods of noninjurious behavior, can also be used. For example, an individual may earn a can of soda daily for not showing SIB; in addition, if the individual exhibits no SIB for a 5-day period, he or she may earn a bonus reward (e.g., going out for a ride).

Step 5: Deciding on a Reinforcement Period

Once the target behavior has been selected and reinforcements have been chosen, a reinforcement period needs to be established. This consists of defining how long the individual needs to present the target behavior before the reinforcement is earned. The length of the reinforcement period is closely linked to the rate of the SIB. In the initial phase of treatment, a reinforcement period should be selected that is appropriate to the individual's ability. For example, if the target behavior is "being calm" (behaviorally defined), the reinforcement period at the beginning of the plan should last about as long as the individual can typically remain calm *without* the use of reinforcement. This will insure that the individual is capable of earning the reinforcement and that he or she begins the reinforcement period with some success.

If an individual shows SIB at extremely high rates (e.g., 30 times per hour), the individual may initially require positive reinforcement as frequently as every 1–2 minutes. A reinforcement period that lasts longer than 1–2 minutes may well be beyond the person's initial capability. In cases where an individual requires very frequent rewards, the demands upon staff members to provide the rewards are great.

In settings that are not highly structured and well staffed, it may be unrealistic to expect the staff to provide rewards every 2 minutes for an entire day. In situations where an individual requires very short reinforcement periods, the plan may need to be put into effect for only a portion of the day. In this way, a staff member may work intensively with a person for a 2-hour period, attempting to gain "reinforcement control" during that period. When the rate of SIB decreased during that 2-hour time, the frequency of reinforcers can be expanded from every 1–2 minutes to perhaps every 5 minutes. Once the reinforcement does not need to be provided with great frequency, the length of time for which the behavioral program is in effect can be expanded without placing impossible demands on the staff.

Step 6: Shaping and Fading

As the rate of SIB decreases and the rate of the target behavior increases, the dispensing of rewards can be spaced further apart. When rewards are given less frequently, they usually need to be made more potent (e.g., more "expensive" and time-consuming). These changes constitute part of a fading procedure, wherein less frequent rewards are used to maintain the behavior change. Intermittent reinforcement of the target behavior becomes possible.

Changing SIB in these populations is usually a slow process. Patience on the part of staff is required. Once changes have been achieved, attempts to shape and fade should be introduced slowly and carefully. If the individual regresses during one of these periods of change, the program should be quickly reevaluated; usually, the change should be modified to prevent continued regression. For many individuals, a year or more of regular reinforcement is required before significant "thinning" of the reinforcement can occur.

The first fading procedure should be to reduce the frequency of the dispensing of concrete or primary rewards. As this is done, social reinforcement will usually become more prominent. The individual will then gradually learn to be maintained by social reinforcement alone as the final step to fading the behavioral program.

Summary of the Steps of the Behavioral Plan

1. Collecting behavioral data on the frequency of SIB.
2. Removing as much positive and negative reinforcement as possible that is inadvertently provided to the SIB.
3. Deciding on a target behavior to be strengthened that is incompatible with the SIB.
4. Selecting reinforcers that will be sufficiently potent to change the individual's behavior.
5. Deciding upon a reinforcement period that indicates how frequently the reinforcement will be provided.
6. Instituting shaping and then fading procedures as behavior begins to change.

Time Out

Time-out procedures are frequently an important complement to the reinforcement procedures outlined above. Time out is often more effective than ignoring SIB in achieving a decrease in the problem behavior. However, recent trends regarding the rights of mentally retarded and emotionally disturbed individuals have resulted in highly stringent criteria for the use of time out and other restrictive responses. As a result, careful consideration should be given to (1) the legality of using time out within a particular setting; (2) the potential danger of self-injury if a client is placed in time out; and (3) the likelihood that less restrictive, positively oriented treatments may be effective without the use of time out.

Examples of Individual Behavioral Plans

To provide more concrete suggestions for developing behavioral plans, three examples are provided here. These examples are intended to show a range of options for use with individuals of diverse levels of functioning.

PLAN FOR AN AUTISTIC TEENAGER IN A CLASSROOM

Description of Individual. Alan is an autistic 17-year-old. He does not have expressive language, but does have some receptive language. He attends a highly structured school program for autistic children. He shows a great deal of self-stimulation, including handflapping and rocking.

Problem Behavior. Alan bites his hand repeatedly. His hand has a large callus from the high frequency of self-biting. He also slaps himself on the side of the head. The cause of the SIB is unknown.

Baseline Data. Frequency counts of both types of SIB during a 1-hour time sample over several mornings show that SIB occurs at an average of once every 3 minutes.

Response to the SIB. Teachers ignore Alan when he shows SIB. They look away from him and do not speak with him for 1 minute after each occurrence of SIB.

Target Behavior. Alan is reinforced for keeping his hands away from his head (no contact between hand and head).

Reinforcements. Alan is given a small food reward. He is also given verbal praise and prompting.

Schedules. The food reward is provided whenever Alan keeps his hands away from his head for 2 minutes. The verbal praise is provided as often as possible.

PLAN FOR A MENTALLY RETARDED WOMAN LIVING
IN A GROUP HOME

Description of Individual. Dawn is a moderately retarded 38-year-old woman who has some expressive and receptive language. She lives in a group home and attends a sheltered workshop during the daytime.

Problem Behavior. Dawn slaps and pinches herself on the face, neck, and arms. She occasionally bangs her head. These behaviors are most likely to occur when demands are placed on her (e.g., in the morning when she is getting ready for her workshop, and in the evening when she takes her bath).

Baseline Data. On average, Dawn engages in SIB four times per week.

Response to the SIB. Dawn is ignored for 5 minutes after she engages in SIB.

Target Behaviors. Dawn is reinforced in the morning for getting ready for her workshop without showing any SIB. She is reinforced in the evening for completing her evening routine, including the bath, without showing SIB.

Reinforcements and Schedules. In the morning, Dawn earns a special snack, which she takes with her to the workshop. In the evening, she earns 15 minutes of individual time with a staff member to do a special task or just to talk. Verbal praise is provided as often as possible. When Dawn goes for 3 consecutive days without showing any SIB, she will earn a bonus reward of going on an outing to shop or to eat.

PLAN FOR A MILDLY RETARDED MAN
LIVING SEMI-INDEPENDENTLY

Description of Individual. Jake is a 44-year-old man living in an apartment with two other mildly to moderately retarded people. Jake is highly verbal and has good daily living skills. He is visited daily by a staff member who provides support, structure, and assistance when necessary.

Problem Behavior. Jake scratches his face with his fingernails. He makes visible scratch marks, some of which bleed. He usually scratches himself when he is frustrated by his inability to succeed at a task or when he is angry at his housemates.

Baseline Data. During a 1-month baseline period, Jake scratched his face three times.

Response to the SIB. When the staff member notices Jake has scratched himself, he is told that he has not earned his reward and that the reinforcement period is beginning over again. On these occasions, the staff member shortens her visit.

Target Behavior. The goal is for Jake to learn to manage his frustration effectively. He is reinforced for expressing his frustrations and anger appropriately and for not scratching his face.

Reinforcements and Schedules. At least twice a week, when Jake has not scratched his face, his worker talks with him, at which time she (1) praises him for not scratching his face; (2) discusses the problem situations he has encountered that might have led to SIB; and (3) suggests ways for Jake to handle these situations effectively. Jake is praised and prompted to make statements about wanting to learn to handle his frustration and anger appropriately. Jake earns going out for a ride with his worker whenever he goes 7 days without scratching his face.

III
Treatment

Chapter 9
Individual Treatment:
Cognitive–Behavioral Techniques

Self-mutilation is a symptom that is but one aspect of a broader psychological problem. When discussing treatment, it is necessary to distinguish between treatment of the symptom of SMB and the treatment of the overall psychopathology. Self-mutilation as a specific symptom can often be reduced or eliminated through treatment. By contrast, the psychopathology that has spawned the self-mutilation is a much more formidable obstacle within treatment, since typically we are dealing with a personality disorder or psychosis. Discussing the treatment of these forms of psychopathology in a comprehensive way would require volumes. As a result, the focus of this chapter is on self-mutilation as a symptom within the larger picture of psychopathology. The treatment suggestions that follow are designed to treat the problem of self-mutilation in a circumscribed way and are not meant to represent a cure of the broader emotional problems or mental illness of the individual.

This chapter addresses cognitive–behavioral formulations and interventions for self-mutilation. Cognitive, operant, and classical conditioning approaches are described in detail. For those unfamiliar with these approaches, a number of excellent introductory texts are available. We particularly recommend Rimm and Masters's (1979) book as a general overview of behavioral techniques, and the works of Beck (1976), Meichenbaum (1977), Beck, Rush, Shaw, and Emery (1979), and Kendall and Braswell (1984) as introductory texts on cognitive techniques.

The Cognitive Basis for Self-Mutilation

Most people find the act of intentional self-injury abhorrent. What is it about the thinking of self-mutilators that allows them to demean and deface themselves through self-inflicted wounds? In summarizing the types of thoughts that lead to self-mutilation, we can say that these fall into four categories:

1. Self-mutilation is acceptable.
2. One's body and self are disgusting and deserving of punishment.
3. Action is needed to reduce unpleasant feelings and bring relief.
4. Overt action is necessary to communicate feelings to others.

The following discussion elaborates on these categories of thinking. We begin with the category of thinking that is easiest to overlook, since it appears to be tautological.

Self-Mutilation Is Acceptable

Self-mutilators injure themselves because they think that it is acceptable, necessary, or advantageous to do so. This truism is easy to overlook, yet is important in understanding and treating SMB. As long as the individual thinks that self-mutilation is acceptable or beneficial, he or she is at risk of continuing the act. These thoughts, whether conscious or unconscious, must be present at some level for the mutilation to occur. These thoughts form, in essence, a value that the mutilator possesses. Like any other value, it prescribes and regulates behavior. Many values are unconscious in the sense that they exist as structures of thought without necessarily being in conscious awareness. As will be discussed later in this chapter, a key goal in treatment is to replace this value with the belief that self-mutilation is unacceptable and unwarranted.

One's Body and Self Are Disgusting and Deserving of Punishment

Not only do many self-mutilators think that the mutilation is acceptable; they believe it is deserved. These individuals have many negative, self-critical thoughts. Especially common are derogatory thoughts about their bodies. (See also Chapter 4 regarding these body image problems.) These mutilators have thoughts such as the following: "I hate my body. I'm so ugly. I'm disgusting. I can't stand looking at myself in the mirror." These negative thoughts about body image are critical, since they establish the person's own body as repulsive and as a likely target for abuse. When guilt or other emotions become intolerable, the mutilator has psychologically established his or her body as a target for self-sacrifice.

The belief that self-injury is deserved derives from a broader condemnation of self. Self-mutilators report that they loathe and hate themselves. Their thinking includes cognitions such as these: "I hate myself. I'm a jerk. Everything about me stinks. I can't do anything right." Low self-esteem is synonymous with this thinking style.

Action Is Needed to Reduce Unpleasant Feelings

The thoughts described above—acceptance of self-mutilation, and disgust for one's body and self—are a dangerous and volatile mixture. Once this combination is in place, other thought patterns act to trigger the emotional explosion of self-mutilation.

When stressed, mutilators often think that some kind of action is necessary in order to reduce tension. They concretize the means of tension reduction into some kind of physical act, such as aggression, substance abuse, or self-directed injury. During times of stress, the thinking of these individuals includes such statements as these: "Something needs to happen. I can't stand this any longer. I have to do something." These thoughts spur the mutilator into action. The stage has already been set for self-mutilation, and these thoughts trigger the response. Coupled with these action-oriented thoughts are cognitions suggesting that the individual will feel better after the act: "I know I'll feel better if I just cut myself. It's what I need to do to relax." These thoughts serve to convince the person that relief is available through a self-inflicted wound.

This orientation toward action for the purpose of tension reduction represents a major obstacle to treatment. Most of the suggestions made in therapy for tension reduction are not sufficiently action-oriented to accommodate the cognitive style of self-mutilators.

Overt Action Is Necessary to Communicate Feelings to Others

Many mutilators use the act of self-injury as a method to communicate intense feelings of anger, despair, or anxiety to others. Without overt action, they fear that no one will fully understand the level of distress they are experiencing. Until the act is visible for others to see, they fear that "No one will know how bad I feel. They'll think I'm OK when I'm really suffering." Cognitions of this kind function to mislead mutilators.

Mutilators also underreact to others who do *not* use action to communicate feelings. For example, a self-mutilating young woman revealed in therapy that a friend was extremely angry for something the client had done. Yet the woman said she did not believe the friend was truly angry, because all the friend did was to say, "I'm really angry." The client discounted and minimized the friend's anger, because, as the client said, "How could she be really angry if all she did was *say* she was angry? She didn't *do* anything!" This shows the perceived need for action to communicate feelings. As another example of this cognitive pattern, consider the thoughts expressed in the following excerpt from a note written by a 17-year-old female:

> I think I'm going to cut myself. Nobody knows what it's like to be me. Everything is going crazy. I feel like a bomb that is going to blow up. I hate myself when I feel this way. . . . I have stopped looking in the mirror. Ugly!! . . . I know I'm going to do something, but I don't know what to do. I want to cut myself so bad.

Cognitive Treatment: Changing Thought Patterns

The thought patterns of self-mutilators constitute a very important aspect of the maintenance and precipitation of SMB. These thoughts are what justify the mutilation and give meaning to the act; they are, therefore, a critical focus of treatment. A cognitive–behavioral approach is a direct and productive means for changing these thoughts, thereby decreasing or eliminating self-mutilation. For cognitive-behavioral treatment to be effective, each of the four categories of thinking described above needs to be changed. As will be apparent in the following pages, the types of thought patterns are so closely linked that it is usually necessary to change them in combination.

Cognitive–behavioral therapy with self-mutilators can be conceptualized as requiring several sequential steps. These steps are outlined below.

Step 1: Demonstrating the Connection between Thoughts and Self-Mutilation

We have just described the typical thought patterns of self-mutilators. As professionals, we think it is generally obvious that thinking patterns lead to self-mutilation. For clients, however, this connection may be a revelation. The first step in cognitive–behavioral treatment is to show clients how thoughts lead directly to feelings and behaviors. Most clients will accept this concept as it becomes clear that there is a direct connection between their frame of mind and their self-mutilation. Each time an individual self-mutilates, the therapist can assist the individual in discovering the exact thoughts that preceded the SMB.

Clients need to learn to monitor their own thinking and to observe the impact of their own thoughts. The therapist can facilitate this process by focusing a client's attention away from environmental conflicts and onto the client's own thinking. This refocusing carries the implied message that the solution to the self-mutilation rests with the client and his or her ability to change. This responsibility may be initially frightening to accept, but the message also contains an element of hope, in that it provides a new direction for achieving control and mastery over the problem.

Step 2: Showing That Self-Respect and High Self-Esteem Are Incompatible with Self-Mutilation

As noted, self-mutilators hurt themselves because they believe it is acceptable or necessary. These thoughts need to be challenged and changed within therapy. One way to accomplish this is to present a client with the concept that self-mutilation is incompatible with self-respect. It is impossible for people with self-respect to debase and disfigure themselves. How could anyone who cared about himself or herself do this? One form of self-respect is demonstrated through concern and protection for one's own body. As long as one's body is thought of as disgusting or ugly, it may be the target of harm. It is logically impossible to respect one's body and to mutilate oneself.

An early intervention in therapy is to label self-mutilation as disrespect for oneself and one's body. The eventual elimination of the acts of self-harm rests on the perception that self-mutilation is unacceptable, since it represents disrespect for oneself. Each episode of self-inflicted harm is labeled as evidence that the client has not yet begun to show self-respect.

Many mutilators have a "mind–body split" that allows the mutilation to occur. They see their bodies as loathsome. They also experience a sense of psychological detachment from their bodies. This schism needs to be reduced so that a mutilator sees mind and body as a unit, in which the mind serves to direct and control the body.

Once this realization is achieved, other changes in thinking become possible. One critical change in thinking is the gradual enhancement of the client's self-esteem. Individuals with low self-esteem do not think about their positive qualities, or even accept that they have any. The therapist must help such a client recognize positive attributes that the client possesses. General questioning about the person may lead to revelation of potential areas of positive self-esteem. Examples of these questions are as follows: "Is there anything at all about your personality that you find acceptable or even likeable?" "Are you a good friend to others?" "Are you loyal?" "Are you sensitive to other's feelings?" When personality or character traits are reduced to component parts, it is almost always possible to find qualities that the mutilator will acknowledge are positive. Once identified, these positive thoughts represent the beginning of a reappraisal of self-image. As positive thoughts of self increase, the risk of SMB decreases.

Another technique for discovering these positive qualities is to ask such clients what other people would list as the clients' positive qualities. Although self-mutilators may initially be uncomfortable identifying their own positive qualities, they may be able to acknowledge that perhaps other people view them as having positive aspects.

When these clients are asked whether they ever think about their positive qualities, the answer is invariably "No." They do, however, think at length about their negative qualities. This imbalance in their thinking constitutes, by definition, a poor self-image. To redress this imbalance, the therapist states to such a client that (1) the client has a negative view of himself or herself; (2) the client has positive qualities that he or she ignores and fails to think about; (3) the client will need to change this imbalance of thoughts to become stable and achieve accuracy of self-perception; and (4) the best way to do this is to begin thinking about the positive qualities of self and to reduce thinking about the negative.

The therapist uses the cognitive–behavioral approach to teach the client how to change the thoughts that are lowering self-esteem and allowing the mutilation to occur. The client is also taught how replacing these thoughts with other thoughts will make a significant difference in self-regard and level of self-protection. The new set of thoughts that the therapist is recommending should be compatible with the client's actual strengths and thinking style, and may require modeling by the therapist. Here is an abbreviated version of possible therapist comments:

> You and I have agreed that it is time you change your thinking. You have a lot of positive qualities that we have discovered together. You are hard-working, generous, and sensitive to other's feelings. It would be great if you could remind yourself of those facts. Why can't you say to yourself, "You know, I'm not so bad after all. There are some things about myself that I do like. I've got to stop being so critical of myself."
>
> We have also agreed that it is time you started telling yourself to stop mutilating. You need to show more respect for yourself. You may not like everything about yourself, but you do not deserve to be harmed and disfigured. Would you recommend to a friend who was unhappy with herself to cut herself? No, of course not, because you have too much respect for her to think she deserved to be injured. But you do not have so much respect for yourself. You need to begin reminding yourself, "I'm going to try to stop hurting myself. I don't want to do this any more. It's not right for *anyone* to hurt oneself. I have to start being more protective of my body."

Step 3: Restructuring the Need for Action into an Active Thinking Style

Since self-mutilators have an action orientation regarding tension reduction, new thinking is required to allow them to "let go" of the

SMB. These individuals believe that "something needs to happen" when they experience intense emotions. It is important that mutilators come to view this belief as faulty. It is not true that something *must* happen. Nonmutilators recognize that unpleasant feelings do not have to lead to action, and accept that these feelings must at times be tolerated. For nonmutilators, feelings are alleviated through changes in thought that accommodate and soften the experience and lessen the intensity of the feelings.

Toleration of unpleasant affect is not comprehensible to self-mutilators. Living with emotional discomfort leads to frustration and the fear of being overwhelmed. Until the thoughts that cause this frustration and fear are restructured, a mutilator feels compelled to act to reduce tension. The fear of being overwhelmed by emotions is linked to a skill deficit: The mutilator lacks alternative means to discharge feelings. When taught other methods for tension reduction, the individual is at least able to choose between self-destructive acts and these new, adaptive strategies.

The cognitive–behavioral approach is one way for these individuals to learn to dissipate intense feelings. First, they must learn to accurately label the type of feeling that is being experienced. This seemingly easy step is often difficult or overlooked, but it is critical that self-mutilators "observe" their feelings and label them. They must think, "I can tell I'm upset. I'm really very angry right now." Second, they need to tell themselves that they must stay in control, even though they have this intense feeling. And, third, they need to develop the ability to think about their feelings only when it is an appropriate and safe time to do so. Feelings can be controlled by allowing the feelings to be experienced and then, after a while, pushing them out of conscious thought. In effect, the feelings are turned on or off by switching thoughts on or off.

Typical thinking for a self-mutilator might run as follows: "I can't stand this. I'm too angry. I'm going to explode unless something happens. How could he do this to me? I'd like to kill him. Something needs to happen. I can't stand this." These thoughts are likely to lead to self-destructive or aggressive action and the sense of being out of control. On the other hand, if the same person is taught to control this thinking, he or she may have the following thoughts: "I'm very angry, but I need to be careful with how I feel so I can stay in control. I know I'm mad at him, but I've got to decide how I can deal with anger in a reasonable way. I don't want to overreact. I also can't deal with this now because I have other things that need to be done. I'll deal with it later when the opportunity is right. I have to learn to tolerate these feelings better than I have before." These thoughts are likely to lead to self-control and a regulated dissipation of the feelings.

The toleration of emotions may be restructured into an accomplishment. Experiencing emotions without having to act or "do something" becomes viewed as progress: "I can learn to tolerate these feelings. It's a good thing that I'm feeling something intensely but not reacting." These are examples of restructured thinking about the tolerance of emotions. These thoughts are incompatible with the thoughts that make the individual desperate for alleviation.

Step 4: Helping the Client to Think Differently about Communication and Relationships

As noted, self-mutilators fear their emotions will not be understood by others unless mutilation or some other extreme action is taken. In this way, mutilation becomes a critical component of communication and a cornerstone of relationships. These mutilators often think, "She doesn't really know how badly I feel. She isn't taking me seriously. I've never been this upset, and she can't even tell. I have to get through to her because I need her so much right now." This type of thinking leads to SMB.

Self-mutilators need to learn to use language rather than actions to communicate feelings. They must remind themselves that communication can occur without action. Examples of these more adaptive thoughts include the following: "I want her to know I'm upset, but I don't want her to think I'm going to kill myself. I'll tell her that I'm depressed and that I could use some support. She'll understand if I just tell her. I don't have to communicate it by hurting myself." These kinds of thoughts help stop SMB.

Giving up SMB changes the nature of mutilators' relationships. Their relationships become less intense and more stable once the symptom stops. Most self-mutilators are ambivalent about this change. On the one hand, they seek stability; on the other hand, they are addicted to the excitement. To help resolve this ambivalence, cognitive restructuring is necessary. The mutilators need to think about the advantages of a lifestyle without mutilation. The more the mutilators are aware of and thinking about the positive aspects of a stable lifestyle, the faster the symptom will be reduced. It is helpful to teach these individuals to think, "I really want to be stable. I want to have relationships that don't revolve around hurting myself. I will like myself and my life much better once I stop mutilating."

Later in the chapter, other alternatives for communication are presented for use by clients. As these new methods are learned, cognitive changes may be incorporated to remind the clients of what alternatives exist and why these are advantageous. Cognitive methods are only one aspect of cognitive–behavioral treatment for self-mutilators. The next sections of the chapter deal with operant and classical conditioning approaches to reducing SMB.

Identifying Reinforcement Patterns for Self-Mutilation

Self-mutilation is reinforced both internally and externally. The internal reinforcement is generally in the form of negative reinforcement. The external reinforcement may be positive or negative. We first examine the internal negative reinforcement that occurs when an uncomfortable emotional state is decreased or stopped by the act of self-injury.

Internal Negative Reinforcement

Self-mutilators are seeking relief and alleviation of tension. Tension is an aversive stimulus resulting from guilt, anger, or self-hatred. Any act that reduces this tension will be negatively reinforced. Self-mutilation reduces the discomfort, and is therefore strengthened as a response. Since for mutilators the level of aversive experience is great and the extent of relief provided by the SMB is substantial, the degree of reinforcement resulting from the behavior is powerful. The pattern of tension buildup, followed by relief, can become firmly established as a result of the internally experienced negative reinforcement. At times, this pattern may be maintained without any external reinforcement. Self-punishing mutilation patterns are maintained in this way. The person feels better after the act because he or she feels punished and relieved of the discomfort. It is not the punishment per se that is sought; it is the effect of the punishment that is satisfying.

External Negative Reinforcement

Negative reinforcement can also be obtained from external sources. SMB causes major reactions in others that can lead to negative reinforcement of the response. For example, self-mutilators may experience criticism, anger, or rejection as highly aversive. They often lack tolerance for these unpleasant interpersonal situations. If the mutilation results in a decrease or elimination of these aversive interactions, then the self-injury will be negatively reinforced.

A brief case example illustrates this point. Two 19-year-old female college students who were rooming together had an intense, overinvolved relationship. Both young women were self-mutilators. At times, the roommates would become hypercritical of each other. Threats of rejection and termination of the friendship would be made by each. An act of self-mutilation by one of the roommates usually occurred during these times of stress. The other would immediately stop the criticism and threatened rejection, thereby providing negative reinforcement for the SMB.

Many types of interactions may be experienced as aversive. Physical abuse, sexual abuse, yelling, and guilt-inducing statements, are all experienced as aversive. However, even love and affection may be experienced as aversive if the affection is felt to be smothering, intense, undeserved, or perverse. Cessation of any of these aversive experiences following a self-mutilating act will strengthen the self-mutilation pattern.

External Positive Reinforcement

The positive reinforcement of SMB by others often goes hand in hand with its negative reinforcement. Self-mutilators have periods when they become desperate for closeness and affection. Alienation and emotional disconnection elicit fear. The mutilator wants to get nurturance from others but feels unable to do so; either he or she lacks the social skills to elicit caring appropriately, or the other person is reluctant to provide the affection. A heightened sense of isolation results, and the individual resorts to coercion in the form of SMB to bring about a positive, caring response. As soon as nurturance, affection, or attention results, the self-injurious act has been positively reinforced.

Significant others in a mutilator's life usually view the mutilator as in danger. They may also feel pity for the mutilator. These feelings allow a sympathetic response to occur. This is why SMB is so much more effective than aggression in eliciting caring and nurturance from others. Aggressive acts usually lead to retaliatory aggressive or punitive responses. When someone hits or yells at others, it is very difficult for "victims" to be warm and pleasant in return. But when a person hurts himself or herself, it is easy to show care and concern, because the act is not viewed as an attack. Others are not physically damaged; the mutilator is hurt. Thus, it is not uncommon that sympathy is provided just as if the mutilator had been hurt in an accident. The mutilator is viewed as an unfortunate victim; the fact that he or she is also the perpetrator of the harm only underscores the apparent extent of the despair.

The provision of positive reinforcement to self-inflicted injuries is very difficult to avoid. Medical attention is often required, and this alone is reinforcing. A parent, nurse, or doctor generally takes care of the wound and probably provides reassurance and empathy, which are usually experienced as positive reinforcement. Mental health professionals also become involved when SMB is discovered. This initiates a series of interviews, assessments, and treatment sessions. Thus, more warmth and attention is provided to the mutilator.

This is not to imply that self-mutilators do not merit or require empathy, interpersonal attention, and medical care. They do, of course. But it is important to note that solicitous attention from family or professionals immediately following the actual injury will reinforce and help maintain the behavior.

Altering the Reinforcement of Self-Mutilation

Eliminating negative and positive reinforcement of self-mutilation is crucial to achieving symptom relief; however, the actual removal of these reinforcements is usually quite difficult. The negative reinforcement that results from the removal of aversive internal feelings is especially problematic. The process is covert, and treatment requires cooperation from the client.

Altering Internal Negative Reinforcement

Since the client will want tension reduction even if he or she does not self-mutilate, the therapist needs to help the client learn alternative methods for discharging and tolerating emotions. This is not an elimination of the negative reinforcement; rather, it changes the response that has previously been negatively reinforced. For example, if the client learns to be more assertive, and this results in tension reduction, then assertion will be negatively reinforced. If the client has previously used SMB for this tension reduction, it is a major accomplishment to have an adaptive behavior replace the maladaptive response. There are several alternative adaptive methods that may lead to tension reduction; these are discussed in the final section of the chapter. The key point about internalized negative reinforcement is that constructive alternative responses need to be learned if the SMB is to be reduced.

Altering External Positive Reinforcement

It is generally easier to eliminate external reinforcement, since it can at least be observed and the environment can then be changed. The first step in eliminating external reinforcement is to identify the sources. Usually several people, including friends, family, and professionals, are reinforcing the act. Whenever possible, inclusion of these people in treatment or planning meetings is helpful, so that they can be educated as to their role in the maintenance of the behavior. In situations where positive reinforcement is being provided, careful instruction is necessary. Most people think it is cruel, insensitive, or unethical to ignore a person who has mutilated himself or herself. The injured party is hurt, emotionally distraught, and asking for help. Most people, including professionals, feel guilty if they withhold care from such an individual. The most important message in this education process is this: The mutilator should be given ample attention, care, and nurturance, but only when he or she is acting in a self-protective manner. The advice, therefore, is not to ignore the mutilator all the time. Rather, the recommendation is to reduce the level of care, empathy, and concern as much as possible for the period immediately following the infliction of the wound. Even necessary medical attention should be provided with as little nurturance as is reasonable.

The same advice applies to mental health professionals. Extra meetings, longer sessions, phone calls, or other responses following acts of self-injury will only reinforce the behavior. The minimum necessary level of contact and assessment should be provided. Of course, assessment regarding a client's safety is necessary, and, as such, some reinforcement by treatment personnel is unavoidable.

Families tend to have great difficulty instituting these suggestions. Family counseling is usually required to help families eliminate positive reinforcement of the act or even the threat of the act. Families provide both social and concrete reinforcement to self-mutilators. The concrete reinforcement is an attempt to "buy off" or placate the mutilators with tangible rewards. These rewards include clothing, money, vacations, or anything tangible that can be used to make the mutilators feel better. These reinforcers must also be removed.

Self-mutilators are used to wielding power. They are accustomed to getting what they want by using self-mutilation. When there is a change in the contingencies and they can no longer get what they want through self-injurious acts, their sense of power and control is threatened. Must mutilators initially respond to the removal of positive reinforcement by an escalation of acts of self-harm. They intensify the mutilation either by hurting themselves more frequently or by making some serious wounds. Their escalation is often successful in reinstating the old set of contingencies, since family members, friends, or professionals become alarmed and feel compelled to respond. When the escalation is successful in eliciting additional positive reinforcement, the self-mutilation is strengthened even further. The message to the mutilators is clear: If mild mutilation is not enough, more severe mutilation will succeed in eliciting caring or attention. For this reason, it is very important that once positive reinforcement has been reduced for SMB, it should not be reinstated for escalation of the problem. This will only serve to create an even more pathological pattern than existed previously.

At the time that positive reinforcement is being reduced, it is worthwhile to predict in advance the anticipated escalation of the

SMB, both to a mutilator and to all significant others. Prediction to the mutilator may work paradoxically to prevent the escalation from occurring. Prediction to others prepares them for the escalation and makes the intensification of symptoms less frightening when and if it does occur. If the escalation of symptoms is severe and dangerous, restrictive intervention such as psychiatric hospitalization may become necessary. Although such interventions are serious, a continuation of positive reinforcement of SMB poses the greater risk to the individual.

Altering External Negative Reinforcement

External negative reinforcement that is the result of interpersonal interactions must also be removed. If a mutilator succeeds in stopping aversive exchanges with others through a self-injurious action, this must be altered. The first step in changing negative reinforcement is to identify the situations where it is in operation. Since detecting negative reinforcement patterns is difficult, seeking professional intervention may be necessary to identify the process as it occurs. This may also involve the use of the additional behavioral techniques outlined below.

Additional Behavioral Interventions

Desensitization

One intervention that is helpful in reducing the negative reinforcement of SMB is to increase the mutilator's tolerance for aversive stimuli. Common aversive stimuli include conflict, criticism, the threat of loss, or guilt-inducing statements from others. These interactions are emotionally painful to the mutilator and cause tension. However, it is unrealistic to expect that all anger, criticism, or guilt will be removed from the mutilator's life. Although it is a worthwhile goal to reduce these unpleasant events, everyone needs to learn to cope with the discomfort of aversive experiences. Mutilators adapt by using SMB to stop the aversive behaviors imposed by others. Nonmutilators adapt by learning to tolerate and then to respond to these aversive experiences.

Developing this tolerance requires desensitization. The mutilator needs to gradually learn to cope with unpleasant feelings. A formal or informal hierarchy is useful in defining incremental steps leading to the desired goal. The hierarchy will vary, of course, across clients. One common way to differentiate the steps on the hierarchy is to use the concept of length of time. Most clients agree that they can tolerate almost anything if it lasts only for a very short period. The hierarchy is defined by increasing the length of time the aversive stimulus can be tolerated. If a mutilator finds criticism extremely aversive and immediately attempts to avoid or escape from the situation, the desensitization progresses by having the client tolerate slightly more of the stimulus before he or she escapes or avoids it. The client is always in control and can regulate his or her own degree of exposure to the aversive experience.

Cognitive interventions serve to complement the desensitization strategy. Clients are assisted in developing a thinking style that increases their tolerance. For example, they may learn to think, "I tend to over-react to criticism. I'm going to try to listen to what she is saying for a little longer than before. I don't want to get aggressive or hurt myself because I'm being criticized. I'm going to listen just a little longer."

The hierarchy may vary according to the *type* of aversive stimulus, in addition to the length of time it lasts. For example, anger may be experienced much more painfully than guilt, or vice versa. The client always begins low on the hierarchy and works toward more stressful, aversive situations. *In vivo* desensitization or the more traditional systematic desensitization (Wolpe, 1973) may be used. The principles are the same, and both may be used in conjunction. Desensitization is necessary for most situations causing stress in self-mutilators. These situations include fear of rejection, intimacy or anger, and feelings of disgust from poor body image.

A case example illustrates how desensitization helped a 17-year-old mutilator cope with a very poor body image. This girl, Melanie, would seldom look in a mirror because she hated her looks. She wore shabby clothes that were dirty and torn. She had poor hygiene and seldom washed or showered. She did nothing to enhance her appearance. Initially, this client was uncomfortable thinking or talking about her body. Self-mutilation was often precipitated by body image issues. If a boy gave her a compliment about how she looked, an impulse to mutilate herself would follow.

In individual therapy, the desensitization procedure was initiated by gradually increasing Melanie's tolerance for discussing body image issues. The therapist regulated this conversation, and over time the client became able to tolerate direct discussion of body image as a problem. The client eventually agreed to take very small steps *in vivo* to improve her hygiene. She agreed to wash her hands and face daily and to brush her teeth. Later on, she agreed to upgrade her clothing by discarding some of her most tattered clothes. She agreed to buy some new clothes, which at first consisted of new T-shirts and jeans. All of these steps were taken quite slowly and at a pace acceptable to the client. She reported feeling very self-conscious whenever she took a new step, such as wearing a new T-shirt. The last thing she said she wanted was for someone to notice and give her a compliment.

As her level of anxiety about her body decreased, Melanie was able to discuss specific parts of her appearance that were "less disgusting" than others. For example, she hated her hair less than she hated her other features. She agreed to wash her hair more frequently and to brush it daily. At one point Melanie, on her own, impulsively set her hair with curlers on a weekend. She was not quite ready for this step. When she took the curlers out of her hair and looked in the mirror, she was repulsed by what she perceived as a hopeless attempt at self-enhancement. She raced from her house to her next-door neighbor's back yard. She had remembered that the neighbors had an above-ground swimming pool that had not been cleaned in a long while. The water had green slime floating on the surface. She dunked her hair in the slime and said to herself, "That's the kind of hair treatment that is more appropriate for me." Although this act was not technically a self-mutilation, the level of self-degradation provided the same function.

This event set the desensitization process back several weeks. However, it progressed again and eventually led to marked changes in Melanie's hygiene habits and willingness to improve her appearance. Her self-concept slowly evolved and improved. She stopped hating her looks and began to accept, and ultimately appreciate, compliments from others. She began getting professional haircuts, got braces for her teeth, and dressed neatly and appropriately. There appeared to be a direct association between her level of self-mutilation and body image. As her body image improved, the degree of self-mutilation decreased and finally stopped.

Developing New Social Skills

Although learning to tolerate aversive stimuli is helpful in decreasing SMB, there is a limit as to how much tolerance for unpleasant events should be developed. Surpassing this limit becomes counterproductive and masochistic. There is a point at which criticism, anger, or guilt induction requires an assertive, active response rather than passive tolerance. This leads to the second set of interventions that is necessary in altering faulty reinforcement patterns: the development of new social skills. Mutilators need to feel powerful and competent in the face of aversive experiences without having to resort to self-mutilation as a weapon. Shaping assertiveness and other interpersonal skills provides an alternative to SMB as a means for coping with problems. When these skills are missing, it is not surprising that mutilators feel overwhelmed and resort to self-injurious acts. Desensitization alone is not enough to change the patterns that result in SMB. New skills must be learned to replace the self-mutilation, in order to give the individual adaptive ways to react to discomfort.

The belief that "something needs to happen" may be channeled in this direction. The "something" should consist of adaptive, healthy, and constructive responses that accomplish all of the positive results achieved with SMB without the accompanying problems. These new responses must therefore include the ability to (1) communicate feelings, (2) reduce tension, (3) enhance power within relationships, (4) induce changes in others, (5) eliminate guilt, and (6) maximize rewards. For a person to be able to respond in all of these ways, a variety of skills are necessary. The client may already possess some of them, but may not use them strategically, since the SMB has been a more consistently effective response.

The shaping and strengthening of these new responses take time. The skills need to be identified, broken down into component parts, practiced, reinforced, and refined. This cycle of events is repeated over and over until the skills are developed and utilized at the correct times.

Shaping of new skills is not only needed in dissipating tension and communicating feelings. Self-mutilators have a generalized skill deficit in building relationships and achieving intimacy. Their low self-concepts make them reluctant to take chances in initiating relationships. They assume that other people will find them unlikeable, foolish, even disgusting. In beginning new relationships, they also fear rejection once their self-mutilation is discovered. Many mutilators believe that their disfigurement makes them physically unacceptable to others. Their scars are lasting reminders to themselves and warnings to others of their stormy history. Like craters or volcanos on a newly discovered planet, the scars are evidence of past upheavals.

Most self-mutilators have little experience with normal, consistent, nurturing relationships. When this kind of relationship finally presents itself, mutilators are confused and distrustful. They assume that such a relationship will ultimately lead to rejection or pain. These fears prevent commitment and intimacy from progressing beyond a superficial level. Predictably, mutilators also have tremendous difficulty forming healthy sexual relationships. They expect others to be repulsed by their scarred, "ugly" bodies. They feel inadequate in experiencing or accepting love.

All of these skill deficits in relationships are obstacles in the path leading away from self-mutilation. Without these various social skills, an individual does not have the behaviors in his or her repertoire to succeed in relationships. Attempting to remove the self-mutilation will not succeed unless other behaviors are developed to replace the mutilation as a coping mechanism.

Social Reinforcement of Self-Control
and New Social Skills

The shaping of these new skills occurs in several ways. Often the first systematic inducement for change is provided in the form of approval by the therapist. If a therapeutic relationship has been established, no other structured sources of reinforcement may be necessary, since naturally occurring reinforcement in the environment will strengthen and maintain the new behaviors. This natural reinforcement occurs when self-mutilators experience success. They master new situations, receive positive feedback from others, and accomplish things that provide satisfaction. Approval from a therapist can, therefore, be a powerful reinforcer that supports the initial changes in behavior. The development of a therapeutic relationship is an obvious prerequisite, yet it may take many sessions before the therapist is acceptable as a reinforcing agent.

The shaping process using social reinforcement by the therapist requires successive approximations. Consider, for example, a client who feels compelled to cut, yet successfully fights the impulse for an hour before finally self-mutilating. For this client, this may be progress, and it thereby requires reinforcement from the therapist. As the shaping process continues, the therapist's expectations of the client increase, and the length of time for which the client resists the impulse must be longer to achieve the therapist's approval.

Similar strategies may be used in shaping the types of wounds from more serious to less serious. If a client has a strong impulse to make deep wounds, yet makes only superficial cuts, this too is progress and worthy of reinforcement. While the client is being reinforced for SMB, there is a simultaneous strengthening of the incipient stages of self-control.

The approval from the therapist should be accompanied by statements suggesting that the client use self-administered reinforcement as well. The therapist may say, "I hope you feel some satisfaction from what you are accomplishing, because you deserve it. You should tell yourself you have done well since you protected yourself more effectively." These suggestions, paired with the therapist's approval, encourage the development of intrinsic self-reinforcement.

Behavioral Contracting

For many clients, social reinforcement from the therapist is not sufficient to change the SMB. For these individuals, behavioral contracting can be a useful technique. Generally, contracts are developed jointly by the therapist, the client, and perhaps family members. The contracts specify the target behavior to be strengthened and the reward to be earned. A contract is written down following a negotiation process to make sure it is acceptable to all parties. The contract is time-limited and is renegotiated when the specified time period is up. The rewards selected must be sufficiently powerful to have an impact on the SMB. If the client is part of a treatment program, money may be available to purchase reinforcers. Otherwise, the family must decide what money is available to buy rewards. Shared activities and recreational events that cost no money are, of course, good alternative choices for rewards when funds are not available.

Figures 9.1, 9.2, and 9.3 are examples of contracts that have been used in treating SMB. These examples are geared toward use with

Figure 9.1. A behavioral contract for directly curtailing SMB.

Name: James Doe
Date Contract Begins: February 3
Date Contract Ends: February 17
Target Behavior: Protecting my body (not hurting myself)
Reward: Money

    I understand that I will receive from my parents $1.00 a day for every day I do not hurt myself in any way. I do not earn money for that day if I injure myself. I also understand I will not receive any additional allowance money from my parents during the next 2 weeks.

Signed: _____   Date: _____

Parent's Signature: _____
_____

Therapist's Signature: _____

---

adolescents and are designed to incorporate family involvement. The target behaviors for such contracts vary and do not always center on SMB directly. Since other skills may be necessary to compete with the SMB, these contracts strengthen alternative behaviors. These external reinforcement strategies are seen as a temporary bridge to the development of new patterns of behavior. Mutilators will give up the SMB

Figure 9.2. A behavioral contract for expressing feelings.

Name: Alice Smith
Date Contract Begins: March 4
Date Contract Ends: March 11
Target Behavior: Expressing my feelings
Reward: Cigarettes

    I need to express my feelings toward others rather than hold them inside. Each time I am able to express any type of feeling, such as happiness, anger, guilt, or frustration, I will make a check mark on an index card. Each morning, my parents will agree to provide me with a pack of cigarettes if I have expressed at least five feelings during the last 24 hours. I understand that it is my responsibility to keep an honest record and to express my feelings sincerely.

Signed: _____   Date: _____

Parent's Signature: _____
_____

Therapist's Signature: _____

Figure 9.3. A behavioral contract for enhancing positive body image.

Name: Donna Jones
Date Contract Begins: April 11
Date Contract Ends: April 18
Target Behavior: Improving how I care for myself by (a) being clean, (b) being neat

    I realize that I have to show more respect for my body. One way to do this is to have good hygiene and to wear neat, clean, unripped clothes. Each day I need to take a shower, wash my hair, brush my teeth, and wear clean, neat clothing. For every 3 days in a row that I do this, my parents agree to give me a ride to a friend's house or a store within a 15-minute drive, and pick me up afterward.

Signed: _____   Date: _____

Parent's Signature: _____

_____

Therapist's Signature: _____

---

after adaptive behaviors have become sufficiently strong to replace it. There are many naturally occurring reinforcers in the environment that will maintain these new, safe behaviors. This allows for the fading of reinforcement strategies implemented by the therapist.

Summary

The cognitive and behavioral techniques that may be used to reduce SMB are summarized below. These steps are listed in the typical order of implementation, although the specific circumstances of each case may result in changes in that order.

1. Identify and eliminate positive and negative reinforcement for SMB.
2. Use cognitive therapy to change cognitive structures that maintain the SMB. Develop and strengthen cognitions that make SMB unacceptable and that increase self-esteem and tolerance of emotions.
3. Develop a hierarchy and use desensitization strategies to increase tolerance of stress-related experiences.
4. Provide social reinforcement through the therapy relationship to shape desired behaviors.

5. Use external reinforcement and behavioral contracts to further strengthen adaptive behaviors. Develop social and coping skills using these reinforcement strategies.
6. Fade external reinforcement as naturally occurring reinforcement in the environment begins to maintain appropriate behavior.

Chapter 10

Individual Treatment:
A Psychoanalytic Approach

Although the cognitive–behavioral approach discussed in the preceding chapter is the one we use most frequently, we also employ psychoanalytic treatment with a variety of self-mutilating individuals. We have a few basic rules as to what type of clients are best suited to psychoanalytic psychotherapy. Since this type of treatment generally lasts 3–5 years and entails meeting once or twice weekly, clients must, first of all, have a reasonable degree of motivation, commitment, and endurance. They must also be capable of introspection and have an interest in exploring their early life histories in detail. Thus, they must be motivated to look at their lives in a sustained, comprehensive manner, and to pursue the interrelated goals of self-understanding and change.

Since adolescents rarely possess these various characteristics, we generally exclude them from psychoanalytic treatment. We also exclude psychotics, since they are unable to endure the demands of long-term, intensive, introspective work. However, we have successfully treated a rather broad range of adult mutilators, including neurotic, borderline, and narcissistically disturbed individuals, using psychoanalytic methods.

In this chapter, we provide a brief overview of a psychoanalytic approach to the understanding and treatment of self-mutilation. We begin by presenting a short review of the psychoanalytic literature on this topic. We then present a theoretical formulation of SMB that is based on a developmental model of Sigmund Freud's. Next, we apply this theoretical explanation in discussing a case of a chronic self-mutilator. Finally, we present a summary of the phases in the psychoanalytic treatment of mutilators with reference to the case example and the theoretical formulation presented here.

Review of the Psychoanalytic Literature

Psychoanalytic explanations of SMB have gone in many different directions. In fact, psychoanalytic interpretations about the meaning of this behavior have been almost as numerous as the references themselves. The earliest paper was Emerson's (1914) case study of a female self-cutter. He contended that the behavior was the result of guilt and repulsion of sexual feelings and inwardly directed anger derived from interpersonal rejections. He also interpreted the cutting act as a symbolic masturbation and menstruation (pp. 45–46). Malcove (1933) explored the link between a child's learning to eat with utensils and an adult's self-cutting. Both behaviors were interpreted as being primitive, aggressive, even cannibalistic.

Menninger's (1935) contribution was the most lengthy and the most influential of the period. He stated:

> [S]elf-mutilation is the net result of a conflict between 1) the aggressive destructive impulses aided by the superego and 2) the will to live, whereby *a partial or local self-destruction* serves the purpose of gratifying irresistible urges and at the same time averting the prelogical but anticipated consequences thereof. The reality value of the self-mutilation varies greatly; the symbolic value is presumably the same in all instances. (p. 465, emphasis added)

The idea of SMB as a "partial suicide" or "focal suicide" has had a sustained influence on psychoanalytic writers from the time of Menninger's report to the present. (A recent example is Pabis *et al.*'s [1980] use of the term.) As noted in previous chapters, Menninger's intent was to identify the similarities and differences between self-mutilation and suicide. He conceived of SMB as a "psychic bargain" that individuals strike with themselves in order to continue a forbidden indulgence (e.g., masturbation or the fantasy of an aggressive retaliation). Menninger viewed SMB as a means of fending off suicide. Thus, he discussed SMB as a variant of suicide in which the need to inflict serious self-harm is satisfied, but not at the extreme expense of ending one's life. Most psychoanalytic writers since Menninger have not addressed the problem of distinguishing between SMB and suicide.

The one important exception is the report by Friedman *et al.* (1972). They stated that SMB is an attack on one part of the body (usually displaced from the genitals) and that a sense of relief is experienced *following* the act. With suicide, the attack is on the whole body, and relief occurs *prior* to the act. What suicide and SMB have in common, they contended, is that both are a reaction to loss: "[W]e have observed an invariable feature in all our patients, namely a constant underlying fear of abandonment" (p. 181). In the case of suicide or SMB, the act is a way of turning a passive circumstance (being left) into an active circumstance (leaving or venting rage). Friedman *et al.* also posited that self-mutilating adolescents have a pathological relationship with their bodies. They reported that many of their patients "talk of hating their bodies intensely and . . . feel forced by their bodies to have these fantasies and carry out these acts" (p. 182).

One of the most intriguing, lengthy, and speculative discussions of a self-mutilating act is that of Lubin (1964). He psychoanalytically explored the most notorious of all self-mutilations—Vincent van Gogh's removal of a portion of his outer ear. Lubin explained the act, in part, as a desperate reaction to two major losses in van Gogh's life: the impending marriage of his older brother and his rejection by Paul Gauguin. Lubin interpreted the ear removal as a symbolic, masochistic self-castration. He contended that the self-inflicted pain was also an attempt at Christ-like self-sacrifice. Athough additional details of Lubin's analysis need not concern us here, the paper deserves mention because of what it represents. Lubin described his paper as an attempt to explain "this particular self-mutilation at this particular time under these particular circumstances" (Lubin, 1964, p. 352). The article is the pre-eminent example of how one act of self-mutilation and its idiosyncratic determinants can be explored psychoanalytically at length and in depth.

However, the limitations of this approach have been noted by Runyan (1981). He identified 13 alternative (and largely incompatible) explanations of van Gogh's ear removal that have been proposed by psychoanalytic writers. As Runyan noted,

In some cases, critical analysis of the range of possible interpretations may enable us to reject all but one of the alternatives, but in other cases, we may end up with a "surplus" of explanatory possibilities, each of which is consistent with the available evidence, and with no apparent means for deciding among them. The psychobiographical enterprise must, it seems, steer between the Scylla of inexplicable events and the Charybdis of phenomena open to a troubling variety of alternative explanations. (p. 1076)

Whether psychobiographical or not, the more recent psychoanalytic contributions have continued to offer highly divergent interpretations of SMB. If there is a common thread, it is the emphasis on loss as a key antecedent to self-mutilating acts. Kafka (1969), for example, likened the self-mutilating act to a child's use of a transitional object. He contended that the appearance of blood following cutting is a pleasant, reassuring security blanket, a protection against deadness and loss. Pao (1969) distinguished between "coarse and delicate [i.e., superficial] self-cutting." He explained that delicate self-cutting is a "self-engrossed, auto-erotic . . . drive-dominated act which [is] simultaneously sadistic and masochistic" (p. 198). He stated that "while conflicts over aggression were the precipitating factor for the act of cutting, conflicts over being abandoned, being left behind . . . paved the way" (p. 201).

Asch (1971) explored the feelings of emptiness or deadness that many individuals have described as characterizing the moments immediately before the self-mutilating act. Asch believed that self-mutilation usually occurs when the perpetrator is experiencing anhedonia, a primitive form of depression. Asch also provided yet another interpretation of the meaning of SMB: "The genetic basis of this disorder may be that the induced bleeding in the cutting is an attempt to undo the current separation by identifying with the bleeding woman (mother), symbolic of this mother–infant unity in the past" (p. 617). Thus Asch also identified loss (separation) as a key antecedent of self-mutilation.

Novotny's (1972) article "Self-Cutting" is particularly helpful because of its heuristic value. He suggested that a complete psychoanalytic formulation of SMB should include the following components: (1) dynamic, (2) structural, (3) economic, (4) genetic, and (5) adaptive. Although Novotny's discussion of these dimensions was too brief to be definitive, his presentation suggested a useful schema for providing a comprehensive psychoanalytic discussion of SMB. To date, no one has attempted to provide such a formulation.

If one were to summarize regarding the psychoanalytic contributions concerning SMB, one could say that the field has manifested diversity regarding interpretations of the *meaning* of self-mutilating acts, but considerable unanimity regarding the *antecedents* of these acts. Interpretations of the meaning of SMB have included symbolic menstruation, masturbation, castration, and mother–infant unity. The behavior has been viewed as guilt-ridden, autoerotic, cannibalistic, a focal suicide, a psychic bargain, a transitional object, a symptom of anhedonia, and a manifestation of bodily self-hatred. From these diverse interpretations, one is hard pressed to identify common characteristics. Perhaps the best one can say is that psychoanalytic writers have agreed that self-mutilators have major problems within the broad categories of anger and aggression, sexuality, and body image.

The one aspect of SMB on which psychoanalytic writers have indicated considerable agreement is the sequence of events that culminates in the self-mutilative act. They have consistently identified loss or separation as the key antecedent to SMB. This consensus is striking, given the divergence of views on almost all other issues concerning SMB. This suggests that psychoanalytic treatment of self-mutilation should focus extensively on experiences of loss.

A Psychoanalytic Formulation of Self-Mutilative Behavior

Given the diversity of explanations already presented for acts of self-mutilation, one might reasonably ask, "Why provide yet another?" There are at least two answers to this question. The first is that it is important to understand the nature of psychoanalytic inquiry. As noted by Bettelheim (1983), psychoanalysis is essentially an idiographic science. This approach focuses on the meaning and interpretability of events and phenomena within the context of individual development and life history. The psychoanalytic approach is in marked contrast to a nomothetic science, which utilizes experimental verification and statistical analysis to test predictions (e.g., the methods employed in Chapters 4 and 5 of this volume).

Since psychoanalysis is idiographic in nature, it is neither surprising nor contradictory that the psychoanalytic reports regarding SMB have provided highly divergent explanations of the same behavior. Each of these reports has been based on the intensive study of a single person, or, at most, several individuals. The fact that these explanations differed markedly from case to case indicates only that the determinants of the SMB were idiosyncratic to these individuals. Until commonalities can be identified across cases (i.e., beyond the issue of loss already mentioned), a more generalized psychoanalytic explanation of SMB is not possible. In the meantime, consistent with the idiographic approach, psychoanalytic knowledge is advanced through the careful presentation and theoretical discussion of select cases. Thus, we provide an additional theoretical discussion of a case here, as a contribution to the overall compendium of cases presented to date.

Beyond this, the discussion that follows deals with an important phenomenon pertaining to the occurrence of SMB. This phenomenon is the sequence of events that begins with loss and culminates with the commission of the self-mutilative act. Many psychoanalytic writers have described this sequence as occurring for their cases (e.g., Pao, 1969; Asch, 1971; Rosenthal *et al.*, 1972; Friedman *et al.*, 1972). However, none have attempted to explain the sequence theoretically.

As the reader may recall from the brief description of the sequence in Chapter 3, it consists of the following: (1) A loss or perceived threat of loss initiates the sequence; (2) mounting, intolerable tension is experienced, which the individual is unable to verbalize; (3) a state of dissociation, or, more specifically, depersonalization then follows; (4) an irresistible urge to cut or otherwise mutilate oneself is experienced; (5) the self-mutilating act is performed, generally with an absence of pain; (6) tension relief and a return to normalcy conclude the sequence.

In trying to understand this sequence, which many of our own clients have reported, we have used a developmental model. For this model we have drawn on a relatively early paper by Freud, "On Narcissism: An Introduction" (Freud, 1914/1953). In this paper, Freud outlined three stages in child development: autoerotism, narcissism, and object love. Although this developmental model is less well known than Freud's psychosexual model (of oral, anal, and phallic stages), its enduring importance has been indicated by psychoanalytic writers as diverse as Kohut (1977) and Lacan (1977). As Freud saw it, the phase of autoerotism is the earliest period of an infant's life. During this period, the infant is a bundle of unintegrated impulses, sensations, and movements. The newborn's experience is one of total dependence, motor incapacity, disjointedness, noncohesion, and fragmentation.

As the infant matures, it passes to the next phase, which Freud termed that of primary or normal narcissism. During this period the infant begins to perceive the relatedness of its own movements, sensations, and vocalizations. In maturing as an organism, the infant comes to view itself as a unit, as a single entity, and as an integrated (as opposed to fragmented) individual. In so doing, the infant takes itself as its first object, as the first focus of libidinal investment; thus, the term *"primary* narcissism" describes this phase in development.

The third and final phase in this developmental schema is that of object love. By this time in its development, the infant is able to perceive not only the unity of itself, but also the unity of its primary caregiver, usually the mother. The infant comes to recognize that the figure who repeatedly responds to its narcissistic demands by feeding it, holding it, changing it, smiling at it, affirming it, and so on is really *one* individual. Thus, the initial experience of the unity of the ego is followed closely by the experience of the unity of another, the mother. Moreover, in time, if the child has been well cared for, it learns to partially renounce and defer its demands and needs in response to this other. This signals the beginnings of the shift from an exclusive narcissistic love to a combination of self-love and object love. If all goes well, this phase concludes with the child's having the nascent capacity to become invested in and intimate with another human being.

However, with disturbed individuals such as self-mutilators, all has generally not gone well during this developmental process. One way to ascertain these problems during childhood is to take a detailed developmental history of the individual. Another way is to study the sequence of events that culminates in the self-mutilating act. Our contention is that the sequence itself reveals major failures in the development of the capacity for self-love and object love. More specifically, our understanding of the self-mutilative sequence is that it represents a profoundly regressive experience. The steps in the sequence reflect important failures in the developmental process described by Freud.

Why does the self-mutilative sequence begin with loss? Because a stable capacity for object love has not been achieved by the mutilator. This crucial step has not been achieved because a significant loss or abandonment has occurred during the early narcissistic or object love phase. As a result, the threat of a loss, or an actual loss in the present, reactivates the profound anguish associated with the childhood loss.

The object relations of these individuals are generally so distorted that they doubt even the basic unity or cohesion of other persons. This is why self-mutilators characteristically are unable to see their therapists as complex human beings capable of a full range of positive, negative, and neutral acts. As a result, mutilators tend to vacillate between idealizing their therapists as all good or denigrating them as all bad. This is also why mutilators are skeptical of the continuity and longevity of the therapeutic relationship. To them, other persons, including the therapist, are just too elusive, partial, and fragmented to be depended on.

The role of loss, therefore, is that it triggers a regressive sequence in which, at the outset, the failure to achieve object love is re-experienced. The new loss is so troubling because a secure form of object love has never been attained. This makes the experience of subsequent separations and loss intolerable. The short-term result is the second step in the sequence: the profound, mounting intolerable tension that cannot be verbalized. If it could be verbalized—that is, if it could be shared and communicated directly with another—then the tension would be considerably diffused. But this sharing is not possible for the same reason yet again: Stable object love and intimacy have not been achieved, thereby precluding the possibility of the communication.

As a result, the tension builds unchecked, with the individual having to respond in some way. The characteristic response for self-mutilators is the third step in the regressive sequence: a reflexive escape into a dissociated or depersonalized state. And what is this state of depersonalization? It is a state in which one loses contact with one's own personal reality. It is an experience of derealization accompanied by feelings of strangeness and alienation. Most importantly, for the self-mutilator the depersonalization entails experiencing "parts of one's body . . . [as] . . . alien or altered in size and one may have the experience of perceiving oneself from a distance" (Reber, 1985, p. 188).

This depersonalized state provides only the briefest of respites from the intolerable tension. It is analogous to the experience of an accident victim whose body goes into shock as a defense against severe physical trauma. The depersonalization does not "cure" the anguish any more than the shock cures the physical damage. It merely removes the pain from consciousness for the moment.

However, the state of depersonalization has its own major risk. As the quotation from Reber (1985) indicates, in some cases the body is

experienced as alien, distant, and fragmented. What this form of depersonalization represents, therefore, is a further regression to the edge of
the first developmental phase of autoerotism. Thus, the individual
regresses almost to the intrapsychic state of the neonate. The psyche
has employed depersonalization to escape the anguish associated with
loss, but the immediate price is the terrifying experience of the disintegration and fragmentation of the ego and body.

As Lacan (1977) has written, when the unity of the ego is threatened, the ego responds with aggressivity—that is, with an aggressive
attempt to protect the ego's view of itself as unified, integrated, and
cohesive (pp. 9–16). But this aggressive explosion must be directed
somewhere, and for a self-mutilator it is directed at the self, and
especially at the body. Self-mutilators direct their aggression inward
for two reasons. First, they punish themselves because (once again) the
object has been lost. The mutilators blame themselves for this loss and
abandonment, and therefore punish themselves. A mutilating act is in
this way an act expressing self-loathing and self-blame.

A self-mutilating act serves a more fundamental purpose as well.
When a mutilator is on the edge of experiencing his or her body as
fragmented, the cut (or other form of SMB) serves to provide a sense of
physical reintegration. By inflicting the cut, the mutilator re-experiences
himself or herself as having one body, one skin. In viewing and sensing
the cut, the mutilator is reassured that the body is whole, or one piece.
Thus, paradoxically, by cutting his or her own body, the mutilator
restores its unity, and with it the unity of the ego.

The fact that the self-mutilation is usually experienced without
physical pain serves to confirm that the individual is in a depersonalized state at the time of committing the self-mutilating act. There is no
pain because, at the moment of inflicting the self-harm, the individual
is out of touch with and distant from his or her own body. It is the act
itself that "reunites" the individual with his or her body. The self-
mutilating sequence thereby concludes with the self-mutilator restored
to whatever form of normalcy he or she is accustomed. The tension is
reduced and the crisis is past.

Of course, this explanation of the self-mutilating sequence is at
this point still rather abstract. To give it a fuller meaning, we need to
apply this explanation to the discussion of a case. This is provided in
the section that follows.

Case Example of a Self-Mutilator
in Psychoanalytic Treatment, Part 1

A young woman, whom we will call Miss O, first came into treatment at the age of 20 for multiple problems. A college student, she was failing all her courses and was on academic probation. She was prone to fits of rage, was overweight (although muscular), and frequently mutilated herself. On entering treatment, she was initially almost nonverbal. She sat with her head buried in her arms, seldom revealing her face and never making eye contact. Her speech consisted of brief statements, such as "I don't know," "I'm so embarrassed," and "I'm a moron."

Within a few weeks of weekly sessions, she began to relax and to speak more actively. She requested that she be seen twice a week and that the treatment be long-term. Noting that she was intelligent, seemed motivated, and was able to discuss her life history, the therapist accepted her provisionally into psychoanalytic psychotherapy. His feeling was that he could transfer her to a more short-term cognitive–behavioral therapist if the introspective work proved too much for her.

Miss O revealed that she had grown up in the Midwest. She was the fifth of seven children raised in a middle-class home. In a conversation the therapist had with an older sister at the time of referral, the sister stated that the five older children had had a "normal upbringing." However, according to the sister, the youngest two children, including Miss O, received "almost no parenting" because of a marked deterioration in the parents' level of functioning. Over time, Miss O herself revealed details regarding her history: Her father was a chronic alcoholic, and her mother had certain bizarre habits that suggested she was psychotic. More specifically, during Miss O's childhood the mother had become a compulsive collector of refuse, newspapers, and discarded items of clothing. The family's 10-room house had gradually become filled with this material until, by the time Miss O left for college, only two rooms in the house were still usable. The kitchen was no longer functional, so meals were cooked on a hot plate and dishes were washed in the bathtub.

Over time during treatment, Miss O described a rather tortured childhood while carefully avoiding direct criticism of her parents. She revealed that she had often been abused by her father. During her childhood and adolescence, her father had abused her sexually on several occasions when he had been drinking heavily and her mother was absent.

Miss O's high school years were comprised of a rather unusual mixture of accomplishments and problems. Her grades were generally B's, and she was also an excellent athlete. In addition, Miss O was able to make several friendships with young women. However, during this period several serious problems began to emerge. During her final 2 years in high school, she began to have difficulties completing written work in school, particularly in courses that required her to express her own opinions. This problem precipitated a pattern of dropping at least one course each semester, which persisted through college. More ominously, she began to experience periods of great anguish and rage. She would often take long-distance bike rides or runs as a means of punishing herself. At other times, she took large doses of laxatives as a weight reduction technique. And she began to cut herself frequently (usually with a razor) on her arms, legs, and abdomen.

Also, during this period, Miss O began to develop a rather elaborate delusion. She became convinced that she had a relationship with a small, bodiless spirit who resided inside her mind and with whom she had long conversations. She stated that he was generally a positive force in her life—that he would encourage her and give her insights and warnings regarding various people she knew. Over time, Miss O said, she learned how to enter the realm of this spirit and to leave her body. At these times, she was able to regard her body from an outsider's point of view, and, while in this state, to feel peaceful and relaxed. Miss O stated that many times she wished to remain outside her body—to die and to join the spirit. However, the spirit would not permit this; he always insisted that she return to her physical self and continue to live.

To accomplish these "out-of-body" experiences, Miss O would often spend many hours a day rocking in a fetal position on her bed. This would produce a rhythmic, lulling effect and eventually "release." At other times, to calm herself, she would cut herself repeatedly and superficially; if she were particularly anguished, however, the cuts would get deeper and more disfiguring.

By the time she was referred for treatment, she was repeating her sophomore year of college. She reported anxiety attacks related to completing written work. She said that "committing herself" in writing exposed her stupidity and left herself open to the ridicule of others. Her self-destructive behavior had also intensified. She reported cutting herself or excoriating her wounds three to four times per week. She had made several suicide attempts prior to entering therapy by riding her bicycle in front of a truck. On another occasion, she had thrown herself into the ocean in wintertime and was saved only "when the spirit showed me a ladder to get out." She also showed her therapist a four-page "Christmas letter," which she revealed afterwards had been written in her own blood. In addition, Miss O reported that she was frequently tortured by nightmares in which machines or animals devoured her or tore her to shreds. She revealed that no people ever appeared in her dreams.

Early in treatment, Miss O's demeanor during sessions was painful to observe. She writhed in her chair and was often unable to speak. When she did speak, she expressed doubt about the validity of anything she said, except when she began one of her favorite streams of self-denigrating invectives (e.g., "I'm retarded, ugly, a fat slob, pathetic"). The close quarters and intimacy of the therapy hours clearly caused her great anguish, yet she never missed or was even late for a session.

Over time, she made slow, gradual progress. She reported that her delusional relationship with the spirit had ceased. She came to recognize that the spirit had probably been "only a part of myself." Her grades improved, and she was no longer on academic probation. She lost weight and assumed a more attractive appearance; she also maintained several long-term friendships. Nonetheless, she was subject to periods of serious regression. During these periods she withdrew from her friends because she became convinced that they hated her. She would frequently mutilate herself, usually with razor blades or glass. She became quite demanding of the therapist, attempting to give him presents, to schedule extra sessions, and to call frequently between sessions.

As an indication of her intrapsychic state at the time of these regressions, we provide the reader with a verbatim report of one of her dreams. This dream occurred in the midst of one of her more regressed periods.

I had a dream I was in the water with someone else and a shark was eating me, tearing me apart. I was being flung all over the place, and finally I slipped through a gate that the shark couldn't fit through. I was surprised

I fit and didn't get stuck. I thought my legs would get in the way; then I realized my legs weren't there. I was all bloody and dangly. I said, "I'm torn to shreds."

After reporting this dream in treatment, she then presented the following associations:

1. "In the water with someone else": This "someone else," Miss O said, was a young woman with whom she was having an intense, fused, ambiguously sexual relationship. They had recently been fighting, and it was unclear whether the relationship would survive. Miss O said, "I feel like my friend has been drowning lately and that she's trying to drag me down with her."

2. "The shark": "My friend was the shark," said Miss O.

3. "Eating me, tearing me apart": Miss O said, "I was terrified; I felt like I was being chewed." Also, a later association was of her friend having oral sex with her (i.e., "eating her").

4. "I slipped through a gate": Miss O said, "The gate was like the black iron gate in front of a cathedral . . . the kind with spears on top. If you fall on it, you'd die."

5. "My legs weren't there": Miss O said, "Everything from the waist down was gone . . . not so bad really . . . it would mean I wouldn't have to deal with anything 'down there' like that time of the month or sex."

6. "Bloody and dangly": Miss O said, "I saw all blood and I couldn't see my body. It was like I was all chopped up. . . . There was blood everywhere, but I was in the water. By the end I didn't need to breathe any more. It was like something took me away. . . . I was in the water . . . I was free. Maybe I died . . . I probably died."

7. "I said, 'I'm torn to shreds'": Miss O remarked, "I wasn't horribly frightened, I said it matter-of-fact."

The first thing that can be said regarding the dream (and its associations) is that it clearly represented a regressive sequence. The dream contained essentially the same components as the six-item self-mutilative sequence (with one notable exception, discussed below). The dream began with a reference to Miss O's dual problems with intimacy and loss. She was experiencing her friend as "tearing her apart." The terror that Miss O reported was due both to her friend's move toward intimacy and to the related threat of loss of the relationship. Miss O was not able to accept either of these outcomes, and this inability on her part reflected her major problems in achieving object love.

That Miss O had problems with this developmental phase was no surprise, given her early life history. It was clear that the psychotic-level functioning of her mother and the primitive, impulse-ridden style of her father had damaged her severely. In fact, she had major problems not only in the area of object love, but in the area of normal narcissism or self-love as well. The fragmented nature of her ego was reflected not only in the frequent experiences that she had had in the past involving "the spirit in her mind," but in the dream as well. In the dream, again and again, the images of missing legs and genitalia, of dismemberment, and of shredded tissue reflected the fragmented nature of her ego and body. As Lacan (1977) says,

> This fragmented body . . . usually manifests itself in dreams when the movement of the analysis encounters a certain level of aggressive disintegration in the individual. It then appears in the form of disjointed limbs, or of those organs represented in exoscopy, growing wings and taking up arms for intestinal persecutions. (pp. 4–5)

Thus, the dream went beyond a fear of losing a valued object. It also indicated her fear that her ego was shattering and that she would be reduced to the chaos of the autoerotic phase.

However, the dream also reflected Miss O's ambivalence about the depersonalization; ambivalence is atypical for most self-mutilators. Mutilators generally fear the experience of fragmentation and mutilate themselves in order to *terminate* it. In contrast, although Miss O feared it, she was also rather *practiced* at depersonalizing. In the past, she had frequently induced such a state. She reported becoming comfortable over time in "escaping" her body and achieving some sort of altered state of consciousness. For Miss O, this state came to represent the attraction and allure of death. Death represented peace and permanent escape from the pain and anguish of living. And yet, despite the temptations of death, she always eventually chose to return to her body and to continue living. These themes were all repeated in the dream in the reference to the gates of a cathedral and her association, "Maybe I died . . . I probably died."

Even though the dream included her passing through the gates of death and escaping the dangerous waters of intimacy and loss, it concluded with her saying, "I'm torn to shreds." What was significant in this concluding sentence was that she *said* it. In speaking the words, she indicated her *wish* to remain a speaking, human subject. To speak, there must be a speaker, an individual, a reintegrated subject. Thus, the act of speaking that concluded the dream was identical with the conclusion of the self-mutilative sequence discussed above.

A Summary of the Treatment Process

In treating individuals such as Miss O, we have found that we generally go through four phases of work. The first is concerned exclusively with relationship building. Given their histories of object loss and object failure, self-mutilators are wary of interpersonal relationships. The anguish that Miss O showed early in her therapy is not unusual, although the particular forms of discomfort vary from client to client. Mutilators typically have difficulty settling into serious discussion. They may be largely silent or may ramble on endlessly, but either way their anxiety about revealing themselves is clear.

In response to this anguish, it is important for the therapist to be warm, empathic, and very active in the early sessions. If the therapist does not clearly convey concern and interest early on, the client is likely to terminate treatment. Mutilators are not able to endure a traditional form of psychoanalytic reserve in these early sessions. The therapist needs to take the risk of "contaminating the transference" if the client is to be kept in treatment.

If the therapist fails to adopt this active stance, clients will often give warnings that they are dissatisfied. They will indicate that their needs are not being met by coming late to sessions, requesting to leave early for "practical" reasons, or missing sessions altogether. These warning signs need to be responded to quickly if the treatment is to survive. The best response is to actively question such clients about the treatment thus far. Is the treatment what was expected? Is it frustrating? If so, how? Naturally, the therapist will not concede to inappropriate requests and demands, but these can be gently deflected.

The goal of this active, empathic approach is, of course, to establish enough of a therapeutic relationship for the real treatment to begin. To be sure, if the relationship itself is sustained, warm, empathic, and consistent, some modest benefit can be achieved. But, if the treatment does not progress beyond this first phase, the likelihood of significant progress in the areas of self-concept, object relations, and the self-destructiveness itself is minimal.

The second phase in treatment entails the therapist's gradually shifting from the stance of an active participant to that of an active and attentive listener. This is a key shift that should be announced in advance to a client. The therapist can explain the shift by indicating that the client has made progress, is now more comfortable, and is ready to speak at length on his or her own. The therapist explains that the advantage of the client's speaking extensively without the therapist's "interruptions" is that the treatment will progress to a new and deeper level. This will permit greater understanding and an increase in the capacity for positive change. Most clients can accept this rationale.

If the therapist does not explain the shift in advance, the risks are considerable. The client may say, "Lately, I've been thinking you want to get rid of me. I think you're bored with me and would rather be doing something else." Although such transferential material can be productively interpreted later in treatment, this is not the case early on. Such statements indicate the risk of the client's discontinuance. An interpretive approach to such material would merely confirm in the mind of the client the therapist's withdrawal and lack of concern.

The proper focus in this second phase of treatment is on the day-to-day problems and successes in the client's current life situation. During this phase, the client is beginning to identify, with the therapist's help, recurring patterns in his or her life. With self-mutilators, there is often a certain similarity from client to client. They tend to identify the following recurrent problems in their present lives: (1) unresolved, primitive relationships with their families of origin; (2) stormy, intense, inconsistent peer relationships; (3) periods of depression and withdrawal from others; (4) problems in enjoying and/ or performing at school or work; (5) disgust with physical appearance, especially concerns with weight, eating, and attractiveness; and (6) major problems in the area of sexuality, which, at this phase, can scarcely be talked about. In addition to these specific issues, mutilators have generalized problems with self-esteem and identity.

The identification of these various important areas of dysfunction is important for two reasons. The first is that clients are generally able to make modest changes in some of the problem areas, once they have identified them. For example, once Miss O discussed in therapy the details of dropping and failing courses in school, she began to discipline herself and to obtain good grades. The support of the treatment was sufficient for her to make gains in this area. Although her academic failure was by no means one of her more serious problems, the progress she made encouraged her to move on to more difficult issues.

The second advantage of the here-and-now focus in treatment is that it lays the groundwork for the third and most important phase. By identifying the recurrent patterns of dysfunction in his or her present life, the client is led inevitably to discussing the past. These dysfunctional patterns reveal key points of entry, therefore, into the client's early life history.

For those clients who make it to the third phase in treatment, the real work begins. The focus in this phase is on uncovering the nodal "events" in the client's childhood history. These "events" are not necessarily dramatic, traumatic occurrences. That is to say, what the client reveals may or may not be based on actual events or occurrences in the client's life. What makes the "events" nodal is the emergence of key chains of associations that reveal themselves to be at the heart of the matter. For self-mutilators, the revelation of these key associative chains generally clarifies the puzzle of the clients' self-loathing and self-destructiveness. An example of the unveiling of key associative chains is provided in some further case material pertaining to Miss O.

Case Example, Part 2

After 3½ years of twice-weekly therapy, Miss O was well into the third phase of treatment. By now she spoke less frequently about day-to-day events in her life. She was able to concentrate quite consistently on discussing material in her early life that she saw as the basis for her present problems. She was also able to associate quite freely to dream material. Miss O became able to talk about her self-loathing, which dated from childhood. This included her conviction that she was "ugly and fat" as a child, even though family photographs revealed otherwise. She recalled the ridicule she experienced as a child from her older siblings, who taunted her with words such as "retard," "stupid," "moron," "fatso," "ugly," and "animal." She also recalled her confusion at her mother's "jealousy," which she could only dimly remember and understand.

During one session, Miss O began to describe a rather hazy memory of an exceedingly uncomfortable experience. She stated that she remembered being in the bathtub at about age 3 or 4. "I was little," she said.

MISS O: My mother and sister were washing me even though I didn't want to be. I was crying, pleading with them not to hurt me. They laughed at me, saying they were only washing me and that it wouldn't hurt. But I was afraid the pain would come back, I was really afraid of the pain . . .

THERAPIST: What pain?

MISS O: The pain in my stomach. It's like the pain I still get some times. [Although Miss O said the word "stomach," she pointed to her genitals.]

THERAPIST: You said your "stomach," but I noticed that you pointed to your genitals.

MISS O: No, my stomach . . . Well, maybe it was my genitals . . . I remember being washed another time. Maybe it was my mother . . . No, my father. I was standing up in the tub and he was being nice, washing me all over, but then there was this pain which shot up inside of me, like right through me . . . into my *stomach*, but it began . . . in my vagina . . .

This particular series of memories and associations became the focus of many subsequent sessions. Miss O reworked the material repeatedly, gradually recalling other important details. She said that while her father was washing her, he had suddenly inserted his finger into her vagina. This had caused her great shock and pain. She had yelled because of the pain, and, as a result, her mother came into the bathroom. Then a strange series of looks or glances occurred. First, the father gave Miss O a "dirty look" for yelling. Next, the mother gave the father and daughter a "suspicious look," which the father avoided. Finally, both parents looked at Miss O angrily and scolded her for "being bad and making a ruckus."

As a result of this material, Miss O pulled together a number of important themes. She came to link her nakedness with being coerced and laughed at. To be naked was to be exceedingly vulnerable to others, both verbally and physically. She connected these thoughts and feelings with her present fears of sexuality and especially of any form of penetration, be it from a tampon, finger, or penis. She also linked her nakedness and her pain with her disgust toward her body. She felt she was to blame for the pain, the conflict, and the yelling. She was naked, embarrassed, in pain, and crying, and her parents were yelling at her, entirely unsympathetic to her bewildered vulnerability. She described herself—using words she had used many times previously in therapy—as "falling apart," "cracking," with no one there to help.

As Miss O presented this material, she was often profoundly upset. She resumed squirming in her chair and hiding her face, as she had done early in the treatment. She reported wanting to cut herself, but at this point in treatment she did not begin self-mutilating again. Instead, she talked about it, and afterward began to express a greater sense of relief. She stated that she now had a better sense of why she had always thought of herself as ugly and horrible, and why she had always avoided sex. She began to express great anger at the unavailability and "collusion" of her parents. Yet she was also able to feel some compassion for them in recognizing how seriously disturbed they too had been.

Material such as Miss O revealed is the type that needs to be articulated during the third phase in treatment. This type of material begins to solve the puzzle of both the SMB and the broader problems with self-love and object love. Such experiences with abuse and victimization begin to explain for the client the loathing of self and body and the profound distrust of others. Even more important than the achievement of insight is the sense of relief that accompanies it. The client comes to recognize that his or her basic sense of unworthiness and ugliness is not intrinsic and fundamental. Rather, it is the result of unfortunate, even tragic circumstances that predate his or her own responsibility. If material of this depth can be reached, the treatment is on the road to success.

The final phase of treatment, of course, is that of termination. There is little that is distinctive or unique in the termination of the treatment of self-mutilators. Like other clients, they tend to regress in anticipation of the ending of therapy. They may briefly become volatile again, both inside and outside the sessions. The self-mutilation itself is unlikely to recur. However, given the sensitivity of these clients to loss, much archaic material regarding childhood loss and abandonment is likely to be raised again. This recapitulation is really no different than that experienced with other, nonmutilating clients. In most cases, the regression is brief. The ending consists of a mutually shared combination of sadness at saying goodbye and a sense of accomplishment at having endured a long, tiring, productive collaboration.

Chapter 11

Family Treatment

Parents have many concerns about the kinds of problems their children will encounter as they pass through adolescence. Common concerns and worries are that children will become involved with drugs and alcohol, will violate family rules, or will have significant school difficulties. Although any of these problems is highly stressful, most families realize that difficulties of some type are likely to occur with adolescent children. Despite these expectations, family members are shocked if a child deviates from "traditional" forms of adolescent turmoil and presents self-destructive behavior. They are unprepared and have no pre-established notions about how to cope with a child who exhibits SMB.

The initial reaction of most families to self-mutilation is fear. A family undergoes radical changes in interpersonal dynamics as the shock of a self-mutilative act pervades the system. Not surprisingly, the self-mutilation may function as a signal that alerts the family to dangerous and pathological family patterns. An alert family is able to recognize that family problems play an important role in a child's self-destructiveness. Rapidly, this type of family seeks to obtain professional help, often telling the clinician that the child "tried to commit suicide." The stream of events following this initial professional contact usually leads to family treatment.

Since the family probably does not, at this incipient stage, have a sensible way of responding to a self-mutilative act, the pathology in the family becomes exaggerated as the family system strains to accommodate the new stress. As time passes, and especially if the self-mutilation is repeated, the family system establishes new patterns to respond to the self-mutilation. Some of these patterns have regrettable consequences, as the responses within the family only serve to perpetuate or precipitate continued self-mutilation acts. The importance of the family therapy is to correct the family patterns that have contributed to the formation or continuance of the self-mutilation.

As in most instances of deviant behavior, there is a reciprocal relationship between the SMB and the family dynamics. Although the self-mutilation has a profound impact on the family, the pre-existing family dynamics may have spawned the self-mutilation. Thus self-mutilation is but one, albeit dramatic, link in a behavior chain of interaction between and among family members. It is very difficult to separate the cause and effect of the self-mutilation within a family.

The present chapter describes the occurrence of self-mutilation within a family context. The intent of this discussion is to show (1) how different types of mutilators reveal or conceal their self-inflicted injuries within their families; (2) what sorts of family dynamics spawn these types of mutilators; and (3) what functions the acts of self-harm serve within the family system. The chapter concludes with a discussion of family therapy techniques that have been designed to assist the different types of self-mutilators. These techniques are then "applied" in the discussion of a case.

The information presented in the chapter is categorized in two ways. First, three dimensions are defined that provide clinicians with a means of conceptualizing the interaction between mutilators and their families. Each of these dimensions pertains to a significant area of family functioning that may be causing or at least maintaining the self-mutilation. Second, we also present a schema of different types of mutilators. Three types of mutilators are discussed in relationship to their family contexts: (1) manipulative self-mutilators, who are generally individuals with personality disorders (especially borderline personalities); (2) self-punishing mutilators, who are typically guilt-ridden and depressed individuals; and (3) psychotic self-mutilators, who inflict self-injuries as a result of thought disorder.

This system of organizing information allows us to examine each of the three types of mutilators in relationship to each of the three family dimensions. Table 11.1 displays this conceptual framework and summarizes some of the recommendations for family treatment.

TABLE 11.1
Summary of Subtypes of Self-Mutilators along Three Dimensions

	Dimensions			
Self-mutilator subtypes	Public vs. private mutilation and type of wound	Emotional response of family	Power issues	Primary treatment goals
Manipulative self-mutilators	Always public. Wounds range from superficial to serious with a tendency to escalate in severity over time.	Highly variable response by family over time, ranging from intense support and nurturing to extreme rejection and withdrawal.	Extremely important to mutilator. Wants to be able to regulate others' responses.	1. Achievement of stability in level of intimacy within family. 2. Removal of SMB's power to cause shift in emotional expression.
Self-punishing self-mutilators	Private at first; may be discovered later. Wounds vary from mild to serious on covered parts of body.	When detected, response of family is to induce guilt in mutilator.	Not a major dynamic, but mutilator generally feels powerless and weak.	1. Consistent detection of the SMB. 2. Improvement of communication, support, and guidance by family.
Psychotic self-mutilators	Regulated by specific nature of psychotic thinking. Wounds tend to be serious and often to vulnerable body parts.	Irrelevant unless part of a delusional system.	Significant if part of delusions of grandeur or persecution.	1. Management of dangerous behavior. 2. Understanding of psychotic process. 3. Clarification of communication.

199

Family Dimensions

Public versus Private Self-Mutilation

Some mutilators go to great lengths to conceal their self-destructive acts. They injure parts of their bodies covered by clothing, avoid exposure of wounds, and do not seek medical attention for their wounds. These individuals take elaborate steps to prevent the discovery of their self-harm. For these mutilators it is imperative that their wounds not be discovered, because nothing is to be gained from others' knowing about their injury.

In contrast to the surreptitious self-mutilators are those individuals who insure that their families and significant others are aware of their injuries. These mutilators injure parts of their bodies that tend to be visible, display their wounds by wearing revealing clothing or rolled-up sleeves, place highly visible bandages on their wounds, and seek medical attention even when it is unnecessary. For these mutilators, it is imperative that their wounds be discovered, because much is to be gained from others' acknowledging their self-mutilation.

This "public versus private" dimension provides valuable information about self-mutilators. When a self-inflicted injury is concealed, it has little or no impact on family or group dynamics. When an injury is exposed, it has a powerful effect on family members and friends. Once individuals begin to mutilate themselves, they quickly recognize the impact of the self-harm. They must immediately decide whether or not to keep it secret. In general, mutilators publicly reveal their self-injuries when they wish to make an *interpersonal* impact. Conversely, a decision to keep the mutilation secret results from *intrapsychic* conflicts, which may be rather far removed from interpersonal considerations.

As noted in previous chapters, the location and type of self-inflicted wounds are important in the assessment of SMB. In evaluating family systems, the type of wound reveals useful information as to the family dynamics. Generally, self-mutilative acts designed for maximum effect on the family tend to be superficial and relatively painless. These wounds differ from those made to inflict self-punishment or to accommodate a bizarre thought process. This latter type of wound is much more likely to be physically damaging and to require medical attention.

There is a linear relationship between the severity of an individual's psychopathology and the severity of the self-mutilative wound. If the psychopathology is relatively mild and the primary motive for the act relates to interpersonal conflict, the wounds will be superficial and confined to relatively "safe" and visible areas of the body. Superficial scratches on the arms are the most common example of this type of self-harm.

In cases of more severe intrapsychic dysfunction, the type of wound is deeper and often more "dangerous." The extreme of this continuum is seen in psychotic individuals, whose wounds may be grotesque and serious, often affecting the eyes or genitals.

Emotional Response of the Family

The response of significant others, especially family members, to the self-mutilation is a key variable in understanding SMB. One would normally expect family members to be highly reactive to a behavior such as self-mutilation. However, in actuality, families show considerable variability in their response. These range from outrage and hostility to depression and guilt, or even passivity and unconcern. Also, the reactions of families may change over time, particularly when the self-mutilation is repeated frequently. Some families eventually become detached and unresponsive to the self-mutilation. Such nonresponsiveness can even reach the point of refusing to provide medical assistance to the wounded individuals. Such families are usually intensely angry about the repetition of the self-mutilation, and attempt to use rejection as a mode of punishing the behavior.

Other families, in effect, are held hostage to repeated threats of self-mutilation. These families remain reactive to and frightened by the act and will go to almost any length to prevent the vulnerable individuals from mutilating themselves. This emotional responsiveness may at times be successful in preventing a mutilative act, but the risk is that the mutilators will be highly reinforced for the threats and actions of self-harm. Paradoxically, although multilators may wish for an emotional response from their families, they are not able to tolerate or respond to the emotions once these are generated.

Multilators are usually seeking an emotional reaction from their families because they feel empty and unloved. For some, the only time they feel cared for is when their families are pushed or coerced to respond to a self-mutilative act. If a mutilation, or simply a threat of one, results in attention and other benefits, it has been useful in meeting a person's emotional needs in a temporary fashion. Even if the family remains detached and uninvolved, the mutilator, while feeling rejected, usually finds some solace from the revenge that has been achieved. This revenge is gained by forcing the family to deal with the practical consequences of the self-mutilative act.

There is, then, a profound disturbance regarding the expression of emotions in many of these families. On one end of the continuum, the dysfunction is a total lack of communication of care and warmth; there is a void that prevents any emotion from entering into the family process. This vacuum is terribly frustrating to the mutilator, who uses SMB to trigger some minimal form of emotional expression within the family. On the other end of the continuum is the family that operates within a field of intense and overwhelming emotions. This affective overload may be temporarily stimulating and exciting for the mutilator, but in the long run, it is incapacitating. There is a sense of drowning in the flood of feelings, which the mutilator experiences as uncontrollable and frightening. In this latter type of family, the self-mutilation is used as a dam to block or modulate the flood of emotions, or as a weapon to punish the family members who have been the initial source of the affective outpouring.

Power Issues

The power issues occurring within a family with a self-mutilating member are highly relevant to family treatment. Adolescents find countless ways to draw parents into power struggles: They rebel by resisting family rules, dressing in unusual ways, refusing to achieve in school, or withdrawing from involvement in family life. Virtually any issue pushed to an extreme will lead to a power struggle.

Self-mutilation may be used as the vehicle for engaging in a power struggle for several reasons, including the following: (1) It is dramatic and almost impossible to ignore (especially at first); (2) it generally induces tremendous anxiety and/or guilt in others; and (3) it is virtually impossible to prevent if the mutilator is determined.

Self-mutilation is often used strategically in multiple ways. The most obvious power issue is the implied or stated message, "You can't stop me." Although parents and professionals may be successful in bringing tremendous pressure to bear by imposing loss of privileges, psychological treatment, and psychiatric hospitalizations, nothing other than total sedation can prevent self-mutilation. Even patients in four-point restraints can bite their tongues and cheeks or dig their fingernails into their hands. Informing determined self-mutilators that they will not be permitted to mutilate themselves is an empty promise.

This type of power struggle is similar to attempts to force patients with anorexia nervosa to eat. Trying to use power and control to make the patients eat will usually fail. Even force-feeding may not be successful if the patient is free to induce vomiting, pull out intravenous tubes, or engage in extreme exercise routines.

Thus, self-mutilation is a conduit for expression of power and independence. The family members, typically parents, desperately seek to find methods for reinstating their dominance and control. Resolution of these power issues rests on the successful negotiation of the child's developmental needs to have sufficient autonomy and control.

Another way in which power and control affect self-mutilation is in cases where the mutilator is trying to change his or her family through the use of SMB. For example, a teenager unhappy about the alcohol abuse of a parent may attempt to use the self-mutilation to force the parent to stop drinking. The same strategy can be employed to stop sexual abuse or any other family pattern in which the child feels powerless. Self-mutilation empowers the child while simultaneously threatening the parents. A child who is otherwise defenseless or without resources can suddenly become a major force in family politics.

Subtypes of Self-Mutilators and Family Dynamics

As noted earlier, for conceptual purposes this chapter has categorized mutilators into three subtypes. Each of these subtypes entails different interactions within a family system. This section of the chapter examines each of these subtypes according to the dimensions outlined above.

Manipulative Self-Mutilators

Manipulative self-mutilators are most commonly diagnosed as borderline or antisocial personalities. When these individuals self-mutilate, the action is usually a manipulative attempt to provoke a response from others. Thus, the primary focus of these acts is interpersonal, in that the self-injury is largely motivated by relationship issues. Although the mutilation may have some self-punishing aspects, these are secondary to the need to achieve a desired response from significant others, especially family members or important caretakers.

Since the aim is to affect others, the self-mutilation in this subtype is always public. There may be manipulative, half-hearted attempts to conceal the wound, but these are calculated to make the SMB seem more dramatic once it is discovered. These mutilators are determined to evoke the reaction of others, for it is the emotional response of their families that satisfies the mutilators' needs.

A well-known pattern of borderline personalities is the dramatic, intense fluctuations in intimacy within their relationships. Borderline individuals appear compelled to seek and perpetuate these constantly shifting unstable relations. Self-mutilation provides such individuals with a very effective tool in satisfying their need to control and modulate interpersonal closeness.

A manipulative mutilator is adept at knowing what effect the self-mutilation will have on family members, even when the reactivity of the family is highly variable over time. For example, a family's reactions to the SMB may vary from great nurturance and support to complete, cold rejection. Such a family regularly shifts back and forth between these polar extremes, spending very little time in the emotional center. The self-mutilation is a catalyst that compels the family to shift from one pole to the other. If the mutilation occurs when the family members have been enmeshed, they are effectively pushed to a distant position by the mutilator, who has become uncomfortable with the closeness. If the mutilation occurs when the family is remote and distant, the mutilation serves to reinstate the closeness of the family and to reassure family members that they are still emotionally affiliated.

This pattern can continue over many years, but over time there is often an escalation in the acts of self-harm because of a process of satiation or desensitization. As a result, the frequency and/or severity of the wounds may intensify over time. For example, self-inflicted injuries that began as superficial scratches may become more serious and numerous wounds, requiring stitches. These deeper and/or more frequent wounds eventually produce the desired changes in the family, but at a greater physical cost.

Power issues within the family are a critical element in this type of pattern. The manipulative mutilator simultaneously uses the acts of self-harm to coerce the behavior of others, while also demonstrating his or her own freedom from the influence of these others. If the family attempts to control and stop the mutilation, the mutilator resists the control and continues the self-abuse. The message to the family is clear: The act cannot be controlled by anyone other than the mutilator.

The first task in treatment of such a family is to achieve a reasonable degree of stability to replace the extreme shifts from emotional overinvolvement to cold rejection. As long as the self-mutilation succeeds in controlling these shifts within the family, it is likely to continue. The challenge for the therapist is to assist the family in accepting the importance of stability and in developing a consistent degree of closeness. This entails arriving at a level of closeness for the family that is neither stifling nor distant.

Sometimes a family, especially if it has more than one pathological member, resists accepting this sameness and consistency. It is a less exciting, less dramatic form of existence, which may seem unappealing and understimulating as a lifestyle. If this goal is not desired by the family, resolution of the self-mutilation is much more difficult.

This family pattern is the one that is most likely to intensify and worsen once treatment begins. The self-mutilator will repeatedly test the limits imposed in treatment and will use incrementally more severe forms of mutilation to re-establish the usual family dynamics. It is often helpful to predict these escalations in advance, in the hope that this prediction will paradoxically prevent the intensification of the self-mutilation.

The manipulative self-mutilator is very trying for the family therapist. Overreaction by the therapist results in the same dynamics as seen within the family. However, a lack of responding by the therapist can encourage a dangerous escalation of acts of self-harm. The therapist must therefore model for the family a balance between responsiveness and dispassionateness. This demonstrates for the family members the balance that they need to achieve.

An example of the treatment of such a family is seen in the following case discussion. The identified patient was a 16-year-old girl, whom we will call Gina. Prior to entering treatment she was a frequent self-mutilator. Gina would cut or burn her arms, hands, and stomach about once a week, and would threaten to do so almost daily.

She always made certain that her parents became aware of her injuries. She would roll up her sleeves so that her injuries were readily observable, would put on larger-than-necessary bandages, and would leave blood-soaked tissues around her home.

Gina's self-mutilation was always connected to a demand for money, cigarettes, privileges, or other concrete benefits. These requests coincided with periods when her parents were angry and distant from each other. Gina used the threat of SMB to stop her parents from arguing. If her parents refused to give her what she asked for, she would threaten to mutilate herself. If they continued to deny her, she would follow through on her threat and injure herself. As time went on, Gina was able to control her parents' arguing and to obtain virtually anything she wanted.

Gina's parents developed polarized reactions to her SMB. Her mother generally tried to set limits and be nonreactive, whereas her father was extremely reactive. He would invariably succumb to Gina's demands and provide her with what she wanted. This situation was symptomatic of profound marital problems that culminated in divorce 2 years after treatment began. The marital problems and associated distress were the root cause of the self-destructive behavior shown by Gina.

Following the divorce, Gina remained with her mother, who was able to terminate the pattern of rewarding the self-mutilation. Gina tried unsuccesfully to use SMB to force a reconciliation of her parents. Although there was initially a period of sharp escalation of the SMB, this was followed by a steady reduction in occurrence of the problem. Within 7 months the self-mutilation stopped altogether.

Self-Punishing Self-Mutilators

The self-punishing self-mutilator is in many ways the opposite of the manipulative mutilator. In the self-punishing pattern, the mutilator is attempting to use the SMB as a weapon against the self. The SMB is designed to inflict punishment, relieve guilt, and express self-hatred. The primary motivation for the act is intrapsychic, not interpersonal. Since the discovery of the self-mutilation may result in unpleasant consequences, such as increased guilt or a psychiatric hospitalization, the wounds are usually kept private for as long as possible. When the wounds are inflicted, they are usually hidden on parts of the body normally covered by clothing; if necessary, extra clothing is worn to conceal the evidence. Such mutilators often wear long sleeves on even the hottest summer days.

If a wound is accidentally revealed to the family, the mutilator will confabulate stories to explain how he or she was hurt. These stories are often naively accepted by the family members, since they are eager to deny the truth regarding the self-mutilation. Some of these families never discover or acknowledge that one of their members has been self-inflicting wounds. However, in most cases the reality of the self-mutilation becomes inescapable as more and more incidents are detected and as the wounds require medical attention.

The family members of a self-punishing mutilator are typically highly reactive to the SMB. Parents react with shock, with anger, and most typically with guilt. After the mutilation has been detected, the family members desperately try to determine the reasons for the act. They pressure the wounded member into revealing *"the* cause" of his or her baffling behavior. Such a family generally responds by using guilt to stop further mutilations. Parents will employ a variety of guilt-inducing measures, ranging from giving lectures to developing their own depressions or psychosomatic illnesses. These responses by the family are designed to make the mutilator feel remorse and to pressure him or her into stopping any further behavior of this type.

Although the self-mutilator in this pattern has sought to keep the mutilation secret, there is ambivalence. He or she hopes that the family will come to the emotional rescue. This ambivalence is what ultimately pushes the mutilator to a degree of self-harm that can no longer be kept from the family. Unfortunately, an attempt at emotional rescue is not forthcoming because of the deficits of the family system. The family usually heaps additional guilt onto the mutilator, who is left again to feel inadequate and isolated. This increases the risk of further mutilations.

Power issues are not centrally important to these self-punishing mutilators. They are indifferent to the potential strategic effects of self-mutilating acts. One exception is a situation in which the mutilation acts both as self-punishment and as a weapon to prevent grossly unacceptable family interaction (e.g., incest). A brief example will serve to illustrate this point.

A 17-year-old girl had been a chronic self-mutilator for several years. She felt tremendous guilt and self-hatred. Much of this self-denigration stemmed from the trauma of ongoing sexual abuse by her father. The family system was very regressed, and the girl was adrift in her desperation, without any recourse within the family. Her self-mutilation provided instant, temporary relief from her feelings of guilt and rage. Although she succeeded in keeping hundreds of self-mutilating acts secret from her family for 2 years, eventually school personnel became aware of her SMB. Family treatment was initiated. As the girl was pressed for answers to the cause of her emotional stress, the truth about the sexual assaults emerged. This resulted in placement outside the home.

This young girl's use of SMB as a means to reveal a family secret developed secondarily to the self-punishing aspects of the mutilation. She mutilated herself for years in private and experienced relief. And she believed she deserved the punishment she was administering. However, the wish to have the incest detected and stopped eventually allowed for the revelation of the SMB.

Although the self-punishing pattern of self-mutilation is primarily precipitated by intrapsychic experience, the family systems of these mutilators are often a cause of the intrapsychic conflict. These mutilators report feeling alienated from their families, misunderstood, and unloved. The primary goals of family treatment in these cases are to open lines of communication and to have parents provide appropriate support, nurturance, and guidance.

These mutilators resist the imposition of family involvement in what has previously been a private dilemma. These individuals want to continue to hurt themselves because they believe they deserve and need the self-mutilation. Bringing their families into the process complicates their actions tremendously. These mutilators do not want their families to suffer. They believe it is necessary and acceptable for themselves to suffer, but not their families. As the self-mutilation is made public, the mutilators become aware that their acts affect others, and the likelihood of further wounds decreases. This is the first step in which these mutilators are brought out of their isolation and back into their family units. From this point on, the various blockages in the flow of thoughts and feelings within these families can be detected and eliminated.

Since many of these families have poorly developed relationship skills, much of the treatment of such a family is geared toward building these skills. Family members may not know how to talk to one another, how to have fun, how to argue, or how to show affection. Each of these tasks needs to be broken down into its component skills and taught to the family. The improvement in the communication allows the mutilator to discuss the feelings that have led to the self-mutilation. The greater the sharing and level of understanding, the safer the situation becomes for the mutilator.

Psychotic Self-Mutilators

Psychotic self-mutilators injure themselves as a result of psychotic thought processes. Since the precipitants of the acts are the results of idiosyncratic, bizarre thinking, the role of families in the SMB is of lessened significance. The issue of public versus private mutilation may be totally irrelevant for these mutilators, unlike other mutilators in other family subtypes. This disconnection of the act from social relationships is the hallmark of psychotic self-mutilation.[1]

In these cases, the reaction of family members has relatively little impact on the mutilators. Even concrete rewards or concessions play little role in the dynamics of these families. Not surprisingly, parents of these mutilators feel helpless in attempting to influence their children. Psychotic mutilators may well be unreachable at times of severe decompensation.

As parents realize that their children are unresponsive, they usually attempt to hospitalize them. It is very rare that psychotic mutilation is allowed to continue for an extended period. This is in contrast to the other subtypes, where parents may be (wisely) reluctant to hospitalize their children. In those instances parents believe they may be able to influence or appease their children and to reinstate a safe environment. In psychotic self-mutilation, the bizarreness and the total lack of control prod families to take quick action.

The types of wounds made by psychotic mutilators also spur a quick response from family members to pursue intensive psychiatric treatment. The self-inflicted wounds are frequently serious, are made on vulnerable body parts, and are accompanied by strange rituals or behaviors. The

1. The only exception to this is when SMB occurs as part of a psychotic transference. This circumstance is described in Chapter 7 on psychotic self-mutilation.

acts are often so bizarre or grotesque that even the most disorganized families are compelled to respond to the safety needs of the mutilators.

Power issues between family members are not major factors in the occurrence of psychotic SMB. However, psychotic processes that are grandiose or persecutory will probably include periods of preoccupation with issues of power and control. These power issues may be highly significant to a psychotic mutilator and may be a direct cause of the mutilation. Thus, the relationship between these power issues and the family system are likely to be linked only tangentially. In other words, power issues within the family are not an important cause of the self-mutilation, although a schizophrenic may have tremendous feelings of powerlessness that are defended against through grandiose or persecutory delusions.

Family treatment of psychotic self-mutilators centers on their families' developing an understanding of psychosis and a reality-based method of interacting with the mutilators. Unlike other mutilators, these individuals may have little control over impulses to harm themselves. Alterations in a family system may increase the coping skills of the family but will usually not stop the mutilation. Successful treatment of the self-mutilation rests on a diminution of the psychotic process, which is best achieved through medication.

The most important role of families during times of dangerous decompensation is to assist professionals in the management of the crises. The family treatment is helpful in teaching families how to recognize psychotic thinking and in setting clear limits with the mutilators as to which behaviors will be tolerated and which will lead to psychiatric intervention. The family therapist must assist such families in following through on these limits.

Since psychotic mutilators are likely to be delusional and to speak bizarrely about self-mutilation, families need instruction as to how to provide reality testing to their disturbed members. Feedback as to what is real, what is delusional, and what is bizarre is helpful for psychotic people attempting to remain in control.

Summary

Analyzing the three subtypes of self-mutilators along the three family dimensions described in this chapter has been proposed as a means of conceptualizing assessment and treatment of self-mutilators and their families. For each self-mutilator subtype, it may be helpful to examine the form of family dynamics; this should assist the therapist in deciding on family interventions. For example, if an individual is engaging in private self-mutilation, one of the treatment goals is to make the mutilation public so that all of the family is aware of the problem. Private mutilation is symptomatic of an alienated and self-punishing individual, and it is important that he or she be drawn out of this autistic self-destruction. The scrutiny of family members to detect acts that have previously been private exerts pressure on the mutilator to stop the self-destructive behavior and to communicate with family members.

Making the act public necessitates teaching other family members how to monitor the mutilator for signs of self-injury. The denial of the SMB by the family must be confronted, so that the family no longer accepts far-fetched explanations for the sudden appearance of wounds. When the family members suspect that a self-inflicted wound has been made, they are expected to tell the mutilator that they are aware of the source of the wound. Once family members are adept at detecting the self-mutilative acts, they are then in a position to help the mutilator and to change their responses in a therapeutic manner. The key point, however, is that the family system cannot change unless the mutilation is uncovered and the denial of the problem is eliminated.

In most situations, the self-mutilation is not private. More commonly, it is a major event that sends shock waves through the entire family system. In such a case, the first goal of treatment is for the family to develop a carefully calculated reaction to the mutilation. The purpose of the mutilation is to manipulate a particular outcome or to induce an emotional change. In either case, the act of self-injury sets in motion a chain of responses by the family that ultimately reinforces the act. The mutilator obtains either a concrete reward or a desired emotional reaction. As long as the mutilation serves such a useful purpose, it will be repeated.

The labeling of these processes within family therapy is a critical goal. Each time a dynamic is displayed, the therapist can point out the repetition of the pattern, predict the likely responses of the family, and discuss alternative methods of responding. If family members remain highly reactive to the act, it will be extremely difficult for them to gain a sense of control. Decreasing the reactivity of the family may require discussion of several issues, including (1) the mutilator's safety (is the mutilator really suicidal, or is there a basic misunderstanding of the acts of self-harm?), (2) the guilt experienced by family members (are they really responsible for the act?), and (3) the motivation of the mutilation (why is the act happening, and does the mutilator have control over the behavior?) The answers to these questions serve to prescribe a family demeanor somewhere between excessive reactivity and apathetic withdrawal.

Case Example of Family Treatment

We conclude this chapter with a synopsis of the family treatment of a case already familiar to the reader—the case of Artha, which was presented at the end of Chapter 6. We discuss the case of Artha again here for two reasons. First, she represents what we believe to be a type of self-mutilator that clinicians commonly encounter: a manipulative individual whose SMB is invariably public and is designed to exercise considerable control over the emotional responses of the family. Second, we employ the case again to indicate how the goals of individual and family treatment can be complementary in nature.

Artha, her mother, and her 24-year-old brother were referred for family treatment at the time of Artha's psychiatric hospitalization. As the reader will recall, Artha had been admitted to the hospital at the age of 18 because of a chaotic lifestyle, including the self-destructive behaviors of wrist cutting and pill ingestions, polydrug use, school failure, frequent battles with her mother, and conflict with her peers. Her battles with her mother generally centered on Artha's coming home in an intoxicated state, her frequent violation of curfews (including staying out all night), her academic failure in school, and her refusal to do any household chores. The mother also expressed concern about Artha's self-destructive behaviors, saying that she feared the family was on the verge of "losing another family member," a reference to the death of her husband 4 years before.

Artha's difficulties could be linked quite directly to the death of her father. In fact, the entire family had struggled since his death, each member in different ways. At the time of the first family interview, the mother appeared to be depressed, perhaps chronically so. She described herself as largely remaining at home. She had not dated since her husband died; she also spent little time with old friends because she felt like a "third wheel around other couples." Financially, her husband had left her reasonably well off. As a result, she had not worked since his death; however, she did express a desire to be more active and to work part-time "if Artha would only settle down."

Artha's brother, Steve, was the best-functioning of the three family members. Still living at home, he had worked for several years at a local garage. He helped out at home and avoided the conflicts between his mother and sister by leaving the house. Still, like his mother, Steve seemed subdued and depressed. He seldom dated anyone and lacked ambition regarding a career, despite having been an excellent student in high school.

At the beginning of the family treatment, the therapist focused on Artha's more disruptive behaviors, including her staying out all night, coming home intoxicated, and being self-destructive. The first goal in family therapy was to reduce Artha's disruptive and pathological control over the family. Since Artha was receiving considerable support in her twice-weekly individual therapy, the family therapist began to challenge her coercive and destructive role within the family. Accordingly, with the therapist's help, the mother and brother agreed that if Artha were to remain at home she would have to get herself under control. More specifically, they decided that any additional occurrences of curfew breaking, intoxication, or SMB would result in her having to live elsewhere. Consistent with this idea, the mother and brother explored the possibility of residential placement for Artha if she defied the new rules. Artha was adamantly opposed to placement, saying that she would not go no matter what they decided.

Within a week of the new rules' being defined, Artha put her family to the test. She came home intoxicated in the early hours of the morning, acting loud and hostile. When her mother and brother confronted her regarding her behavior, she sneeringly cut herself as they watched. In response to Artha's testing, the mother and brother were not able to follow through on their promise of placement. Instead, they reverted to their usual pattern of withdrawing into an immobilized silence. This seemed both to delight and to infuriate Artha.

At this point, the family therapist suspended the family sessions temporarily and met with the mother individually. He did so because he was convinced that until the mother was helped with her depression, the family was unlikely to change. For 2 months, the therapist met with the mother individually, using a cognitive–behavioral approach similar to that described by Beck *et al.* (1979). This work had three foci:

1. Helping the mother begin to express her feelings of loss regarding her deceased husband. (Note that it was important that she only *begin* this work in the individual sessions, and that the majority of this grieving be deferred until the family meetings were reinstated. This permitted the family to grieve together for the first time.)
2. Assisting the mother in identifying and beginning to challenge her chronically negative thoughts and judgments regarding herself, the future of her family, and life in general.
3. Helping the mother to have a life of her own, regardless of how her children were functioning.

The mother proved to be a cooperative and eager client. She worked very hard in the sessions and implemented many changes between sessions. For example, within several weeks she began to leave the house more often, going out to lunch with old friends. She also began to go out in the evenings occasionally whether Artha was home or not. In the past, she would not have left Artha home alone.

At this point, the therapist reconvened the family sessions while continuing to meet with the mother occasionally. Interestingly, both of the children had noticed the change in their mother and did not appreciate the therapist's "meddling." As usual, Artha expressed the family situation effectively, saying, "My mother used to be in her room too much. Now she's out with friends too much." This permitted the therapist to raise the question of whether or not they were functioning as a family together. All three agreed they were not.

This conversation quickly led to a very uneasy discussion of the father's death and how they had ceased being a family at that time. With the mother leading the way, the family members began for the first time to discuss together the unresolved trauma of the husband and father's death. For the first time, they discussed the details of the evening he died, with a powerful sense of sadness and horror. Thus, they talked as a unit about the event that had shattered the family.

This theme of grieving and recovery continued to be the predominant one over the next several months. During this period, Artha's instances of SMB markedly increased. This understandably alarmed and worried the mother. However, the mother was better able to deal with the SMB dispassionately this time. This change was due to the therapist's explaining that the SMB was related to Artha's feelings of sadness and loss, and that it was in all likelihood *not* a preparation for suicide.

The treatment of this family had many additional twists and turns. For present purposes, the most important to be mentioned are the changes the family made in terms of communication, affiliation, and limit setting. Once the mother became less depressed, she became more available to her children. In response to their legitimate complaints, she was able to acknowledge and modify her tendency to withdraw when stressed. She began to go shopping for clothes and art supplies with Artha and to prepare meals for all three of them more regularly. She also encouraged and sponsored her son's returning to school so that he might escape his comfortable but dead-end job.

Although the mother became more available to her children, she also became more demanding. She made it clear to Artha that her self-mutilation and other out-of-control behaviors were no longer acceptable. She encouraged Artha to talk about her frequent troubles with boyfriends, rather than "cutting and slashing away." Also, while the mother was unwilling to take the step of residential placement for her daughter, she did "exile" Artha on two occasions to family relatives. These week-long "suspensions" were mandated by the mother after episodes of intoxication and SMB. Artha was furious about this limit setting, but appeared to gain a new respect for her mother once it had occurred.

Over time, with the help of both the individual and family therapy, Artha made considerable progress. She was able to reduce her impulsive behavior markedly and to remain at home. The other family members benefited as well. The mother eventually obtained her wished-for part-time job, and she became involved in a flurry of community activities. Steve entered school full-time and moved out to live in an apartment near the college he attended.

The common gains that the family had made during treatment included (1) a greatly enhanced sense of affiliation and ability to communicate; (2) a revised power structure within the family, in which the mother assumed her proper place as the head of the family; (3) a clear definition of what was acceptable and unacceptable behavior within the family; and (4) a mutual appreciation of the individual growth and development of each family member.

Chapter 12
Group Treatment and Contagion

As discussed in Chapter 5, self-mutilation may occur in contagious fashion within groups. The interpersonal dynamics within these groups are typically regulated by the mutilation; self-injurious acts have a profound impact on others. This impact varies from fear, disgust, and anger on the one hand to jealousy or sympathy on the other. Group treatment is useful and often necessary to help group members cope with the repercussions of mutilation. Group treatment can also be effective in helping the mutilators to stop the self-injury.

In describing the contagion of self-mutilation in Chapter 5, we have enumerated several key issues in the development of contagion. By way of review, these key issues include the following:

1. Mutilators are especially likely to hurt themselves when they experience a loss. Within groups of mutilators, actual losses or the fear of loss may precipitate a contagion episode.

2. Primitive communication patterns play a role in self-mutilation within groups. The desire to be acknowledged and to be understood are important to everyone. Mutilators use SMB to communicate these needs.

3. Self-mutilation may be used within groups to manipulate or change the behavior of others. This manipulation may result in concrete rewards or, more commonly, in a desired emotional reaction from others.

4. Membership within groups may be dependent upon SMB. Group membership or high status in a group may be achieved through acts of self-injury.

These issues, as well as others, can be dealt with effectively through various forms of group treatment. The discussion of group treatment in this chapter is divided into two sections. The first section presents an overview of the types of people found in groups where SMB is a problem. The interpersonal dynamics of these groups are reviewed. The second section of the chapter discusses a model for structured group therapy.

Group Membership and Dynamics

Self-mutilation is a common and acutely disruptive problem within treatment programs for seriously disturbed individuals. However, self-mutilation occurs in many settings outside of treatment programs as well. Acts of mutilation and even contagious mutilation may occur within tightly knit communities, such as college dormitories, military barracks, or athletic teams.

The first question that should be asked about group membership is why anyone would want to be part of a group where self-mutilation is happening. After all, since most people find self-mutilation to be repulsive, why would anyone want to associate with mutilators? Part of the answer is that some people find dangerous acts to be exciting and attractive, even if the act is also frightening or abhorrent. Some individuals are drawn to the excitement, danger, and deviance of the act. Borderline personalities are especially likely to be attracted to these situations.

Ambivalence toward SMB and self-mutilators is a hallmark of these groups. The ambivalence results in major shifts in the interpersonal relationships between and among members. The mutilators in the group are either tightly embraced by the group or firmly pushed away. There are cycles of close contact and intimacy among group members, followed by periods of pressured retreat and bitter recrimination.

When individuals are drawn in tightly by the group, membership may be intense, intimate, and satisfying. When pushed to retreat, group members may experience "withdrawal symptoms" of loneliness, isolation, and depression. The self-mutilation is the trigger that stimulates emotional changes and usually results in renewed feelings of closeness. If the group goes for long periods without any self-mutilation, the members begin to feel isolated and empty. There is a hidden need to experience the closeness, intensity, and thrill that follow a self-mutilative act. When one member mutilates himself or herself, it provides the catalyst for the group to become reconnected emotionally.

Although SMB is a catalyst in the group's formation and subsequent cycles of intimacy and distancing, other factors are also important. For example, most mutilators engage in other forms of deviance, such as aggression, drug abuse, or alcohol abuse. These other behaviors serve some of the same purposes as SMB. The emotional life of the group feeds off these high-intensity acts. They are what give the group its properties of attraction and repulsion. The general nature of these groups is that deviance generates a tremendous amount of energy within the groups, which leads to drastic variability in the closeness of group members.

Of course, relatively few people are drawn to these types of groups. Several qualities are typical of people who are interested in such membership.

Low Self-Esteem and Intense Need to Be Part of a Group

Most people who belong to these groups feel inadequate and incapable of functioning or competing in "normal groups." Indeed, most have been excluded or rejected by normal peer groups, and this has led to frustration and increased feelings of inadequacy. Deviant groups that center on self-mutilation are appealing for several reasons. The group is seen as highly tolerant of personality or physical flaws; it is untraditional and countercultural in its structure; and members give periodic, strong positive feedback. The deviant group may be the first one that has made a mutilator feel accepted. To be fully accepted by a group, regardless of its deviance, is very meaningful for such individuals. These are people who are outcasts. Their self-esteem is enhanced by the group, but this esteem is entirely dependent on the continuation of group membership. If the group disbands or a member leaves, the loss of self-esteem is profound.

High Tolerance for Deviance

The dynamics of such groups are centered on the deviance of self-mutilation and other acts. To be part of this group requires a considerable capacity to exist within an atmosphere charged by upheavals. During periods of contagion, there is a frenzy of activity, with group members in close, enmeshed contact. Individuals outside the group, such as parents and professionals, may be brought into the situation. Group members often resist this intrusion. There is a total and exclusive involvement of group members at these times. Participation in the group requires a willingness for this type of total emotional commitment.

Group members are usually fascinated by and drawn to the deviance of the self-mutilation. Squeamish or fearful individuals do not feel comfortable in these groups because of the high intensity and bizarreness of the interactions. The self-mutilation, in particular, frightens away some prospective group members; however, those who do not recoil succeed in passing the "initiation rite" of the group.

Deficiency in Sharing Intimacy

A deficiency in sharing intimacy is a major cause of the lack of affiliation of these individuals. A very appealing aspect of these groups in comparison with others is that it is often easier to achieve and tolerate intimacy. Most group members find it easier to be emotionally close to and to share feelings with similarly deviant individuals. For example, mutilators often discuss very personal emotional material after self-mutilating. For them, it may be the only time they feel meaningful connected to others. Nonmutilating members are introduced to new levels of intimacy by the intensity of the mutilators' emotions. They are able to show caring by coming to the rescue of the endangered members. This rescuing of other persons is powerful and allows otherwise inhibited individuals to provide and accept a deep level of intimacy. They are able to feel important, helpful, and needed. Without the crisis of the SMB, the sharing of intimacy is much more threatening or frightening. This is a major cause of the cyclic patterns and addictive properties of these groups.

Members of the group constantly shift between being providers and receivers of the attention of the group. However, self-mutilators receive the lion's share of attention. Jealousy and the desire to be at the focal point of the group drive other members to mutilate themselves, so that they can share in the attention shown to endangered members.

Group Therapy

The essential element that bonds this type of group together is that the members' intimacy and nurturing needs are being satisfied. The mechanism for satisfying the needs is pathological, however, since self-mutilation or some other form of impulsive behavior is necessary to allow the group to be intimate. For group therapy to be successful, group members must be provided with an alternative way to meet these needs, or they will not give up their pathological pattern. Most group members are not willing to end their relationships, but they are willing to consider suggestions for improving their relationships. This, then, is the goal of group therapy: to change the way the group members use social interaction to meet their needs. The establishment of healthy, adaptive interactional patterns is necessary to replace the unhealthy, pathological process involving self-mutilation.

The schema that follows indicates the structured approach we use in providing group therapy. This structured model is conceptualized as occurring in several distinct steps. Each step involves a goal or task that the therapist must help the group accomplish. *These steps describe procedures for use with pre-existing groups in which members have already become affiliated and the group dynamics established. The assumption is also made that the SMB of one or more members has been revealed to the group.*

Step 1: Accurate Labeling of Self-Mutilation

Self-mutilation is often seen as a suicide attempt by group members. This misperception is empowering to a self-mutilator, since the other group members deal with the act as if the self-mutilative "crisis" were life-threatening. This life-or-death mentality insures that the self-mutilator is taken seriously and is provided with the maximum amount of support from group members. Once the crisis passes, the mutilator appears to have been saved from death. This provides the "saviors" with a tremendous sense of accomplishment. The entire group is usually "high" and tightly knit following the successful prevention of the mutilator's "death."

In cases of self-mutilation, these perceptions regarding risk to life are almost always incorrect. If the intent of the act was self-injury and not death, then the entire life-or-death intrigue is revealed to be a sham. Clear understanding of the intent of the act is a very important but difficult step in the group therapy process. The step is difficult, since the group is resistant to giving up the addictive "high" of the life-or-death struggle. Sensitivity and patience are crucial on the part of the therapist as the reality of the self-mutilation is presented. If the issue is pressed too quickly or forcefully, the group will resist and reject the intervention. Careful preparation and groundwork are essential to prepare the group to accept this redefinition of the problem.

The successful labeling of the problem as "self-mutilation" may be especially difficult if, in addition to the mutilators, there are one or more genuinely suicidal members in the group. When suicide attempts are also occurring, considerable time and effort are needed to help group members learn to differentiate the problems so that they can respond appropriately to each. Indeed, it may be necessary when using these interventions to exclude suicidal members from these particular therapy groups.

It is also common that mutilators will escalate the severity of their acts of self-harm in response to the therapist's attempts at redefining the problem. The mutilators may do this to convince the therapist and the group that they are *really* suicidal. This act of resistance serves to discredit the therapist in the eyes of the rest of the group.

Accurate labeling of self-mutilation evolves as a process within treatment; it is not a discrete phenomenon. Several incidents of self-mutilation must be discussed and analyzed before the self-mutilation is correctly perceived by group members.

Step 2: Accurate Labeling of the Group Dynamics after the Act

Treatment is most possible within these groups immediately following a deviant act such as SMB. Group members have recently re-
affirmed their closeness; tension is at a low ebb; and there is a willingness to communicate more openly. It is also easier to label and identify
the group process at these times without threatening the group. The
sharp shift from alienation and distance to closeness and intimacy has
just occurred. The impact of the SMB on the group is blatant and is
difficult for the group to refute.

The change in the level of intimacy is a critical dynamic that must
be labeled within the group. The future success of treatment rests on
the group's ability to recognize that deviance is serving a purpose for
the group. The group is in collusion to allow these acts so that all
of the members may benefit from the tension reduction and increased
intimacy that follow.

Here, again, there is likely to be tremendous resistance and denial
within the group to this process. There is a collective fear that the
therapist will disrupt and endanger the existence of the group. The
therapist may be seen as being insulting or demeaning, since group
members see themselves as having acted nobly in "saving" a member's
life. The therapist's contention that these acts are merely a means to an
end is disconcerting.

For example, in one group, the therapist introduced the notion
that the self-mutilation was the catalyst that led to the relaxed, close
atmosphere. The members quickly acknowledged the change in atmosphere, but focused on the specific events of each particular crisis
that had passed. For example, if the self-mutilative crisis centered on a
dispute between one of the girls and her boyfriend, they saw the
resolution of the boyfriend–girlfriend problem as the reason for
the change in anxiety level. Incident after incident transpired, and the
therapist persistently showed how the self-mutilation was the crucial
element while the members stubbornly discussed concrete "here-and-
now" events as the explanation for the change in group dynamics. The
therapist was willing to acknowledge that these day-to-day events were
important and stressful. He proposed, however, that no matter what
the specific stressor might be, the members used self-mutilation to
reinstate peace and harmony within and between themselves. Ulti-

mately, such a large number of incidents occurred in contagious fashion that it became difficult for the members to continue to deny that they were using these self-mutilations to meet various emotional needs.

Step 3: Predicting the Repetition of the Cycle and Contagion

Since the group process in these cases is cyclic, it is easy to predict in advance that a deviant act will occur again. Furthermore, it is helpful as these acts occur to identify the dynamics that lead up to them. Predictions of recurrence that turn out to be correct enhance the credibility of the therapist. This greatly assists in overcoming resistance and denial on the part of group members.

The labeling of these dynamics begins after a self-mutilative or other deviant act has occurred. The group has already been told that their current closeness is the result of this act. Now the therapist can predict that this feeling of closeness and calmness is only temporary. As time passes, the group will start to feel isolated and tense. These unpleasant feelings will intensify, and distance will develop between group members. The therapist labels these feelings and discusses these experiences as they develop.

The prediction that SMB will occur again and that the group will be closer afterwards has a paradoxical effect: The prediction tends to lessen the likelihood that the cycle will repeat itself. With each successive prediction, the likelihood of repeated acts decreases. However, the needs of the group members usually result in the SMB's occurring for at least several cycles during treatment. With each additional occurrence of SMB followed by the cyclic shifts in intimacy, the paradoxical intervention grows in effectiveness. The resistance and denial of group members will begin to shift, and the reality of the group process becomes inescapably clear.

It is also useful to predict in advance that contagious self-mutilation will occur. Since the mutilators in the group receive the greatest share of nurturance, this role is very appealing. Modeling occurs, and other members are likely to imitate the behavior to gain acceptance within the group and to move into its focal point. Predicting the spread of self-mutilation following an act of SMB also serves the two functions described above. It proves the therapist's contention about the motivation of the self-inflicted injuries, and it works paradoxically to hamper the spread of the behavior to others.

Step 4: Redefining the Actions of Group Members

Once their resistance and denial are overcome, the group members must develop motivation to change the dynamics within the group. By this point in treatment, the self-mutilation is seen by the group as a repetition of a harmful process. It no longer carries the same excitement and aura. When self-mutilation occurs at this stage, all group members will be self-conscious about rallying around the mutilator. They have learned that providing nurturance and attention to self-mutilation is bad for the mutilator. They know that providing nurturance is gratifying in the short term, but that in the long term it guarantees continuation of the problem. This realization creates a dilemma for group members: They want to help fellow members in trouble, but they are now forced to ask themselves whether their former way of "helping" only serves to perpetuate the problem.

The therapist can capitalize on this dilemma by suggesting that each time the group members provide massive support to a self-mutilator, they are harming their friend. Now, instead of seeing themselves as "saving" a group member, they begin to see themselves as participating in a destructive process. This is a drastic redefinition of helping behavior. The results are initially confusion and conflict as each member works to resolve the dilemma. At this point in the group treatment, a few members will take the lead and become more receptive to finding alternative ways to meet the intimacy needs of the group.

By way of example, when this step was reached for one group of mutilators, the members argued that they were morally bound to lend support to a desperate friend. The therapist agreed that support and friendship were of critical importance, but he also stated that friendship meant helping a friend change a destructive pattern. The group had several discussions relevant to this concept (e.g., "Would you give money to friend who was a drug addict so she could buy drugs?"). The critical topics in these discussions were what constituted friendship and when to stop cooperating in something a friend wants that is destructive.

Working through this concept of noncollaboration was critical for the group. Each member began to realize that if one or all of them did not rush to "save" a self-mutilating friend, the lack of response was intended as support rather than rejection. The members began to feel sheepish and guilty on those occasions when they allowed themselves to be "sucked in to" the usual cycle. As they began to provide support in a more appropriate fashion, they used the group therapy to make sure that their actions were interpreted correctly. As one girl said to a friend during a group therapy session, "I hope you realize how hard it was for me not to come to your rescue. I was scared for you, but knew it would not help if I tried to talk you out of cutting yourself."

Step 5: Identifying and Practicing More Adaptive Means of Meeting Intimacy/Nurturance Needs

To give up the mutilation, the group must develop alternative means of communicating and achieving intimacy. Group therapy is an excellent medium for teaching and practicing these alternative skills. At this stage in treatment, most members are ready to shift the focus to skill development. They wish to escape the dilemma identified by the therapist, and they are motivated to maintain the nurturance of the group.

One significant skill that needs to be developed is that of expressing and discharging emotions through talking. This step is difficult, since most mutilators believe that others will ignore their needs if they abandon extreme behaviors such as overtly dangerous actions. Most mutilators and other group members usually report that stable, verbal interaction is initially unsatisfying. They report that it seems stilted, unnatural, or "phony." With practice, however, most group members find that non-crisis-oriented communication can become natural. They realize that the other members will still listen and respond, even though there is no crisis or danger.

If, as the mutilators fear, the group members do fail to respond to non-crisis-oriented communication, the therapist must quickly intervene. Otherwise, this lack of responsiveness serves to confirm the mutilators' fears. The therapist must highlight to the group the absolute necessity of members' responding to each other's expressed needs and feelings. (Responding, of course, is not equated with granting every wish.) The entire group must learn to react to each other at a much lower level of intensity. Although this is less exciting, the change is crucial for the elimination of SMB and other impulsive behaviors.

Communication skills are easy to observe and practice in group therapy sessions. The therapist can facilitate discussions in which anxiety, anger, or guilt is expressed, and then praise the participants for successful non-crisis-oriented communication. The therapist then monitors and encourages support, nurturance, and appropriate intimacy within the group. This guided practice is used to teach the necessary skills. It also allows the group members to support each other in their shared attempt to change their previous deviant patterns.

Many of the precipitants for SMB may be alleviated or avoided by discussion with and support from the group. For example, body image problems, guilt from past experiences, anger over losses, and fear of attack may be dealt with very effectively. Hearing that other members have the same feelings and concerns is a cornerstone for all group therapy. Group members learn that they are not very different from each other and that it feels good to be understood. Closeness develops from these exchanges, yet no crisis has occurred.

Step 6: Generalizing the Skills Outside of the Group

Once the group has begun to use non-crisis-oriented communication to avoid acting out, the therapist can assist the members in using these skills outside of the group therapy. Each member must take responsibility for communicating his or her thoughts and feelings so that crises do not develop. If an individual's crisis leads to SMB, the group needs to discuss how the self-harm could have been avoided if adequate communication and support had been provided before the act. Thus, SMB comes to be defined as a *failure* for the entire group. As a result, when a crisis is successfully avoided, the situation is presented as evidence that these new skills can prevent self-harm and provide support.

Step 7: Fading the Use of Group Therapy

Successful treatment of SMB concludes when group members are able to maintain their new skills while not showing symptoms. If the group has become dependent upon the therapist for eliciting nurturance and communication in lieu of self-mutilation, then the group must learn to interact without the help of the therapist. The therapist first identifies for the group members their reliance on the professional assistance. The therapist then becomes less verbal and directive in the therapy over time. Since the therapist has explained the rationale for becoming less active, the group members are less likely to feel rejected by the therapist's withdrawal. Later, the frequency of meetings can also be gradually faded to insure a smooth transition of the group away from therapy. As with any termination process, there will be a need to discuss the termination and to watch for a return of any symptoms that may relate to the ending of therapy. A fitting conclusion to the group involves recognition that relationships can come to an end without a need for acts of self-harm or other impulsive behavior.

General Comments about Group Treatment

The steps presented here serve as a general outline for providing group treatment to those who frequently mutilate themselves. Of course, the actual events and steps in treatment vary widely from group to group. One major reason for this is that we do not run groups that deal with self-mutilation exclusively. As a result, a group may go in many directions that do not concern self-mutilation and contagion.

In doing actual treatment, it is common to combine steps or to move on to a later step before the preceding one has been completed. Thus, for example, predicting the repetition of the cycle of contagion (step 3) is often helpful in changing the group dynamics that occur after the act (step 2). Blending two steps together in this way provides for more continuity and is less awkward than clinging too rigidly to the step sequence.

Resistance to specific steps differs markedly across groups. This resistance is of critical importance to the therapist in deciding how quickly to move through the sequence. Factors entering into this resistance include the level of denial and insight of group members, their trust of and familiarity with one another, and their motivation to change. As with any group therapy, these factors are critical in deciding how to proceed.

Throughout this volume, we have stressed several key precipitants of self-mutilation, such as body alienation, loss, and interpersonal conflict. We have found group therapy to be an especially effective means for remediating these problems. Teenage self-mutilators in particular are responsive to hearing about similar problems that are encountered by peers. Knowing that a peer also feels bad about his or her body or that a friend was also sexually abused often provides great relief.

On the other hand, group treatment, especially with teenagers, presents certain problems that other modes of treatment do not. Group sessions can be exploited for the purposes of showmanship and rebelliousness, and can deteriorate into members' trying to outdo each other in being provocative and outrageous. Although it is desirable for a group of teenagers to affiliate with one another, such groups can become no more than a powerful deviant force. Thus, the therapist has to be very careful in setting appropriate limits in the group meetings on impulsive, destructive behaviors.

For example, it is not uncommon for mutilators to use a group session to express an intent to mutilate themselves, thereby initiating the contagion process. A mutilator may actually mutilate or threaten to mutilate during a session. We have had instances where individuals have cut themselves or have held cigarette lighters to their fingers during group meetings. Such behavior clearly goes beyond the bounds of acceptable conduct. When such an act occurs, the perpetrator is removed from the group for the remainder of the session. The other members of the group continue to meet so as not to give the self-destructive member undue control over the treatment process. Such self-destructive behavior is then discussed and confronted in the *next* session, with an emphasis on what the perpetrator was attempting to communicate to the group.

Another issue to which we pay special attention is supporting group members who have resisted or stopped mutilating. This support is important beyond just reinforcing this safe behavior. Frequently there is subtle peer pressure against those individuals who are changing. This pressure comes from those resistant members who are not yet ready to give up their deviance and who fear a change in the existing group dynamics. It often takes courage for a member to decide to break from the pack and not succumb to the pressure to act impulsively. Thus, the therapist must be very sensitive to helping individuals to maintain change in the face of peer opposition.

Chapter 13
Multimodal Treatment

The preceding chapters on treatment have provided guidelines for individual, family, and group treatment of self-mutilation. We believe that this discussion has provided a reasonably comprehensive overview of the treatment of SMB. However, as with any theoretical overview, details have not been provided about doing actual treatment. In this chapter, we provide more details about the practicalities of treating self-mutilators. We emphasize that the combination of services a mutilator receives must be tailored to the specific needs of the individual. Not all people will require or be appropriate for the entire range of services reviewed in Chapters 9 through 12.

This chapter presents three in-depth case examples that are designed to show how treatment decisions are based on the specific needs of individual cases. The intent of this chapter is to show how various treatment approaches can be integrated into a comprehensive, individualized treatment plan.

General Comments

A few general comments are in order before we turn to these case examples. In our experience, self-mutilation and the forms of psychopathology that accompany it are difficult to treat and resistant to treatment. The forces that spawn the problem are usually powerful and entrenched.

As such, clinicians are usually faced with long-term treatment that will be rocky and slow. We have suggested many different treatment techniques in this volume because we have found that it is usually necessary to try many approaches in combination to achieve successful outcomes. The use of one theoretical perspective, one treatment modality, or one practical technique is not sufficient to alter SMB. Rather, we have consistently found it necessary to use a multimodal approach.

Our clinical work has progressed to the point where we have developed a rather broad-based armamentarium of principles and techniques. We have only begun to test the effectiveness of these various approaches empirically, and we are still a long way from answering the basic clinical question of what specific technique is indicated for what self-mutilator at what point in time. Thus, our treatment suggestions are still within the realm of clinical inference, intuition, and personal judgment. Our decided preference in most cases is for the use of individual, family, and group therapy in combination. We use these modalities together unless it is impractical or impossible to do so (e.g., when family members are deceased or unavailable, or when a peer group does not exist).

Another important part of treatment can be the use of psychotropic medication. Of course, there are no medications that are specific to the symptoms of self-mutilation. However, many self-mutilators have more broadly defined disorders and symptoms that are responsive to medications, including antianxiety agents, antidepressants, antipsychotics, and others. Decisions regarding medication are always made in this broader context of psychopathology.

In selecting among various treatment approaches, the clinician must include many factors in decision making. The mutilator's motivation, insight level, intelligence, and other personality traits play a major role in matching treatment strategies with the individual. Likewise, the individual's world view is relevant. For example, some individuals find a psychoanalytic approach too time-consuming and nondirective; others report that the exploration of past events in their life history and the achievement of insight are meaningful and curative. Similarly, some individuals find cognitive–behavioral interventions too simplistic and facile; others report that the straightforward, problem-solving, here-and-now focus of such interventions results in satisfying, consistent, measurable progress. Thus, a process of matching individual needs with treatment approach is very important.

Some general guidelines that we use in providing treatment are worth stating. With adult self-mutilators, we tend to emphasize individual treatment. For adults who are reasonably bright, motivated, capable of introspection, and not psychotic, we recommend psychoanalytic treatment. This treatment is likely to be time-consuming, ranging from 2 to 5 years in length. Also, this treatment tends to be broad in scope, going far beyond the specific problem of SMB into the areas of early life history and the individual's present lifestyle as a whole.

For less motivated or more disturbed self-mutilators, we tend to recommend cognitive–behavioral treatment. This approach ranges in length from 6 months to 2 years. The cognitive–behavioral approach is much narrower in scope and targets specific problems, such as the SMB, an eating disorder, body image distortion, or a problem with assertiveness.

Regardless of the theoretical perspective employed, we tend to emphasize individual treatment with adults. Family treatment is generally ancillary in nature, with an emphasis on addressing unresolved adolescent issues of rebellion and differentiation. In a similar vein, group treatment may be used to help move an individual away from a pathological peer group and into a healthier one.

With adolescent self-mutilators, we emphasize a combination of behavioral contracting and family and group treatment. We rarely recommend psychoanalytic treatment for adolescents; in our experience, they are rarely patient and introspective enough to employ this approach. Even a more time-limited and simplified cognitive therapy is not typically useful with adolescents, because they are not generally able to cooperate with the tasks of identifying antecedent cognitions and modifying rigid thought patterns. As a result, we tend to employ a form of individual treatment with adolescents that stresses the dispensation of social reinforcers and the devising of individualized contracts.

Family and group treatment are much more central in our treatment of adolescent mutilators. Since these adolescents are typically troubled by major family and peer group dilemmas, they tend to accept family- and group-oriented approaches as having more relevance. These modalities focus extensively on issues of communication, differentiation, and limit setting within the family treatment, and on issues of affiliation and conflict resolution within the group treatment.

It should be noted again that in managing our cases, we rarely use psychiatric hospitalizations in response to self-mutilation. Psychiatric hospitalizations are certainly indicated for that minority of mutilators who become suicidal or for those who are decompensating. However, the act of self-mutilation per se seldom requires an admission to an inpatient unit. Once the self-mutilation has occurred, the individual is generally quiescent; the crisis has passed, and a psychiatric hospitalization is therefore contraindicated.

Indeed, our overall orientation to self-mutilative acts is to show a low-key response. Although we expend a great deal of effort trying to understand and eliminate the symptom, we are careful not to allow an individual to manipulate our attention through self-destructive threats or actions.

At this point, let us turn to the case examples, which illustrate how we select and integrate treatment modalities in reducing SMB.

Case Example of Family and Individual Treatment

Background

Brian B first mutilated himself when he was 13 years old. At this age, Brian had his first girlfriend, whom he was generally seeing every day. The relationship quickly became quite intense. Brian and his girlfriend, Ali, began having sexual intercourse 2 months after they began "going out." The relationship was also quite stormy; they frequently argued with each other, each threatening to break off the relationship. A power struggle often ensued in order to see who would give in first and apologize. After one particularly bitter argument, Ali broke up with Brian and refused to accept his apologies for 3 days. Brian became increasingly frantic over Ali's rejection and feared the relationship was truly over. He went to her home and tearfully begged her to forgive him. She continued to refuse.

That night, filled with despair, Brian cut Ali's name into his arm. He later reported that it didn't even hurt—it had actually felt "kind of good." The next day in school Brian did not approach Ali, as he had for the previous several days. Instead, he stayed just far enough away that she could see him looking sullen and depressed. On his forearm, she noticed he was wearing a gauze bandage.

By the end of the day, Ali's curiosity got the better of her, and she approached Brian to ask about his arm. He said it was "nothing." She sensed there was more to the story and pushed him to discuss the injury. After feeling sufficiently pressured, Brian removed the bandage and showed Ali her name carved into his forearm. The result was just as Brian had hoped. Ali was shocked, angry, and "grossed out." Yet she also felt guilty and secretly flattered by this dramatic demonstration of Brian's love. She accepted Brian back, and they resumed their relationship.

Over the next 5 months, Brian cut his arms two more times in reaction to incidents with Ali. Each time a similar pattern ensued as the injuries succeeded in reinstating the boyfriend–girlfriend relationship. Brian began to say he felt like killing himself whenever he and Ali argued.

Brian's parents were aware of each of his wounds. They scolded him for cutting Ali's name into his arm. They told him that he would be "scarred for life" and asked, "How is your next girlfriend going to like it when she sees another girl's name cut into your arm?" They inquired about the other self-mutilations once they were detected, but Brian gave some excuse about how the injuries had occurred. Although his parents were suspicious, they initially accepted his stories. However, one day Brian's mother was cleaning her son's room and "accidentally" found a long note that Ali had written to Brian. The note revealed that they had been having intercourse and that Brian's wounds had been self-inflicted.

The parents sought counseling for their son, and a meeting was scheduled. The therapist saw all the family members together for this first session. Brian refused to talk and sat silently except for occasional one-word answers to questions addressed directly to him. Mr. and Mrs. B told the therapist about the note and also provided background information. They had been having great difficulties in contending with Brian's behavior. He was argumentative and noncompliant, and he acted so independently that the parents felt as though they had no control over him. They were frustrated, angry, and frightened about the self-mutilation and feared he was headed for major emotional problems.

It was revealed during this session that Mr. B was a recovering alcoholic. He had not consumed alcohol for 3 years, but had been a very heavy drinker during most of Brian's life. When drunk, Mr. B had been withdrawn, sullen, and occasionally verbally abusive. During the years that Mr. B was drinking, the marriage was quite poor; Mr. and Mrs. B rarely even communicated. However, during this time, Brian's behavior was quite good. Brian and his mother were extremely close and could "talk about anything" with each other. During the years Mr. B was drinking, Mrs. B found Brian to be more of a support to her than her husband.

As Mr. B began to control his drinking, the family dynamics changed. Mr. B became much more involved in family life, and all the relationships within the family shifted. Mrs. B pulled away from Brian and reinstated her long-lost intimacy with her husband. Mr. B also attempted to develop a closer relationship with his son. However, much to the parents' surprise, the more Mr. B overcame his alcoholism and reintegrated himself into the family, the worse Brian's behavior and mood became. Mr. B commented, "I got along much better with my son when I was drinking than when I was recovering." Mrs. B said it reminded her of stories she had heard about sailors in the Navy who would spend several years away from their families. While the father was off at sea, the remaining family members would learn to adapt to life without him. Then, when the father returned home, the family would have difficulty accepting him as a decision maker.

Course of Treatment

In selecting the modes of treatment that were best suited to this case, several factors were considered. Some modes of treatment were ruled out fairly quickly. For example, it was decided not to use psychotropic medication; although the identified patient was somewhat depressed, there were no psychiatric symptoms that were severe enough to require treatment by medication. Group treatment was also ruled out for a practical reason: Brian was not part of a treatment program, and there were no ongoing outpatient groups available for adolescents in his geographic area.

Individual and family therapy were clearly indicated. However, Brian was reluctant—indeed, opposed—to both forms of treatment. He stated that he would not talk in sessions if his parents forced him to come. The decision was made by the therapist and Mr. and Mrs B to begin with family therapy exclusively and to have Brian participate, albeit passively, in the treatment. It was hoped that after several sessions Brian would begin to participate more actively and would become desensitized to the idea of individual sessions.

Several key points seemed important to pursue in the family treatment. The self-mutilation was, of course, a concern. Indeed, it became more of a concern over the first several months of treatment, as Brian began to mutilate himself in response to conflict with his parents, much as he had with Ali. The family treatment for the self-mutilation focused on many of the issues outlined in Chapter 11. Brian's mutilation was always public; the mutilation was designed to effect interpersonal changes, which then indirectly reduced his intrapsychic discomfort.

The family treatment revealed the role of Brian's self-mutilation within the family context. Over time, it became clear to the family that Brian used self-mutilation strategically to manipulate others when he felt angry and rejected. The family treatment focused on how Brian could more adaptively communicate with and influence his family. With the therapist's help, the family decided to use a contingency management approach to the self-mutilation. Brian was seen as having control over this symptom. The parents, with some eventual cooperation from Brian, agreed that whenever Brian injured himself he would be "grounded" for 3 days following the action. However, every week he went without mutilating, Brian earned a later weekend curfew than his parents had previously granted. The rationale for this contract was that if Brian were going to act in an unsafe manner, he belonged at home where his parents could scrutinize his behavior. Conversely, when Brian was acting in a safe manner, he deserved increased independence and freedom.

This contingency management approach was used for several reasons. Brian was still, at this point in treatment, not particularly compliant and cooperative with treatment. This behavioral approach allowed the parents to feel as though they were doing something to help their son, despite his lack of participation. Also, this approach was the most palatable one for Brian, since it required little from him in the way of active discussion or participation. He could begin to participate and change without having to lose face. He also could earn something he desperately wanted—a later curfew.

The symptom of self-mutilation was, of course, intricately related to other aspects of the family dynamics. Major changes had occurred within the relationship of this family; simply addressing the symptom of SMB without confronting these very important family issues would have been ineffective. Brian had experienced a great deal of loss and rejection during his childhood. His father had been largely unavailable and rejecting during the years that he had been drinking. Brian was no doubt hurt, rejected, angry, and confused by his father's lack of involvement. However, Brian's mother, trying to compensate for her own and her son's loss, had tried to fill the void left by the father's emotional absence. She formed an intense, enmeshed bond with her son, which helped both of them to feel buffered from the pain caused by Mr. B's alcoholism. Although this intense mother–son bond satisfied some needs, it also created other hidden conflicts that were destined to surface. When Mr. B stopped drinking, Mrs. B and Brian were expected to return to a more "normal" relationship and to allow Mr. B to assume the role of husband and father.

Family treatment focused on these themes for several months. As time passed, Brian began to participate more actively in the sessions. He expressed anger toward his mother for "turning her back on him" and toward his father for being "a drunk." When an episode of self-mutilation occurred, it was discussed within the context of Brian's anger and his relationship to his parents. He eventually acknowledged that he used the act of self-injury to hurt others.

Brian also agreed to have "a few meetings" with the family therapist individually, ostensibly to discuss some problems with his girlfriend. However, a fair amount of trust had developed between Brian and the therapist, and Brian was now quite willing to communicate and talk about most issues. The individual treatment focused on several themes, including the relationship with Ali. Brian admitted that he felt extreme anxiety when Ali threatened to break up with him. He said he felt incapable of maintaining control of himself in regard to this possible loss. He described the self-mutilation as both an outlet for this extreme anxiety and as a successful means of showing his love and commitment to Ali.

The "few meetings" were extended to regular weekly meetings, and Brian worked on learning to communicate more directly with Ali. He also discussed his feelings toward his parents and was willing to accept that his desperate fear of losing Ali might be related to his family experiences in early life. As his obsessive need to be accepted by Ali developed, his perceived need to have his mother's attention decreased. However, his anger toward his father persisted.

Brian's issues can be analyzed from a variety of perspectives. The therapist recognized that a psychodynamic interpretation fit the situation quite well, but he decided to minimize the interpretive aspects in his dealings with Brian. Although Brian's level of cooperation had increased, it seemed unlikely that he would remain in treatment for an extended period. Also, although Brian was now comfortable discussing his relationship with his parents and his feelings toward Ali, he still had major difficulties with complex, abstract, psychological interpretations.

The positive relationship that developed between Brian and the therapist was quite useful. Initially, Brian was much more willing to accept communication from the therapist than from his father. The therapist used his relationship with Brian to help Brian learn to view his father in a less hostile manner. The therapist discussed Mr. B's alcoholism and provided empathy for the pain Brian had suffered; Brian was also allowed to vent his anger about his losses. Ultimately, Brian became much more comfortable in expressing these same feelings directly to his father. Finally, the therapist helped Brian to see the need to protect his body from injury. The therapist said that he respected Brian and didn't think Brian deserved to be hurt. Brian's actions indicated that Brian showed little self-respect and self-protection.

As time passed, Brian's self-mutilating decreased and then stopped. The meaning of the self-mutilation had become more clearly understood by everyone involved. The act was not seen as suicidal; it was seen as a desperate attempt to communicate with and to control others. Once Brian and his family achieved this realization, the self-mutilation lost its power to control others. Brian had improved his communication skills and did not need to use SMB to express his feelings.

Brian's relationship with his father improved, although they did not become close. Brian's anger at Mr. B subsided; he was able to accept his father as a father and to recognize that Mr. B held a place in the family for which Brian should not compete.

Case Example of Individual, Group, and Family Treatment in a Residential Setting

Background

Colleen O, aged 19, had a long history of psychiatric problems and treatment. Her psychiatric history included several overdoses of over-the-counter medications, temper outbursts, occasional complaints of hearing "slurred" voices talking to her, extreme conflict with teachers and peers, and school failure. These problems required treatment in a variety of psychiatric hospitals and programs, beginning when Colleen was 14. At age 16, she was placed in a group home and attended a high school and after-school program for emotionally disturbed teenagers. It was at this placement that Colleen first mutilated herself when she was 17 years old.

Prior to this placement, Colleen had lived with her mother. Her parents had divorced when Colleen was 8, and she saw her father thereafter only once every couple of years. Her relationship with her mother was enmeshed and conflictual. Colleen had extreme emotional outbursts that were usually triggered by her perception that her mother had become distant or authoritarian.

When she was 13 years old, Colleen was sexually assaulted by an uncle. She was pressured into having intercourse with him on several occasions. Colleen revealed the sexual abuse to her mother, who prevented further episodes of abuse; however, the mother was angry and rejecting toward her daughter for several months following the revelation.

Colleen's acting out increased. She became involved with a deviant peer group and began smoking marijuana, staying out all night, and having sex with boys. Mrs. O became more angry and rejecting toward Colleen. Mrs. O reported feeling depressed and overwhelmed by her daughter's behavior; she tried to "wash her hands" of her daughter's problems by having Colleen placed permanently in care through the state agency responsible for social services. Following Colleen's overdoses and school failure, the state ultimately assumed responsibility for her care and placed her in long-term treatment.

Once in treatment, however, Colleen remained highly unstable. She reported suicidal ideation, threatened to overdose, and occasionally did take over-the-counter medications in sublethal doses. She frequently requested to be hospitalized for depression, and occasionally complained of hearing the "voices." She was frequently tearful, yet showed marked variability in her mood within the same day.

Colleen had very refined social skills and was frequently perceived as a "best friend" by the other teenagers in her program. They would confide in Colleen and tell her secrets about boyfriends and various family and personal problems. After hearing their secrets, however, Colleen would share the information with other friends, making especially sure that she told the person whom the secret concerned (when this was possible). Inevitably, her sharing of this information caused major disruptions within the peer group. At first, Colleen escaped much of the anger as the various parties fought vociferously, usually using Colleen as an intermediary. In time, however, the group recognized the central role Colleen played in these intense conflicts and saw her as untrustworthy.

The peer group contained several self-mutilators who frequently became involved in epidemics of self-mutilation. The mutilation served many purposes within this group, including the simultaneous punishment of others and the rallying of support for oneself. Colleen's actions often precipitated these outbursts of mutilation within the group. For example, one time she revealed to a girlfriend that "Tom said he doesn't like you any more and he is going out with Sandra now." This message induced the girlfriend to mutilate herself. Colleen comforted the mutilator and then went to Tom to let him know that he had caused the mutilation. Tom was upset and expressed his guilt to Sandra, who, seeing Tom so upset over another girl, also mutilated herself. Colleen then approached Sandra to lend support and to gather new information, which she then revealed to the others.

The group began to resent Colleen more and more. She became isolated and lost her central role with her peers. Colleen herself then engaged in SMB for the first time. The act had a significant impact on the other group members: They were responsive and nurturing toward her for the first time in quite a while, and allowed Colleen to resume her place within the group. However, the pattern then began to repeat itself. The group would tire of Colleen's meddling and instigation of conflict, and she would be rejected. Colleen would feel isolated and alone, and would use self-mutilation as a means to be reinstated within the group. After several repetitions of this cycle, Colleen was forced to dramatically intensify her acting out to achieve readmission. Her self-mutilation became more frequent and more serious; she also made many more threats of suicide.

Course of Treatment

Colleen was seen by a psychiatrist as part of her treatment. Several medications were tried over the course of treatment. Usually there seemed to be initial improvement in her symptoms after a new medication was prescribed, but the benefits were always short-lived, and the medication ultimately would be discontinued. Over a 2½-year period she was tried on an antianxiety agent, an antidepressant, an antipsychotic, and lithium carbonate. Eventually all medication was discontinued except for an "as-needed" order for Mellaril. Her final diagnosis by the psychiatrist was BPD.

As part of the treatment program, Colleen received individual, family, and group treatment. Colleen was motivated to participate in these treatments. Indeed, she often requested additional meetings with her individual therapist beyond those that were scheduled. Colleen's treatment team worked collaboratively to integrate her therapy so that maximum impact could be made on several themes.

Colleen had a desperate need to be accepted and wanted. She felt rejected by her mother and eventually by her peers. She constantly needed reassurance that her peers and the staff liked her, and, even more, that she was seen as special. She wanted to be everyone's best friend and the staff's most important client. She regulated her behaviors to manipulate the wished-for relationships. Deviance played an important part in this manipulation. The self-mutilation was the most extreme attempt to induce a nurturing response from others.

Some of Colleen's desperate need to be loved came from a deep self-hatred. The sexual abuse she had experienced traumatized her and resulted in a mutifaceted self-hatred. She especially hated her body, which had been forced to participate in this horrid act. When her peers or significant adults liked Colleen or complimented her for her appearance, she was able to gain some temporary improvement in her self-esteem. When she acted out sexually with boys, she likewise achieved a feeling of being liked and desired, although these sexual encounters also frightened her and brought back the painful memories of the sexual abuse.

Colleen used the individual therapy to discuss and analyze these issues. She was anxious to please her therapist. At first she believed that the therapist was most available and caring when she was in crisis; she frequently sought him out and was histrionic in her presentation of symptoms and experiences. She requested longer meetings and would become especially upset just as the time was about to run out in the session, in the hope that this emotional display would lead to longer sessions.

The therapist worked very hard not to overreact to these crises. He worked with her to show her that their relationship was not based on crises, and that he was just as available to her when she was stable and making progress. It was very difficult for Colleen to accept the idea that she would be valued by him if she were doing well. She acted out for many months in an attempt to intensify and control the therapy relationship. Eventually, she realized that the therapist was more interested in her learning to control herself than he was in her deviance. She came to accept that she would probably please the therapist and herself the most if she were more responsible in her behavior.

It was difficult for Colleen to trust her therapist because he was a male. She feared (and wished) that he would cross the therapist–client boundary and be her "father." Her acting out continued until it became clear that both the wish and the fear were impossible outcomes. Once this was realized, Colleen markedly reduced her manipulative behavior with her therapist. The relationship became very supportive and helpful to her, and served as a model for many of her other relationships. She was able to recognize the value of boundaries, trust, and stability in a relationship. She worked with her therapist to bring these types of characteristics into play with other people.

Colleen also came to trust her individual therapist enough to discuss the sexual abuse by her uncle. She talked about her feelings of degradation and the resulting impact on her body image and overall self-esteem. Colleen's thinking frequently included negative cognitions about herself. She was very self-critical in her thinking, often swearing and sneering about herself in her own thoughts. Cognitive-behavioral therapy was helpful to Colleen in changing this pattern. She began to accept that she wanted and deserved to like herself.

Changing her thinking represented one avenue toward accomplishing this end. As her thoughts of herself evolved toward the positive, she became more willing to take care of her hygiene and physical appearance. She also became less dependent on the compliments or affection of other people for achieving self-esteem.

As her trust in her therapist developed, Colleen discussed the ways she consciously manipulated her mother and friends through acting out. The self-mutilation in particular was addressed as a purposeful method of accomplishing desired outcomes. Colleen expressed the desire to learn alternative ways to communicate and interact with others. She still wished for closeness and intensity, but accepted the necessity of using more adaptive means to achieve these ends.

In group treatment, many of these same issues were addressed, but from the interactive perspective of the peer network. The group therapist helped Colleen and her peers to recognize the destructive pattern that had evolved. As a group, they were addicted to the powerful dynamics that ebbed and flowed as alliances shifted and deviant acts were perpetrated. These dynamics were identified and labeled as they occurred. Colleen's role within the group was identified, and the group members were encouraged to discuss their ambivalent feelings toward her.

The group therapist became important to the group members as they used this structured and relatively safe medium to communicate with one another. This replaced much of the maladaptive communication (some of which was being channeled through Colleen) with healthier, direct communication.

The role of self-mutilation and contagion was discussed in the group, using the model described in Chapter 12. The group initially resisted the notion that the self-mutilation was a group ritual used to obtain closeness and to punish others. They denied any imitative aspects of the behavior. The pattern continued, however, and each successive episode of contagion made it less feasible for group members to deny the interrelationship among their self-destructive acts. Colleen, in particular, was helpful in confronting other group members with the truth about their self-mutilation. Colleen was eager to have her peers accept her again, and she also wanted to stop mutilating herself. She hoped that if the group stopped mutilating, it would improve her chances of being accepted within the group and would enable her to stop her own self-destructive behavior.

Three other girls in this group were also sexual abuse victims. These girls shared many of Colleen's feelings about being abused; they also had low self-esteem and poor body image. The group therapy was helpful in that these girls were able to identify with each other, to validate each other's feelings, and to provide support and comfort. They were all willing to try to boost each other's self-esteem and to compliment each other for improvements in appearance.

Many of the group therapy sessions were intense and emotional. Colleen seemed at her best in these types of sessions; they seemed to satisfy her need for emotional intensity and responsiveness from others. In general, the level of acting out in the group was reduced as the members learned to communicate without having to self-mutilate or perform some other deviant act as part of their interactions.

In addition to the intrapsychic and peer problems that Colleen manifested, she also had major difficulties in dealing with her mother. Although the individual and group therapy addressed these problems to some extent, family therapy was the primary mode for working on these issues. Mrs. O was willing to come in for family meetings only once a month. This was typical of her relationship with her daughter; she stayed involved, but only in a distant fashion.

Mrs. O was direct in stating her limited willingness to be involved with her daughter. She felt she had been "burned" too many times by Colleen and that she had a hard time trusting her daughter. She feared that to get close to her daughter again was inviting disaster. She recounted incident after incident of overdoses, drug use, staying out all night, and so forth, during which Mrs. O would be emotionally distraught. During these incidents, she had feared for daughter's safety and, at times, even for her life. Eventually, Mrs. O had begun to pull back because she felt so emotionally taxed, and she feared she would break from the strain. She was a single mother who had relied on her daughter as a support, and she felt she was losing both her daughter and her friend. The strain and fear were too great, so she emotionally distanced herself from Colleen as a means of self-protection.

When Colleen heard her mother say all these things, she became upset and angry. She accused her mother of abandoning her when Colleen needed her most. Colleen said she acted out because she felt rejected by her mother, and resented the mother's notion that Colleen was the cause of her mother's pulling back. It was the proverbial chicken-and-egg argument, with each saying that the other's actions had come first and caused the other's response.

Colleen continued to seek a return to a closer relationship with her mother. She wanted to leave the group home and return home. Mrs. O resisted these attempts. She allowed Colleen to visit on weekends twice a month, but she used any arguments, disputes, or acting out to justify her unwillingness to allow Colleen to move home.

It took almost 2 years for Colleen to finally accept that her mother was not going to change her mind and let Colleen live at home. Before Colleen could accept this reality, she expressed tremendous rage at her mother. This rage was derived not only from her mother's rejection, but also from Colleen's anger at the other suffering she had experienced during childhood. This included the overwhelming pain from the sexual abuse, the trauma of the conflict between her parents, and the loss of her father. Colleen retained great anger toward her father, but still fantasized that he would someday meet her needs. She minimized the blame and anger toward her father, and directed these feelings toward either herself or her mother.

As Colleen expressed these feelings in the family meetings, Mrs. O fought to keep her composure. She seemed determined not to show Colleen how much all of Colleen's feelings and recollections upset her. Colleen resented her mother's lack of response and saw this as further indication of her mother's lack of caring. Mrs. O said she was afraid that if she let herself feel too much, she would weaken and once again be caught in the same emotional trap.

Neither Colleen nor her mother fully achieved her stated goals in the family therapy. Colleen was not able to return to live with her mother. She wished to resume their relationship at a point much earlier in time and to recreate a close child–mother relationship. Her mother knew that this was unrealistic, and instead sought a more differentiated and mature relationship with Colleen. Mrs. O hoped that Colleen would become more adult and stop acting impulsively, and that the two of them could have a friendly, nonintense, comfortable, but loving relationship.

When Colleen graduated from the treatment program, she went on to live in a less structured but still supervised living situation. She continued to visit her mother on weekends. Her impulsive behavior had greatly decreased; she no longer showed self-destructive behavior in any form. Her relationships with her peers were more stable than before, but remained stormy at times. She graduated from high school and was working in the food service field. She was on friendlier terms with her mother and accepted that her mother would not take her back; however, an underlying resentment and sense of emptiness remained.

Case Example of Treatment of a More Severely Impaired Client in a Residential Setting

Background

Tammy M was a participant in the same treatment program as Colleen; however, they were in different peer groups. Tammy's level of functioning was low in several areas. Her intelligence level was in the borderline range; her social and daily living skills were also relatively undeveloped. She lived in a group home for disturbed adolescents and attended the same special school and after-school program as Colleen. She was accepted into these programs after showing a long history of emotional difficulties and school and placement failures. She had a reported history of aggression, "self-abusive" behavior, mood swings, and auditory hallucinations.

Mrs. M, Tammy's mother, reported that Tammy had been a problem since infancy. Tammy's biological father was never part of the household, and his whereabouts were unknown; Tammy had never met her father. Mrs. M had had great difficulty in raising Tammy and her two older daughters. The household was disorganized and chaotic. Mrs. M had problems with setting limits and meeting the ordinary demands of parenting. The state department of social services closely monitored the family and eventually removed Tammy from her home at age 7; Tammy was put into the custody of the state until her 18th birthday. She had very limited contact with her mother during these years. Mrs. M moved about 100 miles away and saw Tammy once every couple of years.

Most of Tammy's childhood was spent in a series of foster homes and special programs. Her placements lasted an average of 1½ years, and usually ended when Tammy's lack of socialization or aggressive behavior proved too demanding for her caretakers.

Tammy first reported auditory hallucinations at age 16; she reported hearing a man's voice call her name. The hallucinations occurred episodically. As time passed, the hallucinations included commands for Tammy to hurt herself. Some of Tammy's self-mutilation developed in response to these voices.

The record material compiled over the years regarding Tammy was voluminous. Instances of SIB were noted from the time Tammy was 9. During temper outbursts Tammy would bang her head; this frequently resulted in the need for physical restraint to prevent injury. She began scratching her wrists superficially when she was 15 years old, after she saw a peer showing this behavior. Although Tammy's self-mutilative acts were at times quite frequent, the wounds were generally quite mild and only occasionally required more medical attention than a Band-Aid.

Tammy's mental status was variable. Her thinking was concrete, and her associations ranged from direct and fully oriented to tangential and disorganized. Her moods varied from giddy, silly, and hypomanic to depressed. Her judgment and insight were generally poor. Her memory was fair, and her concentration span was quite limited. She was usually friendly and pleasant except when she had an outburst of anger; the outbursts typically concerned a frustration of one of her demands.

Many psychiatric diagnoses were given to Tammy over time. These diagnoses included conduct disorder, undersocialized aggressive; bipolar disorder, mixed; schizoaffective disorder; and several others. As Tammy got older, her psychopathology seemed to worsen, and many clinicians who worked with Tammy believed that it would be very difficult to establish an accurate diagnosis until she reached adulthood.

Staff members who worked with Tammy on a daily basis saw her as extremely needy and demanding of attention. She sought out staff interaction in multiple ways, ranging from appropriate requests for contact to outrageous actions designed to force staff response. She was very suggestible, and was thus easy prey for more sophisticated teens who set Tammy up to act inappropriately. For example, one peer told Tammy that she should pull a fire alarm if she wanted to get excused from the school for the day. Tammy accepted this piece of advice and set off the false fire alarm. If other youngsters were in crisis and staff members were preoccupied with them, Tammy had a hard time accepting the lack of staff attention. As such, it was a common occurrence for Tammy to show dangerous behavior in the middle of someone else's crisis situation.

Whenever self-mutilation was performed by another client in the program, Tammy was likely to mutilate herself shortly thereafter. Although she was not considered a friend by many of the other mutilators, Tammy wished to be accepted by her peers and tried to emulate them in any way possible, including acts of deviance.

As noted, Tammy's self-mutilation was limited to superficial and mild lacerations. A self-injurious act was usually accompanied by great theatrics: She would announce her intention to cut herself, would show the instrument she had chosen for the act, and would try to extend the length of the event until she had mustered as much attention as possible. Her affect at these times was usually inappropriate; she often smiled through the whole affair, even while she was reporting depressive or bizarre thought content.

Course of Treatment

Psychotropic medications were prescribed for Tammy throughout her involvement in the treatment program. Although there were several changes in the type and dosage of the medications she was taking, she received lithium carbonate and a low dose of antipsychotic medication for most of her treatment. This combination seemed to have the most beneficial effect on her mood and thought processes. Tammy enjoyed meeting with her psychiatrist and would become agitated if an appointment for medication review was canceled or delayed. Attempts were periodically made to reduce (and even to stop) her medications, but these always resulted in a sharp deterioration in her mental status and behavior.

Individual therapy was initiated for Tammy, and she enjoyed this form of one-to-one attention. However, because of her intellectual and psychological impairment, Tammy did little problem solving in her individual sessions. She liked to talk about what transpired on a day-to-day basis; she had little interest in reflecting or capacity to reflect on the causes and effects of her thoughts, emotions, and behavior. She was not motivated to learn new skills such as cognitive restructuring or assertiveness. When these types of approaches were recommended, Tammy would say she was not interested or would make very half-hearted attempts to learn the new skills.

Tammy was interested in the relationship with her therapist, and she seemed to enjoy having this exclusive time. Pleasing her therapist was important to her, although there was a limit to how hard she was willing to work to obtain her therapist's approval. The therapist was able to use the relationship and his approval as a reinforcer to help change Tammy's behavior. Using a simple strategy, the therapist responded differentially to Tammy's reporting of her daily events: When Tammy reported acting responsibly and maturely, the therapist was animated and expansive and praised Tammy for her positive efforts; when Tammy acted aggressively, mutilated herself, or in other ways was irresponsible, the therapist showed much less interest and merely expressed concern over the negative impact these events had on Tammy's life.

This same strategy was used throughout the various components of the treatment program. Staff members in the residence and school program used concrete and social reinforcement strategies to increase the occurrence of Tammy's appropriate and self-protective behavior. The staff developed behavioral contracts that reinforced Tammy for showing respect for her body. These contracts were altered frequently over time, for several reasons. There was a concern that Tammy would become satiated with certain rewards, and she seemed to tire of similar behavioral plans. She also enjoyed the process of renegotiating the contract, and this allowed her to have a large degree of control over the contracting process. A typical contract for Tammy was as follows:

> I agree to protect myself. I will not hurt myself on purpose in any way. For each day that I do not hurt myself, I will receive a soda in the evening from the staff. After 5 days in a row of not hurting myself, the staff will take me out for 2 hours to go shopping.
> This contract will last for 3 weeks.
>
> Signed _____

Daily rewards were usually necessary with Tammy. Her ability to delay gratification was limited; contracts that scheduled rewards after more than 1 day were often ineffective. Thus, the combination of a small daily reward and a larger reward after several days seemed to work best.

Family treatment was indicated for Tammy, but was almost impossible to provide. Mrs. M and Tammy's sisters lived a long distance away and were unable to attend sessions regularly. As a result, during Tammy's entire course of treatment, only three meetings between Tammy and her mother were possible. These sessions were scheduled during each of the occasions that Mrs. M made the trip to see her daughter.

The sparse family contact proved to be of little therapeutic value. The three sessions were superficial in nature, as mother and daughter appeared to want to have pleasant visits without discussing past upheavals. They talked of the future in a similarly casual way. They both said that someday they would be reunited and live together, or at least near each other. But neither mother nor daughter made specific plans. Although family issues seemed to be a critical component in helping Tammy, it was not realistic to use family therapy as a way to assist her.

Tammy was seen in group therapy, and this mode of treatment was quite helpful. Early in group treatment, Tammy was victimized by the group. As previously noted, she was an easy target, because her functioning level prevented her from being able to compete verbally with many of her peers. She was teased and blamed by her peers for a long list of inadequacies. This teasing in the group reflected much of what Tammy was forced to cope with in her daily unsupervised interactions with peers.

One of the goals of group treatment was to label this process and help Tammy develop assertiveness skills to cope with her peers. Tammy often acted explosively in response to provocations from peers. Self-mutilation or other behaviors were used by Tammy to reduce her tension, to communicate her feelings, and to inflict revenge on others. She required new, adaptive skills to accomplish these same goals. Group treatment proved to be a much more effective medium than individual treatment for Tammy; since the interactions with her peers were occurring *in vivo* in the sessions, Tammy was more motivated and more able to learn new ways to respond.

The therapist gave Tammy considerable support during group meetings. The therapist helped Tammy to express her feelings and opinions to her peers, and protected Tammy as much as possible from backlash when she stood up for herself. The therapist also continually labeled the group attacks on Tammy as unfair, and noted that the attacks tended to escalate when Tammy tried to assertively protect herself.

As time passed, the therapist was able to enlist support for Tammy from some peers. This was a major breakthrough, since Tammy had previously been unaffiliated with the members of the group. These supportive peers began to stand up for Tammy when she was picked on, and they started to include Tammy in their friendly banter during the group sessions. This inclusion was very helpful in boosting Tammy's self-esteem and in making her a less obvious target.

Tammy was most vulnerable within the group when she mimicked the deviant behavior of her peers. In particular, she was attacked when she showed imitative self-mutilation. The group as a whole had been working on self-mutilative contagion. They all understood the concept and were at a stage where they resented it when the therapist pointed out the contagion process. The peers attempted to blame Tammy for the appearance of the contagion effect. They claimed that they did not imitate each other's self-mutilative acts, but that Tammy always copied them. She was invariably chastised by the group for making them "look bad" by following suit with a self-mutilative act.

Since Tammy's imitative behavior was so blatant, it allowed the group to resist accepting responsibility for their own imitative behavior. Tammy herself readily acknowledged that she copied the other youngsters, and this further strengthened their claims that Tammy was the main reason for the appearance of contagion. This began to change, however, as Tammy's self-mutilation decreased. It became impossible for the group to blame Tammy for self-mutilative contagion when she was not participating. Each time a contagious episode occurred and Tammy was not involved, the therapist was quick to help Tammy point this out. As a result, other peers were now identified as the imitators. They were acting "just like Tammy," which was not a positive attribute. Being linked with Tammy was, for the peers, a real embarrassment.

When Tammy was able to refrain from participating in these contagion episodes, she felt superior; she felt she was above the others. Now they were the "copycats," and she was the one who had changed and become independent of the peer pressure. She enjoyed this role and felt it gave her some status within the group. These changes, coupled with the other treatments, had a substantial impact on the incidence of Tammy's SMB.

Tammy graduated from high school and left the treatment program. She moved into a community residence for young adults. At the time of her discharge, she had not mutilated herself for 5 months.

Summary

In this final chapter, we have presented three detailed case examples in order to demonstrate how we match treatment modalities with the needs and circumstances of individual self-mutilators. As the case summaries indicate, clients receive varying configurations and combinations of treatment. It should be clear by now that it is rare for us to provide a mutilator with only one form of treatment.

The first client described here, Brian, received two forms of therapy. In his case, the primary emphasis was on family work; relationship issues were emphasized, and reasonable progress was made. Brian came to be more accepting of his recovering alcoholic father's reassuming a more central role in the family system. Also, the family work successfully targeted Brian's SMB for reduction. Especially central in the treatment was a behavioral contract that rewarded Brian with extended weekend curfews for not harming himself. An ancillary form of treatment in this case was short-term, individual cognitive–behavioral therapy. Brian accepted this treatment grudgingly, but was able to make use of it in regard to several girlfriend and family issues. Brian's treatment did not involve the use of psychotropic medication, nor did he receive any group treatment.

The second client described here, Colleen, received residential treatment, and, within that context, individual, family, and group therapy. Her individual therapy was cognitive–behavioral in orientation. In this treatment she worked extensively on issues of self-esteem, body alienation, and trust in relationships. Her group therapy was particularly important. Within the group, she learned to correct her manipulative use of others. She was also able to share and to some extent alleviate her very painful feelings about having been sexually abused. Colleen's family work was not successful in achieving her stated goal—namely, to return home to live with her mother. Nonetheless, the family treatment permitted Colleen to face this major disappointment without reverting to her previous pattern of SMB and substance abuse.

The third case described here was that of Tammy. Like Colleen, Tammy lived in a residential treatment program. Tammy was the only one of the three cases for whom medication was a part of ongoing treatment. For Tammy, medication was important in controlling psychotic symptomatology and in stabilizing her moods. Tammy's use of individual therapy was rather limited; it essentially consisted of the therapist's socially reinforcing adaptive, non-self-destructive behavior and ignoring (or extinguishing) her deviant behavior. No attempt was made to achieve insight in these sessions, and even rather simple cognitive–behavioral goals were not possible to accomplish.

For Tammy, the most important form of treatment was clearly her group therapy. Within the group, she accomplished several significant goals. She improved her ability to avoid peer victimization, and she became considerably more assertive in protecting herself. She also became far more affiliated with peers, and markedly reduced her self-mutilation with the help of peer support. Tammy did not receive any ongoing family therapy because family members were not available.

In short, these three cases illustrate our contention that mutilators typically need and respond to multimodal treatment. This treatment attempts to address the needs of the clients in a comprehensive, individualized fashion. As a result, treatment is designed to meet the entire spectrum of an individual's needs, including biological, intrapersonal, familial, and social facets.

Conclusion

In bringing this discussion to an end, we would like to summarize the recommendations made throughout this book. Each section of the book has included suggestions for future discussion, exploration, and research. More specifically, in Part I we have reviewed the forms of SMB, discussed SMB as a clinical problem, and attempted to determine the incidence of the behavior—at least within a broad range. As noted in Chapter 1, epidemiological studies to date have been either overinclusive or underinclusive with regard to SMB. We have argued that to consider forms of self-mutilation (e.g., wrist cutting, self-burning, excoriation) in the same category as other forms of self-destructiveness (e.g., overdosing and gas inhalation) is ill advised. We have recommended that self-mutilation be considered a separate and distinct category of behavior and that it be studied as such. This in turn has led to the recommendation that epidemiological studies be performed to determine more precisely the incidence of self-mutilation. Until such studies are done, we are substantially in the dark as to the true extent and severity of the problem.

A major emphasis in this book has been on distinguishing between self-mutilation and suicide. Important findings have already been obtained in making this distinction along the dimensions of lethality/physical damage, methods employed, repetition/chronicity, and intent. We look forward to future studies that may identify new dimensions to refine this distinction further. One suggestion presented

here is that researchers "borrow" from the more sophisticated cognitive–behavioral assessment strategies (see Kendall & Hollon, 1981, and
Kendall & Braswell, 1984). These techniques may allow us not only to
tap the dimension of intent more effectively, but also to identify some
new cognitive influences that are instrumental in triggering SMB.

Equally important is the need to study further a subgroup of self-
mutilators identified in our own research—mutilators who also manifested seriously suicidal behavior. Additional studies are needed to
establish whether or not this subgroup was idiosyncratic to our study.
If it is found that this subgroup is prevalent elsewhere, it will be
desirable to identify both the intrapersonal characteristics and the
environmental determinants that precipitate the life-threatening behavior. Such findings pertaining to these internal and environmental
antecedents would in all likelihood have immediate clinical significance and utility.

Also related to this topic is our recommendation that clinicians
become more attentive in their practice to the specific differences
between these two forms of self-destructive behavior. We believe that
the era of mislabeling acts such as superficial wrist cuts as "suicide
attempts" is rapidly drawing to a close. We also believe that the
practice of using psychiatric hospitalization for all but the most extreme forms of self-mutilation should end as well.

In Part II of the book, we have focused on SMB as it occurs in
different clinical populations. We have indicated a variety of approaches for conceptualizing, categorizing, and assessing self-mutilation within these specific populations. Since the etiology and function
of SMB differ within these various groups, we have recommended
tailoring interventions to the specific needs of each group.

One of the groups that has received extended attention is that of
seriously disturbed adolescents. A recommendation that has emerged
from the empirical study reported in Chapter 4 is the need for additional studies of teenage mutilators. This age group is especially
important because self-mutilation typically begins during adolescence. If primary prevention of SMB is to occur, interventions will
have to target this age group or those even younger. Also, additional
findings regarding adolescent mutilators should be useful in learning
to treat SMB before it becomes a sustained, chronic problem in adults.

Another suggestion presented in Chapter 4 concerns the relationship between body alienation and SMB. Our study of adolescents

indicates that much can be learned about the fundamental determinants of SMB by studying body alienation. Findings regarding the body image of self-mutilators should have considerable clinical utility. For example, if researchers were to find that mutilators characteristically have distorted views regarding their body size, proportion, or appearance, clinicians could employ cognitive–behavioral strategies (as reviewed in Chapter 9) to alter these dysfunctional cognitions.

Another important need is for longitudinal studies of self-mutilators. To date, there have been no well-designed studies regarding how mutilators fare over extended periods of time. Important questions include the following: Do mutilators gradually cease the behavior as they enter middle age? Do they shift to other forms of self-destructive behavior, such as alcoholism, drug addiction, or suicide? What is their prognosis as to general level of psychosocial functioning? These questions presently go unanswered.

Another issue that we have highlighted in this book is self-mutilative contagion. Indeed, Chapters 5 and 12 have been largely devoted to this intriguing phenomenon. For a variety of reasons explored in those chapters, SMB is readily modeled across individuals. It is a behavior that can be quickly learned and easily performed. Not infrequently, it is performed by individuals in treatment settings who have no previous history of acts of self-harm. This is an alarming feature of SMB that has important ramifications for clinicians and administrators of treatment programs.

The last 25 years have seen a dramatic increase in the establishment of community-based treatment programs for seriously disturbed individuals. The establishment of these programs must be lauded for providing humane care to the mentally ill and for returning as many of these individuals to the community as is possible. However, there is also a risk pertaining to SMB that is increased by the establishment of such programs. Our research indicates that self-mutilation is more readily learned through modeling than are many other forms of deviant behavior. Our concern is that treatment programs that bring together in one place substantial numbers of disturbed individuals may be serving as breeding grounds for self-mutilation. This contagion phenomenon may in part explain the rising incidence of SMB over the past 25 years. The topic of contagion of SMB within treatment programs is certainly one that merits additional clinical and research attention.

In Part III of the book, we have focused on treatment modalities. We have reviewed individual, family, group, and multimodal treatment, employing several theoretical orientations. In our experience, we have found that if the specific antecedents of SMB are correctly identified, the behavior can usually be successfully treated, especially when multimodal treatment is employed. This final section of the book has been designed to be clinically pragmatic in regard to such assessment and treatment. Our intention has been to share with other clinicians a variety of techniques we have used to reduce and eliminate SMB.

Although it is our belief that SMB can be successfully treated, there is little in the way of research that documents treatment effectiveness. There have, of course, been a few outcome studies that have focused on unusual individual cases or small samples (e.g., Azrin *et al.*, 1975; Roback, Fryan, Granby, & Tuters, 1972). Studies such as these have tended to focus primarily on SIB occurring in retardates. A major gap in the present knowledge base is the lack of information regarding treatment effectiveness, particularly with psychiatrically disturbed individuals.

In sum, much remains to be learned regarding the fascinating and distressing topic of self-mutilation. In closing, we would like to quote a teenage self-mutilator who once described for us the process leading up to a self-mutilative episode. Given the nature of this book, it seems appropriate to give a mutilator the last word.

> All weekend I was going through something. I felt gross, wicked, totally meaningless. It was like there was nothing going on, but there was really so much going on inside.
>
> I kept trying to push the feelings away. I'd feel like I was going to freak out or something, so I'd have to push it away again.
>
> Finally it came down to it that I couldn't push it away any more. It felt like a frenzy in my brain. I began to think really morbid thoughts. I imagined the razor knife in my art supplies . . . that I'd get it . . . and then it would be really vivid—a slice down my arm or my stomach. The scene got quicker and quicker, until I thought, "Why not my whole body?"
>
> And so I did it. I cut my arm in those places. But I knew I didn't want to die. I know that now. There is always that surge of hope that says, "Cut it out."

References

Akhtar, S., & Hastings, B. W. (1978). Life threatening self-mutilation of the nose. *Journal of Clinical Psychiatry, 39*, 676–677.

American Psychiatric Association. (1987). *Diagnostic and statistical manual of mental disorders* (3rd ed., revised). Washington, DC: Author.

Asch, S. S. (1971). Wrist scratching as a symptom of anhedonia: A predepressive state. *Psychoanalytic Quarterly, 40*, 603–613.

Azrin, N. H., Gottlieb, L., Hughart, L., Wesolowski, M. D., & Rahn, T. (1975). Eliminating self-injurious behavior by educative procedures. *Behaviour Research and Therapy, 13*, 101–111.

Bach-y-Rita, G. (1974). Habitual violence and self-mutilation. *American Journal of Psychiatry, 9*, 1018–1020.

Ballinger, B. R. (1971). Minor self-injury. *British Journal of Psychiatry, 118*, 535–538.

Bandura, A. (1969). *Principles of behavior modification.* New York: Holt, Rinehart & Winston.

Bandura, A. (1973). *Aggression: A social learning analysis.* Englewood Cliffs, NJ: Prentice-Hall.

Bandura, A. (1977). *Social learning theory.* Englewood Cliffs, NJ: Prentice-Hall.

Beck, A. T. (1976). *Cognitive therapy and the emotional disorders.* New York: International Universities Press.

Beck, A. T., Rush, A. J., Shaw, B. F., & Emery, G. (1979). *Cognitive therapy of depression.* New York: Guilford Press.

Bettelheim, B. (1983). *Freud and man's soul.* New York: Knopf.

Betts, W. (1964). Autocannibalism: An additional observation. *American Journal of Psychiatry, 121*, 402–403.

Bille-Brahe, U. (1982). Persons attempting suicide as clients in the Danish welfare system. *Social Psychiatry, 17*, 181–188.

Blacker, K. H., & Wong, N. (1963). Four cases of autocastration. *Archives of General Psychiatry, 8*, 169–176.

Blos, P. (1962). *On adolescence: A psychoanalytic interpretation.* New York: Free Press.

Browning, D. H., & Boatman, B. (1977). Incest: Children at risk. *American Journal of Psychiatry, 134,* 69–72.

Carr, E. G. (1977). The motivation of self-injurious behavior. *Psychological Bulletin, 84,* 800–816.

Carr, E. G., Newsom, C. D., & Binkoff, J. A. (1976). Stimulus control of self-destructive behavior in a psychotic child. *Journal of Abnormal Child Psychology, 4,* 139–153.

Carroll, J., Schaffer, C., Spensley, J., & Abramowitz, S. I. (1980). Family experiences of self-mutilating patients. *American Journal of Psychiatry, 137,* 852–853.

Clark, R. A. (1981). Self-mutilation accompanying religious delusions. *Journal of Clinical Psychiatry, 42,* 243–244.

Clendenin, W. W., & Murphy, G. E. (1971). Wrist cutting. *Archives of General Psychiatry, 25,* 465–469.

Cohen, E. (1969). Self-assault in psychiatric evaluation. *Archives of General Psychiatry, 21,* 64–67.

Corte, H. E., Wolf, M. M., & Locke, B. J. (1971). A comparison of procedures for eliminating self-injurious behavior of retarded adolescents. *Journal of Applied Behavior Analysis, 4,* 201–213.

Crabtree, L. H. (1967). A psychotherapeutic encounter with a self-mutilating patient. *Psychiatry, 30,* 91–100.

Crabtree, L. H., & Grossman, W. K. (1974). Administrative clarity and redefinition for an open adolescent unit. *Psychiatry, 37,* 350–359.

Cross, H. A., & Harlow, H. F. (1965). Prolonged and progressive effects of partial isolation of the behavior of macaque monkeys. *Journal of Experimental Research in Personality, 1,* 39–49.

Crowder, J. E., Gross, C. A., Heiser, J. F., & Crowder, A. M. (1979). Self-mutilation of the eye. *Journal of Clinical Psychiatry, 40,* 420–423.

Deitz, S. M., & Repp, A. C. (1973). Decreasing classroom misbehavior through the use of DRL schedules of reinforcement. *Journal of Applied Behavior Analysis, 6,* 457–463.

Delgado, R. A., & Mannino, F. V. (1969). Some observations on trichotillomania in children. *Journal of the American Academy of Child Psychiatry, 8,* 229–246.

Dennis, W., & Majarian, P. (1957). Infant development under environmental handicap. *Psychological Monographs, 71*(7, Whole No. 436).

Dizmang, L. H., & Cheatham, C. F. (1970). The Lesch–Nyhan syndrome. *American Journal of Psychiatry, 127,* 671–677.

Duker, P. (1975). Behavior control of self-biting in a Lesch–Nyhan patient. *Journal of Mental Deficiency Research, 19,* 11–19.

Eisenhauer, G. L. (1985). Self-inflicted ocular removal by two psychiatric inpatients. *Hospital and Community Psychiatry, 36,* 189–191.

Emerson, L. E. (1914). A preliminary report of psychoanalytic study and treatment of a case of self-mutilation. *Psychoanalytic Review, 1,* 41–52.

Erikson, E. H. (1963). *Childhood and society.* New York: Norton.

Farberow, N. L. (Ed.). (1980). *The many faces of suicide: Indirect self-destructive behavior.* New York: McGraw-Hill.

Ferster, C. B. (1961). Positive reinforcement and behavioral deficits of autistic children. *Child Development, 32,* 437–456.

Frankel, F., & Simmons, J. Q. (1976). Self-injurious behavior in schizophrenic and retarded children. *American Journal of Mental Deficiency, 80,* 512–522.

French, A. P., & Nelson, H. L. (1972). Genital self-mutilation in women. *Archives of General Psychiatry, 27,* 618–620.

Freud, S. (1953). On narcissism: An introduction. In J. Strachey (Ed. and Trans.), *The standard edition of the complete psychological works of Sigmund Freud* (Vol. 14). London: Hogarth Press. (Original work published 1914)

Friedman, M., Glasser, M., Laufer, E., Laufer, M., & Whol, M. (1972). Attempted suicide and self-mutilation in adolescence. *International Journal of Psycho-Analysis, 53,* 179-183.

Gardner, A. R., & Gardner, A. J. (1975). Self-mutilation, obsessionality and narcissism. *International Journal of Psychiatry, 127,* 127-132.

Gardner, D. L., & Cowdry, R. W. (1985). Suicidal and parasuicidal behavior in borderline personality disorder. *Psychiatric Clinics of North America, 8,* 389-403.

Geist, R. A. (1979). Onset of chronic illness in children and adolescents. *American Journal of Orthopsychiatry, 52,* 704-711.

Gelles, R. J. (1980, November). Violence in the family: A review of research in the seventies. *Journal of Marriage and the Family,* pp. 873-885.

Gilgotti, R., & Waring, H. G. (1967). Self-inflicted destruction of the nose and palate. *Journal of the American Dental Association, 76,* 593-596.

Goodwin, J., Simms, M., & Bergman, R. (1979). Hysterical seizures: A sequel to incest. *American Journal of Orthopsychiatry, 49,* 698-703.

Goldney, R. D., & Simpson, I. G. (1975). Female genital self-mutilation. *Canadian Psychiatric Association Journal, 20,* 435-441.

Graff, H., & Mallin, R. (1967). The syndrome of the wrist cutter. *American Journal of Psychiatry, 124,* 36-42.

Green, A. H. (1967). Self-mutilation in schizophrenic children. *Archives of General Psychiatry, 17,* 234-244.

Green, A. H. (1968). Self-destructive behavior in physically abused schizophrenic children. *Archives of General Psychiatry, 19,* 171-179.

Greilsheimer, H., & Groves, J. E. (1979). Male genital self-mutilation. *Canadian Psychiatric Association Journal, 36,* 441-446.

Griffin, N., Webb, M. G. T., & Parker, R. R. (1982). Single case study: A case of self-inflicted eye injuries. *Journal of Nervous and Mental Disease, 170,* 53-56.

Gross, M. (1979). Incestuous rape. *American Journal of Orthopsychiatry, 49,* 704-708.

Grunebaum, H. U., & Klerman, G. L. (1967). Wrist slashing. *American Journal of Psychiatry, 124,* 527-534.

Gunderson, J. G. (1984). *Borderline personality disorder.* Washington, DC: American Psychiatric Press.

Gunderson, J. G., Kolb, J. E., & Austin, V. (1981). The diagnostic interview for borderline patients. *American Journal of Psychiatry, 138,* 896-903.

Hall, G. S. (1904). *Adolescence.* New York: Appleton.

Hamilton, J., Stephens, L., & Allen, P. (1967). Controlling aggressive and destructive behavior in severely retarded institutionalized residents. *American Journal of Mental Deficiency, 71,* 852-856.

Harlow, H. F., & Harlow, M. K. (1971). Psychopathology in monkeys. In H. D. Kimmel (Ed.), *Experimental psychopathology.* New York: Academic Press.

Hawton, K., Fagg, J., Marsack, P., & Wells, P. (1982). Deliberate self-poisoning and self-injury in the Oxford area: 1972-1980. *Social Psychiatry, 17,* 175-179.

Hendin, H. (1950). Attempted suicide: A psychiatric and statistical study. *Psychiatric Quarterly, 24,* 34-46.

Herzberg, J. (1977). Self-excoriation by young women. *American Journal of Psychiatry, 134,* 320-321.

Holdin-Davis, D. (1914). An epidemic of hair-pulling in an orphanage. *British Journal of Dermatology, 26,* 207–210.

Holding, T. A., Buglass, D., & Kreitman, N. (1977). Parasuicide in Edinburgh—a seven year review, 1968–1974. *British Journal of Psychiatry, 130,* 534–543.

Hughes, M. C. (1982). Chronically ill children in groups: Recurrent issues and adaptations. *American Journal of Orthopsychiatry, 52,* 704–711.

Johnson, E. H. (1973). Felon self-mutilation: Correlate of the stress in prison. In B. L. Danto (Ed.), *Jail house blues.* Orchard Lake, MI: Epic.

Johnson, F. G., Ferrence, F., & Whitehead, P. C. (1973). Self-injury: Identification and intervention. *Canadian Psychiatric Association Journal, 18,* 101–105.

Johnson, F. G., Frankel, B. G., Ferrence, R. G., Jarvis, G. K., & Whitehead, P. C. (1975). Self-injury in London, Canada: A prospective study. *Canadian Journal of Public Health, 66,* 307–316.

Jones, F. H., Simmons, J. Q., & Frankel, F. (1974). An extinction procedure for eliminating self-destructive behavior in a 9-year-old autistic girl. *Journal of Autism and Childhood Schizophrenia, 4,* 241–250.

Jones, I. H., Congin, L., Stevenson, J., Strauss, N., & Frei, D. Z. (1979). A biological approach to two forms of human self-injury. *Journal of Nervous and Mental Disease, 167,* 74–78.

Kafka, J. S. (1969). The body as transitional object: A psychoanalytic study of a self-mutilating patient. *British Journal of Medical Psychology, 42,* 207–211.

Kahan, J., & Pattison, E. M. (1984). Proposal for a distinctive diagnosis: The deliberate self-harm syndrome (DSH). *Suicide and Life-Threatening Behavior, 14,* 17–35.

Kendall, P. C., & Braswell, L. (1984). *Cognitive–behavioral therapy for impulsive children.* New York: Guilford Press.

Kendall, P. C., & Hollon, S. D. (Eds.). (1981). *Assessment strategies for cognitive–behavioral interventions.* New York: Academic Press.

Kohut, H. (1977). *The restoration of the self.* New York: International Universities Press.

Krauss, H. R., Yee, R. D., & Foos, R. Y. (1984). Autonucleation. *Survey of Opthamology, 29,* 179–187.

Kreitman, N. (Ed.). (1977). *Parasuicide.* Chichester, England: Wiley.

Kreitman, N., Philip, A. E., Greer, S., & Bagley, C. R. (1969). Parasuicide [Letter to the editor]. *British Journal of Psychiatry, 115,* 746–747.

Krieger, M. J., McAninch, J. W., & Weimer, S. R. (1982). Self-performed bilateral orchiectomy in transsexuals. *Journal of Clinical Psychiatry, 43,* 292–293.

Kroll, J. C. (1978). Self-destructive behavior in an inpatient ward. *Journal of Nervous and Mental Disease, 166,* 429–434.

Krupp, N. E. (1977, June). Self caused skin ulcers. *Psychosomatics,* pp. 15–19.

Lacan, J. (1977). *Écrits: A selection* (A. Sheridan, Trans.). New York: Norton.

Lesch, M., & Nyhan, W. L. (1964). A familial disorder of uric acid metabolism and central nervous system function. *American Journal of Medicine, 36,* 561–570.

Lester, D. (1972). Self-mutilating behavior. *Psychological Bulletin, 2,* 119–128.

Litman, R., Farberow, N., & Wold, C. (1974). Prediction models of suicidal behavior. In A. Beck, H. Resnick, & D. Lettieri (Eds.), *The prediction of suicide.* Bowie, MD: Charles Press.

Lovaas, O. I., Freitag, G., Gold, V. J., & Kassorla, I. C. (1965). Experimental studies in childhood schizophrenia: Analysis of self-destructive behavior. *Journal of Experimental Child Psychology, 2,* 67–84.

Lovaas, O. I., & Simmons, J. Q. (1969). Manipulation of self-destruction in three retarded children. *Journal of Applied Behavior Analysis, 2,* 143–157.

Lubin, A. J. (1964). Vincent van Gogh's ear. *Psychoanalytic Quarterly, 30,* 351–384.

Lystad, M. H. (1975). Violence at home: A review of the literature. *American Journal of Orthopsychiatry, 45,* 328–345.

Maclean, G., & Robertson, B. M. (1976). Self-enucleation and psychosis. *Archives of General Psychiatry, 33,* 242–249.

Malcove, L. (1933). Bodily mutilation and learning to eat. *Psychoanalytic Quarterly, 2,* 557–561.

Malmquist, C. P. (1978). *Handbook of adolescence.* New York: Jason Aronson.

Masterson, J. F. (1967). *The psychiatric dilemma of adolescence.* Boston: Little, Brown.

Matthews, P. C. (1968). Epidemic self-injury in an adolescent unit. *International Journal of Social Psychiatry, 14,* 125–133.

McCrea, C. W., Summerfield, A. B., & Rosen, B. (1982). Body image: A selective review of existing measurement techniques. *British Journal of Medical Psychology, 55,* 225–233.

McKerracher, D. W., Loughnane, T., & Watson, R. A. (1968). Self-mutilation in female psychopaths. *British Journal of Psychiatry, 114,* 829–832.

Meichenbaum, D. (1977). *Cognitive–behavior modification.* New York: Plenum.

Menninger, K. A. (1935). A psychoanalytic study of the significance of self-mutilations. *Psychoanalytic Quarterly, 4,* 408–466.

Menninger, K. A. (1938). *Man against himself.* New York: Harcourt, Brace.

The Merriam–Webster dictionary. (1974). New York: Pocket Books.

Mintz, I. C. (1960). Autocannibalism: A case study. *American Journal of Psychiatry, 120,* 1017.

Morgan, H. G. (1979). *Death wishes?* Chichester, England: Wiley.

Morgan, H. G., Barton, J., Pottle, S., & Burns-Cox, C. J. (1976). Deliberate self-harm: A follow-up study of 279 patients. *British Journal of Psychiatry, 128,* 361–368.

Morgan, H. G., Burns-Cox, C. J., Pocock, H., & Pottle, S. (1975). Deliberate self-harm: Clinical and socio-economic characteristics of 368 patients. *British Journal of Psychiatry, 127,* 564–574.

Myers, E. D. (1982). Subsequent deliberate self-harm in patients referred to a psychiatrist: A prospective study. *British Journal of Psychiatry, 140,* 132–137.

Neil, J. F. (1958). Self-mutilation of the tongue. *Journal of Laryngology and Otology, 72,* 947–950.

Nelson, S. H., & Grunebaum, H. (1971). A follow-up study of wrist slashers. *American Journal of Psychiatry, 127,* 1345–1349.

Noles, S. W., Cash, T. F., & Winstead, B. A. (1985). Body image, physical attractiveness, and depression. *Journal of Consulting and Clinical Psychology, 53,* 88–94.

Novotny, P. (1972). Self-cutting. *Bulletin of the Menninger Clinic, 36,* 505–514.

Offer, D. O., & Barglow, P. (1960). Adolescent and young adult self-mutilation incidents in a general psychiatric hospital. *Archives of General Psychiatry, 3,* 194–204.

Pabis, R., Mirza, M. A., & Tozman, S. (1980). A case study of autocastration. *American Journal of Psychiatry, 137,* 626–627.

Panton, J. H. (1962). The identification of predispositional factors in self-mutilation within a state prison population. *Journal of Clinical Psychology, 18,* 63–67.

Pao, P. E. (1969). The syndrome of delicate self-cutting. *British Journal of Medical Psychology, 42,* 195–206.

Patterson, G. E. (1976). The aggressive child: Victim and architect of a coercive system. In E. J. Mash, L. A. Hamerlynck, & L. C. Handy (Eds.), *Behavior modification and families.* New York: Brunner/Mazel.

Pattison, E. M., & Kahan, J. (1983). The deliberate self-harm syndrome. *American Journal of Psychiatry, 140,* 867–872.

Peterson, R. F., & Peterson, L. R. (1968). The use of positive reinforcement in the control of self-destruction behavior in a retarded boy. *Journal of Experimental Child Psychology, 6,* 351-360.

Phillips, R. H., & Alkan, M. (1961). Some aspects of self-mutilation in the general population of a large psychiatric hospital. *Psychiatric Quarterly, 35,* 421-423.

Podvoll, E. M. (1969). Self-mutilation within a hospital setting: A study of identity and social compliance. *British Journal of Medical Psychology, 42,* 213-221.

Reber, A. S. (1985). *Dictionary of psychology.* Baltimore: Penguin Books.

Repp, A. C., Deitz, S. M., & Deitz, D. E. D. (1976). Reducing inappropriate behaviors in classrooms and in individual sessions through DRO schedules of reinforcement. *Mental Retardation, 14,* 11-15.

Rimm, D. C., & Masters, J. C. (1979). *Behavior therapy* (2nd ed.). New York: Academic Press.

Rist, K. (1979). Incest: Theoretical and clinical views. *American Journal of Orthopsychiatry, 49,* 680-691.

Roback, H., Fryan, D., Granby, L., & Tuters, K. (1972). A multifactorial approach to the treatment and ward management of a self-mutilating patients. *Journal of Behavior Therapy and Experimental Psychiatry, 3,* 189-193.

Roper-Hall, M. J. (1950). Self-inflicted conjunctivitis. *British Journal of Opthalmology, 34,* 119-120.

Rosen, D. H., & Hoffman, A. (1972). Focal suicide: Self-mutilation by two young psychotic individuals. *American Journal of Psychiatry, 128,* 1367-1368.

Rosen, P. M., Walsh, B. W., & Lucas, P. (1988). The effects of unstable clients on treatment milieu: Contagion versus continuity. *Adolescence, 23,* 29-34.

Rosenbaum, A., & O'Leary, K. D. (1981). Children: The unintended victims of marital violence. *American Journal of Orthopsychiatry, 51,* 692-699.

Rosenthal, R. J., Rinzler, C., Walsh, R., & Klausner, E. (1972). Wrist-cutting syndrome: The meaning of a gesture. *American Journal of Psychiatry, 128,* 1363-1368.

Ross, R. R., & McKay, H. B. (1979). *Self-mutilation.* Lexington, MA: Lexington Books.

Roy, A. (1978). Self-mutilation. *British Journal of Medical Psychology, 51,* 201-203.

Runyan, W. M. (1981). Why did van Gogh cut off his ear? The problem of alternative explanations in psychobiography. *Journal of Personality and Social Psychology, 40,* 1070-1077.

Schaefer, H. H. (1970). Self-injurious behavior: Shaping headbanging in monkeys. *Journal of Applied Behavior Analysis, 3,* 111-116.

Schaffer, C. B., Carroll, J., & Abramowitz, S. I. (1982). Self-mutilation and the borderline personality. *Journal of Nervous and Mental Disease, 170,* 468-473.

Schmidt, E. H., O'Neal, P., & Robbins, E. (1954). Evaluation of suicide attempts as guide to therapy. *Journal of the American Medical Association, 155,* 549-557.

Sgroi, S. M. (1982). *Handbook of clinical intervention in child sexual abuse.* Lexington, MA: Lexington Books.

Shneidman, E. S. (1973). Suicide. In *Encyclopaedia Britannica* (Vol. 21). Chicago: William Benton.

Shneidman, E. S. (1985). *Definition of suicide.* New York: Wiley.

Shore, D. (1979). Self-mutilation and schizophrenia. *Comprehensive Psychiatry, 20,* 384-387.

Siegel, S. (1956). *Nonparametric statistics for the behavioral sciences.* New York: McGraw-Hill.

Simpson, M. A. (1975). The phenomenology of self-mutilation in a general hospital setting. *Canadian Psychiatric Association Journal, 20,* 429-433.

Simpson, M. A. (1976). Self-mutilation and suicide. In E. S. Shneidman (Ed.), *Suicidology: Contemporary developments*. New York: Grune & Stratton.

Simpson, M. A. (1980). Self-mutilation as indirect self-destructive behavior. In N. L. Farberow (Ed.), *The many faces of suicide*. New York: McGraw-Hill.

Smith, A. J. (1972). Self-poisoning with drugs: A worsening situation. *British Medical Journal, iv*, 157–159.

Smith, J. S., & Davison, K. (1971). Changes in the pattern of admission for attempted suicide in Newcastle-upon-Tyne during the 1960's. *British Journal of Psychiatry, 140*, 132–137.

Smolev, S. R. (1971). Use of operant techniques for the modification of self-injurious behavior. *American Journal of Mental Deficiency, 76*, 295–305.

Steinmetz, S. K. (1980). *Behind closed doors: Violence in the American family*. Garden City, NY: Doubleday.

Stengel, E. (1964). *Suicide and attempted suicide*. Baltimore: Penguin Books.

Straus, M. A. (1979). Family patterns and child abuse in a nationally representative American sample. *Child Abuse and Neglect: The International Journal, 41*, 75–78.

Strober, M. (1981). The relation of personality characteristics to body image disturbance in juvenile anorexia nervosa: A multivariate analysis. *Psychosomatic Medicine, 43*, 323–330.

Stroch, D. (1901). Self-castration. *Journal of the American Medical Association, 36*, 270.

Sweeny, S., & Zamecnik, K. (1981). Predictors of self-mutilation in patients with schizophrenia. *American Journal of Psychiatry, 138*, 1086–1089.

Tate, B. G., & Baroff, G. S. (1966). Aversive control of self-injurious behavior in a psychotic boy. *Behaviour Research and Therapy, 4*, 281–287.

Walsh, B. W. (1987). *Adolescent self-mutilation: An empirical study*. Unpublished doctoral dissertation, Boston College Graduate School of Social Work.

Walsh, B. W., & Rosen, P. M. (1985). Self-mutilation and contagion: An empirical test. *American Journal of Psychiatry, 141*, 119–120.

Weissman, M. (1975). Wrist cutting. *Archives of General Psychiatry, 32*, 1166–1171.

Whitehead, P. C., Johnson, F. G., & Ferrence, R. (1973). Measuring the incidence of self-injury: Some methodological and design considerations. *American Journal of Orthopsychiatry, 43*, 142–148.

Wolf, M. M., Risley, T., Johnston, M., Harris, F., & Allen, E. (1967). Application of operant conditioning procedures to the behavior problems of an autistic child: A follow-up and extenstion. *Behaviour Research and Therapy, 5*, 103–111.

Wolf, M. M., Risley, T., & Mees, H. (1964). Applications of operant conditional procedures to the behavior problems of an autistic child. *Behaviour Research and Therapy, 1*, 305–312.

Wolpe, J. (1973). *The practice of behavior therapy* (2nd ed.). New York: Pergamon Press.

Worden, J. W. (1980). Lethality factors and the suicide attempt. In E. S. Shneidman (Ed.), *Suicidology: Contemporary developments*. New York: Grune & Stratton.

Yaroshevsky, F. (1975). Self-mutilation in Soviet prisons. *Canadian Psychiatric Association Journal, 20*, 443–446.

Index